A Teacher's Guide to American Urban History

A TEACHER'S GUIDE TO AMERICAN URBAN HISTORY

by

Dwight W. Hoover

ILLUSTRATED

Chicago

Quadrangle Books

1971

To Polly, Sara, and Elizabeth—my daughters—
in the hope that they may find their urban environment
as stimulating, challenging, and rewarding
as I found my rural environment

Acknowledgments

This book owes so much to so many people that it is difficult
to select some for special mention. I have profited through the
years from my conversations with Charles N. Glaab and A.
Theodore Brown. Allen Wakstein graciously sent me a bibliography which he used in editing a collection of readings. Park
Dixon Goist stimulated my interest in Lewis Mumford and Benton MacKaye. C. Warren VanderHill pointed out the ideas of
William Goetzmann on the Mountain Man as urbanite. My wife's
enthusiastic dedication to social work has improved my limited
knowledge of this area.

In the preparation of the manuscript I owe a debt of grati-
tude to Ed Andrews, who helped with the bibliographical materials,
to Pat Struve, who provided information on games, to J. Paul

Mitchell, who read parts of the manuscript, and to Danea White, who typed the manuscript and who frequently deciphered the undecipherable.

Finally, I wish to thank Ivan Dee whose wisdom and human qualities made a difficult task easier.

Contents

A Teacher's Guide to American Urban History

Chapter I

THE USES OF URBAN HISTORY
TO THE TEACHER AND THE STUDENT

To say that the United States has become an urban nation is now a banal observation, but like most banalities this one reflects what has become conventional wisdom. American citizens do live primarily in cities, and the characteristic American experience is an urban one. Yet these truisms are not reflected to any great extent in school curricula today. There has been some attempt to reflect urban ways in elementary reading texts by placing the protagonists in city settings, substituting urban or suburban scenes for rural ones. Elementary social studies units quite often start with the local community and its municipal services and work toward the larger communities of state, nation, and world. But in the junior and senior high schools the earlier bow to local institutions is forgotten, especially in United States history courses, and even in state history courses which are quite frequently offered.

The result is that there is no coherent point of view with which to confront the phenomenon of city development. Somehow cities grow, and suddenly they are there. Usually the city appears as a post–Civil War development in company with the increase in immigration from Europe, and it appears as a problem in American society. The teacher's emphasis is upon problems of city life, with the suggestion that this life is somehow abnormal or undesirable. By the time the student reaches 1900, the preoccupation has switched to the issue of reform. The city appears briefly again in the 1920's and in the post–World War II world, if it appears at all, but the context in which the city appears in these eras is again one in which problems are paramount. In the post–World War II period, and to a lesser extent in the 1920's, the city seems to be a malignant growth uncharacteristic and somehow at odds with the values of American life. Consciously or unconsciously, history texts and teachers have assumed this anti-city bias, retaining an older view of America as an agrarian nation of husbandmen.

This guide hopes to correct the rural bias by suggesting other possibilities for including urban history in the standard American history course. In so doing, the aim is to make the growth of urban America seem as natural and familiar as the growth of American nationalism. A further goal is to provide room for innovation in the classroom and to make possible independent learning on the part of the student. Nowhere does the possibility for research into local history seem brighter than in the urban arena. Here there are materials that can be exploited, historical remains, opportunities for discovery in learning that have not been worked over many times before. A real concern with urban problems also allows the teacher to begin at the present and work back into the past, exploring along the way the interrelationships between various urban problems. A good example is the problem of racial tension in the United States. In many ways this is a function of overall urban problems—the decline of the center city, the inability of the city to annex suburbs and thus spread the tax load, and the city's lack of political strength in a system where state and federal funds are not available except through political strength. Particularly since 1900, urban history and Negro history may be merged.

The intent of this guide is not to supplant the regular United States history course, nor to make the history of America solely the history of the city. United States history courses have several functions, among them the inculcation of national values and a sense of identity with the national past, and one could not expect urban history to fill all of these functions. But the history of our cities certainly can help to explain the American past and can, perhaps, help to convince students that city life is not an aberration. Urban history is a necessary part of the total history of our society. Like Negro history, it should be integrated into the larger American history.

With these assumptions in mind, this guide includes several different kinds of units and materials. The teacher should be selective and use them as the time and situation permit. Considering the pressures on the curriculum from various interest groups, it is admittedly impossible to include all of the following units in an integrated history course. Therefore the units have been constructed so that they may be used separately and independently. Ideally, the school would have a year-long course in American urban history, but the ideal is most often not realized. Granted that most teachers will be unable to use all of the units, how many are necessary to achieve a sense of urban change? The answer depends upon you as a teacher or as a curriculum specialist.

In addition to its use in United States history classes, this guide is designed for use in core courses and in other social studies classes, particularly geography, sociology, and economics. The city as an organizing concept for core courses offers considerable potential. A number of disciplines can be brought together to bear on the development, problems, and management of urban life. For those students who are interested in literary approaches, the novel of the city or the biography of the city dweller can be used to show various reactions to the city. For others who are interested in visual imagery, the design and planning of cities and structures in the cities can be fruitful. Thus parts of humanities courses—English, art, and design—might well be combined in a study of the city. The units involving the image of the city should be particularly appropriate for this kind of approach.

Similarly, other units are suitable for use in classes in the social studies. Geographers are trying to return geography as a discipline to the high schools and are focusing upon urban geography as the key for that return. The emphasis which urban geography most often employs is one of natural growth, and the metaphor is organic development. Urban geography thus highlights the unplanned nature of urban development and shares with urban sociology a belief in ecological models. The applicable units in this guide do suggest how some cities have grown, but the historical dimension reveals more planning and rationality than the ecologists allow. This guide can help to provide a partial antidote to the belief that American cities just grew and are a product of an equilibrium achieved by competing forces. It can also show how values enter into the determination of land use and how American values are reflected in the structure of American cities.

Classes in sociology may use other units in the guide. The study of social organization and social structure is facilitated by the population concentration in cities, and the comparison of past organization and structure with the present may offer insights that are often overlooked. Urban history in this sense can be social history which touches upon class division in past societies and upon the social roles available at various times in our history.

The city also has value in economics classes, where it can be taken as an economic unit which shares characteristics of other economic units—division of labor, competition and cooperation in a market framework, multiplier effects, marginal utility, balance of trade, allocation of resources, and provisions for production, trade, and distribution. Urban history can show differing examples of these principles in action, in different epochs under varying circumstances. Decisions on where to locate cities and how to develop them rest in large part on economic factors which may be studied from past examples.

Finally, some of the units may be appropriately used in civics or government classes. These are the units concerned with the governance of the city, the question of elites in the city, and the professionalization of employees within the city. An understanding of various kinds of decision-making can be gained through examples of past successes and failures, and the connection between the larger society and the local community can be demonstrated.

Whether urban history is used to integrate the social studies, to serve as a core for a humanities curriculum, or as an adjunct to established history, geography, sociology, economics, and civics courses, or standing on its own, it should be part of the intellectual baggage of every teacher and student of American history.

Chapter II

WAYS OF INTEGRATING URBAN
HISTORY WITH OTHER DISCIPLINES

This chapter explains basic concepts in the various disciplines—
other than history—that can apply to the study of the city in
American history. As such, the concentration is upon terms and
concepts as tools that may be used to understand the urban scheme.
Each discipline ought to be considered as a way of looking at the
city—but not necessarily the only correct way.

a. geographical concepts

The "new" geography which is suggested for the high schools
has a number of concepts that are useful for considering cities
in time. They are:

1. *central place:* the location of population and services in an
area which forms the base for development of cities.

2. *man-land relationship:* the interaction of man, and his skills and culture, with the natural resources of a particular area.

3. *regions:* an area which shares either common physical or cultural characteristics for purposes of comparison. The central business district in a city would be a region.

4. *space relations:* the interrelationship between all features of a geographic area—physical, social, economic, political, and cultural. As applied to cities, this would show why some cities grew and why others declined.

5. *spatial interaction:* the interaction of regions with one another through services, so that regions are interdependent. In the study of urban affairs, this could show how satellite areas are related to central cities.

For further reading in the field of geographical concepts, the teacher will find these helpful:

Broek, Jan O. M., *Geography, Its Scope and Spirit,* Charles E. Merrill Social Science Seminar Series, Raymond H. Muessig and Vincent R. Rogers, eds. (Columbus, Ohio: Charles E. Merrill Books, 1965), paperback.

Cressey, George B., "Geography," in Gordon B. Turner, ed., *The Social Studies and the Social Sciences* (New York: Harcourt, Brace and World, 1962).

Kohn, Clyde F., "The Geography Component," in *Focus on the Social Studies* (Washington: National Education Association, 1965).

Murphy, Raymond E., *The American City: An Urban Geography* (New York: McGraw-Hill, 1966). This is a standard textbook in urban geography designed for the college student. The book does not use complicated statistical methods, though it does use some mathematical devices. Murphy's work is helpful because of its wealth of definitions and summaries of research. The book also has an excellent bibliography.

Hall, Peter, *The World Cities* (New York: McGraw-Hill, 1966), paperback. This book is in the World University Library series, published simultaneously in Britain, France, Germany, Holland,

Italy, Spain, Sweden, and the United States. Hall, an English economic geographer, discusses seven major metropolitan cities of the world—London, Moscow, New York, Paris, Tokyo, and the Randstad and Rhine-Ruhr (two complexes of cities in Holland and Germany). The book puts the American city in a world perspective and is suitable for the advanced student. It is visually attractive with many colored schematics and black-and-white photographs of cities and areas of cities.

b. city planning

The rise of city planning to the status of a profession and the growing demand for planners—in part because of planning standards for cities receiving federal funds—has resulted in the creation of a new vocabulary. The terminology of planning borrows liberally from political science, geography, and economics.

1. *planning:* the art and science of environmental development through democratic choice and the implementation of these choices through deliberate design.

2. *cities:* dynamic human systems whose future can be changed and influenced.

3. *natural region:* an interdependent area that includes both city and country and combines needs and resources.

4. *land use:* the systematic study of various urban areas with the intent of discovering and classifying the human employment of the resources in those areas.

There are many works available on city planning. None of them are easily grasped and can only be recommended for advanced students. The single exception is:

Altshuler, Alan, *The City Planning Process: A Political Analysis* (Ithaca: Cornell University Press, 1965). This college textbook is frankly aimed at those readers who plan to work in city planning.

Delafons, John, *Land-Use Controls in the United States* (Cambridge, Mass.: Harvard University Press, 1962). Delafons' book shows how planning, a collective enterprise, was put to private use.

In particular, he demonstrates that planning was employed to protect single-family suburban units from the encroachment of the city and to stratify residents by income brackets.

Firey, Walter, *Land Use in Central Boston* (Cambridge, Mass.: Harvard University Press, 1947). In this pioneering, detailed analysis of Boston, Firey proved that urban land value was a function of community sentiment as well as a matter of location, thus rebutting ecological claims. Advanced students might dip into Firey for his insights into the role of cemeteries and historical landmarks in a city.

Gruen, Victor, *The Heart of Our Cities* (New York: Simon and Schuster, 1969), paperback. While primarily concerned with the inner city, Gruen's work is also valuable for its attention to traffic flow. Not so difficult reading as most of the others in this list.

Lubove, Roy, *Community Planning in the 1920's* (Pittsburgh: University of Pittsburgh Press, 1963), paperback. Lubove traces the history of the Regional Planning Association of America, one of the original groups interested in planning in the twentieth century.

Reps, John W., *The Making of Urban America: A History of City Planning in the United States* (Princeton: Princeton University Press, 1965). Rich in graphic material, this book is the most complete, full-scale study of planning published. The author ranges from European backgrounds to 1910. As a resource book, *The Making of Urban America* ought to be available in school libraries and could be used with profit by students who are visually and design oriented. Princeton University has published an abridged paperback edition of this book which is largely concerned with city planning in the West.

Walker, Robert Averill, *The Planning Function in Urban Government* (Chicago: University of Chicago Press, 1950). Walker's book discusses the historical growth of planning in the United States and the relationship between the planning and governmental functions.

Walker, Robert Averill, *The Urban Community* (Englewood Cliffs: Prentice-Hall, 1967). This is one of the books in the American Historical Sources series and is a collection of readings designed for student inquiry. While it is probably difficult for the average student, accelerated classes should be able to put this study of planning in the Progressive era to good use.

George Braziller has published a Planning and Cities series in both paperback and cloth. These books are historical in nature and reflect upon the development of city planning. Two representative titles are Norma Evenson's *Le Corbusier: The Machine and the Grand Design* and Françoise Choay's *The Modern City: Planning in the Nineteenth Century,* translated by Marguerite Hugo and George R. Collins.

Scott, Mel, *American City Planning* (Berkeley: University of California Press, 1969). This book was commissioned to celebrate the fiftieth anniversary of the American Institute of Planners. As such, the book is a valuable historical study which traces the beginnings of urban planning through interviews with early planners and through careful scrutiny of documentary evidence. This book is essential for an understanding of the growth of the planning profession.

Meyerson, Martin, and Edward C. Banfield, *Politics, Planning and the Public Interest* (New York: Free Press, 1964), paperback. The authors studied the problems inherent in planning public housing in Chicago. Their analysis of the political factors that come into play make this paperback an important one.

Whyte, William H., *The Last Landscape* (Garden City: Doubleday, 1968), paperback. This view of city planning and land use by a nonprofessional planner is not technical and it is highly useful for a consideration of the principle of planning.

c. sociology

The sociologist's interest in the city dates at least from 1915 and from the activities of the "Chicago School," which included such individuals as Robert Park, Louis Wirth, Ernest W. Burgess, and Harvey Zorbaugh. Urban sociology has been somewhat eclipsed by the recent interest in small groups, but discussion of larger groups and whole communities still goes forward.

Some of the concepts, disputed and otherwise, that urban sociologists use are as follows:

1. *city:* "a relatively large, dense, and permanent settlement of socially heterogeneous individuals" (Louis Wirth, 1938).

2. *institutions:* groups, found in most societies, which are not temporary but which persist through generations. Examples would be the family, government, and schools.

3. *social structure:* the total character of all groups in a society, and the relations within and among them.

4. *social stratification:* the arrangement of groups, permanent or temporary, into varying levels of prestige based upon the values of the society and the power possessed by the group.

5. *role:* the total expectations of a society as to how persons should behave. An example would be the role of a policeman or a city mayor.

6. *demography:* the study of the growth and distribution of human populations.

7. *ecology:* the study of the interrelation of living organisms with their environment.

For further reading in the area of sociological concepts as they apply to the city, the teacher and the advanced student should consult:

Bendix, Reinhard, and Seymour Martin Lipset, eds., *Class, Status and Power: A Reader in Social Stratification* (New York: Holt, Rinehart and Winston, 1961).

Reshers, James M., *Urban Social Structure* (New York: Free Press, 1962). A statistical study of the structures of social groups in cities and towns. An advanced book for teachers only.

Hawley, Amos H., *Human Ecology* (New York: Ronald Press, 1950). Hawley's book was one of the first to stimulate interest in human ecology and to apply principles of animal ecology to man's behavior. Again, a relatively difficult book.

Merton, Robert K., Leonard Broom, and Leonard S. Cottrell, Jr., eds., *Sociology Today: Problems and Prospects* (New York: Basic Books, 1959), Harper paperback.

Reissman, Leonard, *The Urban Process: Cities in Industrial Society* (New York: Free Press, 1964). Reissman's book contains an excellent short description of the more prominent urban sociologists along with an emphasis upon four variables in the urbanizing process: urban growth, industrial development, the emergence of a middle class, and the rise of nationalism as an ideology.

Rose, Arnold M., ed., *Human Behavior and Social Process: An Interactionist Approach* (Boston: Houghton Mifflin, 1962). See particularly Herbert J. Gans's chapter entitled "Urbanism and Suburbanism as Ways of Life: A Re-evaluation of Definitions," which questions Wirth's definition of the city and also attacks the belief that ecology is a key to looking at the city. Gans does not believe that the city and the suburbs are different entities, nor that they offer different ways of life. Gans's book *The Levittowners: Ways of Life and Politics in a New Suburban Community* (New York: Pantheon, 1967) demonstrates his thesis, as does his *The Urban Villagers* (New York: Free Press, 1962), a study of Italian Americans in Boston. The West End of Boston which Gans studied no longer exists; it was demolished in 1958–1960 by urban renewal.

Rose, Caroline B., *Sociology: The Study of Man in Society,* Charles E. Merrill Social Science Seminar Series, Raymond H. Muessig and Vincent R. Rogers, eds. (Columbus, Ohio: Charles E. Merrill Books, 1965).

Schnore, Leo R., *The Urban Scene: Human Ecology and Demography* (New York: Free Press, 1965). This book by a noted sociologist is a sophisticated treatment of ecology and demography, suitable only for those familiar with the statistical and sociological vocabulary.

Suttles, Gerald D., *The Social Order of the Slum: Ethnicity and Territory in the Inner City* (Chicago: University of Chicago Press,

1968). This book received the C. Wright Mills Award of the Society for the Study of Urban Problems in 1969. One in a series, Studies of Urban Society, edited by David P. Street, whose purpose is to continue the pioneer work of Chicago sociologists in studying urban areas. The study concerns the Hull-House area on the near west side of Chicago, a community of Italians, Mexicans, Puerto Ricans, and Negroes. In the book, Suttles tries to discover the standards of behavior in an area of high delinquency, and succeeds in doing so. He disproves the idea that slums are totally disorganized, claiming rather there is an attempt to find a moral order to which residents may cling. Suttles says the order produces "ordered segmentation" in a number of social relationships made up of age, sex, ethnic, and territorial units. Not an easy book, but a rewarding one.

Valentine, Charles A., *Culture and Poverty: Critique and Counter-Proposals* (Chicago: University of Chicago Press, 1968), paperback. Oscar Lewis' concept of a "culture of poverty" comes under attack in Valentine's book as a middle-class view of urban poverty which reflects an inability to look at the social structure as it is. Valentine suggests that sociologists ought to study the urban scene on its own terms. He then projects a program which can overcome poverty through "positive discrimination" in favor of the poor. While this is a controversial book, it deserves the praise given it by Ralph Ellison as "one of the most important works of social anthropology to have been published in this country."

d. literature

The city has been a major theme in literature, and ideas about the city can be gleaned from novels, poems, and essays. Images of the city of the future are often contained in the imaginative literature of the day. Most often the city has been portrayed as a blight on the American landscape: American literature has, in general, been pro-nature or pro-rural. Some of the useful literary concepts are:

1. *metaphor:* a figure of speech denoted by a word or phrase used in place of another to suggest a likeness or analogy between them. The city may be used in this sense, or the country.

2. *myth:* the collective belief of a group in a proposition which cannot be proven but which is important in holding the group together.

3. *agrarianism:* the belief that rural life is a superior life and that Americans may have had superior moral values because of a rural background.

4. *image:* a symbolic representation of the reality in such a way that an individual or group may grasp it. Quite often images are metaphors—for example, Chicago, Hog Butcher to the World.

5. *urbanity:* the cluster of traits which seem to be associated with living together in cities.

Teachers and students can read works already assigned in English classes with a view to looking for the author's attitude toward the city or for the images of the city implicitly or explicitly drawn. The novels of Theodore Dreiser, John Dos Passos, James T. Farrell, Frank Norris, Sinclair Lewis, J. D. Salinger, and Philip Roth reflect particular American assumptions about the city. In addition, these books specifically centered upon views of the city may be used:

Cowan, Michael H., *City of the West: Emerson, America, and Urban Metaphor* (New Haven: Yale University Press, 1967). This book is a necessary reference work for delineating the metaphor of the city. The book is wider in scope than the subtitle indicates.

Dunlap, George A., *The City in the American Novel, 1789–1900* (New York: Russell and Russell, 1965). This book correctly points out that the first American novel was written with an urban background. The author has limited his book more than the title would indicate, as the book covers only Eastern cities.

Gelfant, Blanche H., *The American City Novel, 1900–1940* (Norman: University of Oklahoma Press, 1954). Miss Gelfant applies sociological insights to such writers as Dreiser and Dos

Passos. The book nicely complements a course on writers of the period.

Marx, Leo, *The Machine in the Garden* (New York: Oxford University Press, 1964), paperback. Marx's book shows how much our ideas of cities are based upon a view of the good life as a pastoral one. Marx draws heavily from nineteenth-century literary efforts, though he devotes some time to F. Scott Fitzgerald.

Strauss, Anselm L., ed., *The American City: A Sourcebook of Urban Imagery* (Chicago: Aldine, 1968).

Strauss, Anselm L., ed., *Images of the American City* (Glencoe, Ill.: Free Press, 1961). Strauss's books are an attempt to catalog the images of the city. His sources are mainly the reactions of individuals to the cities of their times; he does not rely greatly on imaginative literature.

White, Morton, and Lucia White, *The Intellectual Versus the City: From Thomas Jefferson to Frank Lloyd Wright* (Cambridge, Mass.: Harvard University Press, 1962), Mentor paperback. The Whites focus specifically upon anti-urban sentiment and rely upon thinkers like Emerson, Henry Adams, and Henry James. While this book is difficult, it is useful in providing a long overview.

e. architecture and landscape design

The architectural and design images of the city neatly complement those of city planning and literature. But architecture and design are perhaps more specific and less inclusive, more aesthetic and less earthbound, more visionary and less concerned with mundane details. Again, the visually proficient student may well be stimulated to do original and creative work. Useful concepts are:

1. *city as artifact:* a view of the city as essentially a physical container, with necessary maintenance services, where men live and relate to one another.

2. *structure of a city:* the way a city is organized spatially so as to function and provide the necessary services for the citizens who live in it.

3. *urban form:* the shape of a city because of its structure as perceived by individuals, singly and collectively.

The books previously mentioned, particularly those of John Reps and Anselm Strauss, are applicable here. In addition, these books are recommended:

Andrews, Wayne, *Architecture, Ambition and Americans* (New York: Harper, 1955), Free Press paperback. Andrews tries to show how architecture and social pretensions interact. The book is comprehensive, profusely illustrated, and can be used by better high school students.

Bacon, Edmund N., *Design of Cities* (New York: Viking Press, 1967). Bacon traces the evolution of city design from Greece to the present day, emphasizing form, function, and their interrelation. A useful reference tool for libraries, but too expensive for general use.

Burchard, John, and Albert Bush-Brown, *The Architecture of America: A Social and Cultural History* (Boston: Little, Brown, 1961). A history of architecture authorized by the American Institute of Architects, this is nonetheless a valuable work. An abridged version is available in paperback.

Giedion, Sigfried, *Space, Time, and Architecture* (Cambridge, Mass.: Harvard University Press, 4th ed., 1962). A standard work in architectural history and design, this book should be included as a reference work for students in art, design, and history.

Hirsch, Werner Z., ed., *Urban Life and Form* (New York: Holt, Rinehart and Winston, 1963), paperback. This collection of essays centers upon the design element in urban life and on the connection between form and planning.

Kouwenhoven, John A., *The Arts in Modern Civilization* (Garden City: Doubleday, 1962), Norton paperback. Illustrated and suitable for better high school students. Kouwenhoven weaves technological development and design together in an interesting, understandable way. The book is valuable for its discussion of the balloon frame house and cast-iron fronts. *Made in America* ought to help round out students' general education.

Lynch, Kevin, *The Image of the City* (Cambridge, Mass.: MIT Press, 1960), paperback. This book is a must for a theoretical approach to urban form. Touching on theories of perception, Lynch documents the images of specific cities in the United States. A slim volume for use by advanced students.

Mumford, Lewis, *Art and Technics* (New York: Columbia University Press, 1952), paperback.

Mumford, Lewis, *The Brown Decades: A Study of the Arts in America, 1865–1895* (New York: Dover, 1955), paperback.

Mumford, Lewis, *The City in History* (New York: Harcourt, Brace and World, 1968), paperback.

Mumford, Lewis, *The Culture of Cities* (New York: Harcourt, Brace, 1938).

Mumford, Lewis, *Sticks and Stones: A Study of American Architecture and Civilization* (New York: Dover, 1954), paperback.

Mumford, Lewis, *Technics and Civilization* (New York: Harcourt, Brace, 1934), paperback.

Mumford, Lewis, *The Urban Prospect* (New York: Harcourt, Brace and World, 1968), paperback.

Lewis Mumford stands alone as a theorist on the city. *Technics and Civilization, The Culture of Cities,* and *Sticks and Stones* are seminal works which have influenced the thinkers of the day. They attempt to explore many facets of city life and are wide-ranging—from technology to ideas and back again. *Sticks and Stones* may be used to advantage by good students; it is illustrated and lively. Mumford's speculations and generalizations are especially useful in an inquiry method and a discovery approach.

Scully, Vincent, *American Architecture and Urbanism* (New York: Frederick A. Praeger, 1969). Scully, who teaches at Yale, considers the concept of urbanism in American architectural history. He evaluates architects who have contributed to the urban experience and ties the whole package together neatly. This is an essential book for anyone interested in the American design of cities.

Spreiregen, Paul D., *Urban Design: The Architecture of Towns and Cities* (New York: McGraw-Hill, 1965). A history of urban design which emphasizes principles and contains sketches of what the author considers to be good city design.

Trachtenberg, Alan, *Brooklyn Bridge: Myth and Symbol* (New York: Oxford University Press, 1965). By concentrating on one structure, Trachtenberg has shown how technology and values intermix and how the construction of a bridge can be taken to characterize a society. This is a provocative book for better students.

Tunnard, Christopher, and Henry H. Reed, Jr., *American Skyline: The Growth and Form of Our Cities and Towns* (Boston: Houghton Mifflin, 1955), Mentor paperback.

Tunnard, Christopher, *The City of Man* (New York: Scribner's 1953).

Tunnard, Christopher, *The Modern American City* (Princeton: Van Nostrand, 1968), paperback.

Tunnard was professor of city planning at Yale University; his books are valuable and interesting. *American Skyline* and *The Modern American City* can be used for advanced students. *American Skyline* is primarily a design history of American cities and is organized in a manner that may be useful for students as a counterweight to the conventional organization of political history. *The Modern American City* is a mixture of narrative and documents. It treats of recent city design but goes to the background of American cities.

f. political science

The interest of political scientists in the city as a representative political unit dates back to the beginnings of the discipline. Like the economist and the sociologist, the political scientist views the city as a microcosm where theories of political behavior can be observed in practice. Part of the interest in cities stems from the origin of democracy in the Greek city states, and part from the question of how power is shared and used. Some of the concepts political scientists use in looking at urban centers are:

1. *city:* a corporate body with a legal personality, which historically served as a prototype of the state.

2. *balance of power:* the product of the resolution of conflicting interests in the making of political decisions.

3. *polity:* the formal organization and administration of a group which provides order and allocates resources in keeping with group values.

4. *local political elites:* those people who control wealth and investment, the channels of information, and political control.

The books in this section are of two kinds. The first are theoretically oriented toward political analysis, particularly definition and projection of future trends. The second are more specifically concerned with the city. As in the section on geography, the teacher should also check the publications of the National Council for the Social Studies.

Crick, Bernard, *The American Science of Politics* (Berkeley: University of California Press, 1959). Crick's book, though eleven years old, is a useful summary of the general field.

Lasswell, Harold, *The Future of Political Science* (New York: Atherton Press, 1963). Lasswell has been one of the seminal figures in American political science, and his projections carry the weight of his authority in the field.

Lipset, Seymour Martin, *Political Man* (New York: Doubleday, 1959), paperback. The same holds for Lipset who, though a sociologist, ranges widely into other areas. This book looks at politics as an exercise in socialization.

Riddle, Donald H., and Robert E. Clearly, eds., *Political Science in the Social Studies,* 36th Yearbook, National Council for the Social Studies (Washington, D.C., 1966), paperback. A valuable and necessary reference guide for the social studies teacher.

Sorauf, Francis J., *Political Science: An Informal Overview,* Charles E. Merrill Social Science Seminar Series, Raymond H.

Muessig and Vincent R. Rogers, eds. (Columbus, Ohio: Charles E. Merrill Books, 1965), paperback.

Agger, Robert E., Daniel Goldrich, and Bert E. Swanson, *The Rulers and the Ruled: Political Power and Impotence in American Communities*. (New York: John Wiley, 1964). The authors studied decision-making in four communities between 1945 and 1961 in an effort to discover how political decisions were made and who made them.

Banfield, Edward C., and James Q. Wilson, *City Politics* (Cambridge, Mass.: Harvard University Press and MIT Press, 1963), Vintage paperback. A product of the Joint Center for Urban Studies, this book is a useful discussion of political life in cities.

Bollens, John C., and Henry J. Schmandt, *The Metropolis: Its People, Politics, and Economic Life* (New York: Harper and Row, 1965). This book is interdisciplinary in its approach to decision-making. While only suitable for advanced students, this book ought to be helpful for understanding the interweaving of factors in urban development.

Dahl, Robert, *Who Governs?* (New Haven: Yale University Press, 1961), paperback. Widely acclaimed, this book is regarded as the best study of local political power. Dahl's findings suggest that there is no one political elite but rather a number of elites which operate in different areas and which compete and conflict with each other. These findings, although questioned by some, have become orthodoxy in community studies.

Greer, Scott, *The Emerging City* (New York: Free Press, 1962).

Greer, Scott, *Metropolitics: A Study of Political Culture* (New York: John Wiley, 1963). Scott Greer has been one of the political scientists most actively involved in urban studies. His work is stimulating and well written, thoughtful and rewarding. *The Emerging City* attempts a kind of interdisciplinary analysis that makes sense and is not filled with technical jargon.

Hyman, Herbert H., *Political Socialization: A Study in the Psychology of Political Behavior* (New York: Free Press, 1959), paperback. Hyman focuses on how children and adults learn political behavior, how they gain insights, understandings, and values. Recommended for teachers who are concerned with the dynamics of this process.

Williams, Oliver P., and Charles R. Adrian, *Four Cities: A Study in Comparative Policy Making* (Philadelphia: University of Pennsylvania Press, 1963). Surveying the decision-making efforts of four communities, this book offers case studies of problems facing political leadership in cities.

g. economics

The economist has been a late-comer to the study of the city, but has found that, in many ways, the major problems of cities lie on an economic axis. Economic insights are valuable in seeing the reasons behind city development and in relating the city to the larger society. While not all vital economic principles appear in the city, enough do so that the city can be used as a unit to illustrate economic principles.

1. *city:* a matrix of business and industry where the nation's economy is collectively put together.

2. *city:* an economic unit where market conditions apply, where *limited resources* are allocated by these market conditions, where there is *division of labor* and provisions for the *production* and *distribution* of goods, where there is a balance of trade with other areas which may result in *deficit* or *surplus* accounts, where investment may have a *multiplier effect.*

3. *city government:* a firm which makes economic decisions in order to maximize benefits from limited resources. It may prosper or it may go bankrupt. Its voters are customers and may compel the firm to do business at a constant loss.

The following books are divided into two groups. The first are concerned with economic theory, the second with the economic aspects of the city. The teacher can also use the materials offered by the National Council for the Social Studies, the appropriate pamphlets in the Oxford Social Studies Series, the D. C. Heath

Studies in Economics Series, as well as those offered by the Committee for Economic Development. The latter's *Economic Literacy for Americans* (New York, 1962) contains an excellent bibliography of inexpensive materials suitable for high school use. Also useful is the Committee's *Economics Education in the Schools* (New York, 1961). Other books are:

Boulding, Kenneth, *Principles of Economic Policy* (Englewood Cliffs: Prentice-Hall, 1968). Boulding is one of the most imaginative of the present generation of economists who can speak to a general public.

Galbraith, John Kenneth, *Economics and the Art of Controversy* (New York: Vintage Books, 1959), paperback. Galbraith writes extremely well. This paperback may be used to advantage by advanced students.

Heilbroner, Robert L., *The Making of Economic Society* (Englewood Cliffs: Prentice-Hall, 1962), paperback. Heilbroner's writings are clear, well reasoned, and based on historical perspective.

Stead, William H., *Natural Resource Use in Our Economy* (New York: Joint Council on Economic Education, 1960). This short pamphlet is inexpensive and is simple enough for average students. The concepts used here are necessary for a foundation of economic knowledge.

Wingo, Lowdon, Jr., and Harvey Perloff, eds., *Issues in Urban Economics* (Baltimore: Johns Hopkins Press, 1968), paperback. The result of eight years of work by the Committee on Urban Economics of Resources for the Future, this book attempts to delineate the important problems in urban economics. For advanced students, but also a useful reference tool for the teacher.

Abrams, Charles, *Man's Struggle for Shelter in an Urbanizing World* (Cambridge, Mass.: MIT Press, 1966), paperback. Abrams, a well-known urbanologist, looks at shelter and urban land use throughout the world. His book is nontechnical and, while limited to housing, is an excellent introduction to part of the economic problems of the cities.

Thompson, Wilbur R., *A Preface to Urban Economics* (Baltimore: Johns Hopkins Press, 1965), paperback. Despite its title, this book is not for the uninitiated. It does consider urban growth based upon inter-urban and extra-urban and employment analysis. This is a good theoretical place to begin if the teacher has a solid economics base.

Chapter III

A BASIC TEACHER REFERENCE LIBRARY

The concern with urban problems has led to a flood of materials of varying quality. While historians have been thinking in terms of urban history at least since the time of Channing, the development of a discipline of urban history has been largely the work of the present generation. This means that there is available a large amount of recent material.

Books

This section consists of general works of value to teachers and students.

1. Glaab, Charles N., and A. Theodore Brown, *A History of Urban America* (New York: Macmillan, 1967), paperback. The central theme of this book is that "From the beginning, the ten-

sions and impulses of America's cities had given direction to the growth of the nation." Especially strong on the nineteenth century, this general survey is informative and interpretive, and is arranged topically. It does not go beyond World War II.

2. Green, Constance McLaughlin, *The Rise of Urban America* (New York: Harper and Row, 1965), paperback. A good general survey, not particularly interpretive. Suitable for the upper-level high school student.

3. McKelvey, Blake, *The Emergence of Metropolitan America: 1915–1966,* (New York: Free Press, 1968). This is probably the most detailed study of this period of urbanization in the United States. A valuable reference source because of its detail and extensive bibliography, but probably unsuited to general class use.

4. McKelvey, Blake, *The Urbanization of America, 1860–1915* (New Brunswick, N.J.: Rutgers University Press, 1963). This is the first volume of McKelvey's two-volume study of American city growth. It examines the development of cities and towns as well as the economic conditions which contributed to this development. The book was one of the first to deal with pre–World War I urban forces in America. While there is some description of the city as a social organism, the main thrust is factual and bibliographic.

5. McKelvey, Blake, *The City in American History* (New York: Barnes and Noble, 1969). This is Volume IX of Barnes and Noble's Historical Problems: Studies and Documents series. As such it is a survey of city growth through analysis and primary sources. The collection is an excellent one which ought to be in a basic library of urban history. It is suitable for students as well as teachers.

6. Mowry, George E., *The Urban Nation: 1920–1960* (New York: Hill and Wang, 1965), paperback. Mowry traces the impact of mass production, mass consumption, and urbanization during this period, and discusses the effect of foreign affairs on the domestic scene. There is little theoretical discussion of the

problems of urbanization and urban development. Suitable for high school students as a supplementary text.

7. Schlesinger, Arthur M., Sr., *The Rise of the City: 1878– 1898* (New York: Macmillan, 1933). One of thirteen volumes in A History of American Life series edited by Schlesinger and Dixon Ryan Fox. This pioneer effort in the field of urban history still has value if one has access to the other books in the series. Using the idea of city growth as his theme, Schlesinger had few urban studies to guide him in his work and hence is somewhat more general than McKelvey.

8. Weber, Adna F., *The Growth of Cities in the Nineteenth Century* (Ithaca: Cornell University Press, 1963), paperback. Weber's book was first published in 1899 and was remarkable at the time for its sophisticated statistical analysis of city growth. It still is valuable for the present-day student, both as a reference work and as a view of past historical study.

9. Jaher, Frederick C., ed., *The Age of Industrialism in America* (New York: Free Press, 1968), paperback. A collection of essays that combines history, economics, and political science. The essays cover the period from 1870 to 1940 and are on such diverse topics as changing social structures and cultural values, urban elites in Denver and San Francisco, and a comparison of the World's Fairs of 1876, 1893, and 1933. The above-average student will be interested.

10. Warner, Sam Bass, Jr., *The Private City: Philadelphia in Three Periods of Its Growth* (Philadelphia: University of Pennsylvania Press, 1968). This book is included because it presents a conceptual basis for examining the American city through the example of Philadelphia. Warner studies Philadelphia in the years 1770–1780, 1830–1860, and 1920–1930. His conclusions are that American failure to meet urban problems is historical and revolves around the failure of the idea of community to contain "privatism" and the search for wealth.

11. Schnore, Leo F., *The Urban Scene: Human Ecology and Demography* (New York: Free Press, 1965). Schnore is an in-

fluential sociologist who has contributed to the theory of urban and suburban growth. In these essays he illustrates his ideas by showing three different patterns of racial, economic, and educational development in American cities in the period from 1950–1960.

12. Schnore, Leo F., *Social Science and the City: A Survey of Urban Research* (New York: Frederick A. Praeger, 1968), paperback. Another of Schnore's works which is suitable for use because of its theoretical and bibliographical material. Like Schnore's other works, not for the average student.

13. Schnore, Leo F., and Philip M. Hauser, eds., *The Study of Urbanization* (New York: John Wiley, 1965). Schnore teams here with Philip M. Hauser, a University of Chicago sociologist, to look at the process of urbanization from the standpoint of five academic disciplines: history, geography, political science, sociology, and economics. The essays are not easy but, like Schnore's other works, contain valuable theoretical and bibliographical materials which can be used for further reading and for developing projects.

14. Meadows, Paul, and Ephriam H. Mizruchi, eds., *Urbanism, Urbanization and Change: Comparative Perspectives* (Reading, Mass.: Addison-Wesley, 1969). Another collection of theoretical essays which attempts to define and classify urban phenomena —and another difficult book.

15. Burchard, John, and Oscar Handlin, eds., *The Historian and the City* (Cambridge, Mass.: MIT Press and Harvard University Press, 1963), paperback. A noted historian and an architect have collaborated on this book on the problems of urban history. Essential as a starting point for those interested in theory and in what historians have done in the past. Again, for advanced students.

16. Hirsch, Werner Z., ed., *Urban Life and Form* (New York: Holt, Rinehart and Winston, 1963), paperback. This collection of essays contains, among other excellent ones, an article by Rich-

ard Wade which puts fórth a strong claim for the primacy of cities as a cause of innovation in American life.

17. Smith, Wilson, ed., *Cities of Our Past and Present* (New York: John Wiley, 1964). Another useful collection of documents, Smith's book has more material on contemporary problems than does Glaab's (following).

18. Glaab, Charles N., ed., *The American City: A Documentary History* (Homewood, Ill.: Dorsey Press, 1963), paperback. This collection of documents on the city in America is quite strong on the nineteenth century, as is Glaab's text. This book could serve as a primary source for class research.

19. Weimer, David R., ed., *City and Country in America* (New York: Appleton-Century-Crofts, 1962), paperback. This document collection is concerned with visual elements and the distinction between urban and rural landscapes.

20. Callow, Alexander B., Jr., ed., *American Urban History* (New York: Oxford University Press, 1969), paperback. An excellent collection of interpretive articles. Organized chronologically, it contains a number of theoretical as well as factual essays.

21. Wakstein, Allen, ed., *The Urbanization of America: A Reader* (Boston: Houghton Mifflin, 1970), paperback. A collection of interpretive essays of the same high quality as Callow's. The organization is also similar to Callow's. The book should be useful to the teacher and the advanced student.

22. Jones, Emrys, *Towns and Cities* (New York: Oxford University Press, 1966), paperback. A short, well-written, and interesting history, suitable for the general student. Written by an English geographer, it treats both pre-industrial and modern cities and urbanization as well as social problems.

23. Senesh, Lawrence, *Our Working World: Cities at Work* (Chicago: Science Research Associates, 1967). This resource unit concentrates on the economic side of city life (Senesh has been working on putting economics into the curriculum on the elementary level). Probably too simple for high school classes, but it might be useful as an introduction to the city as an economic unit.

24. Wade, Richard C., Howard B. Wilder, and Louise C. Wade, *A History of the United States* (Boston: Houghton Mifflin, 1966). This textbook was written by an urban historian and the book thus concentrates heavily on urban history. Recommended as an alternate or primary text.

25. Peattie, Roderick E., *The City* (New York: H. Schuman, 1952). This is part of the Man and His World series designed for junior high and high school students. A fairly easy book which may be used as an introductory volume for a unit on the city.

26. Thomas, Eleanor, with Ernest W. Tiegs and Fay Adams, *Your Town and Cities* (Boston: Ginn, 1967). This elementary text may be useful for a slow reader.

27. Washington Square Press has a series of inexpensive paperbacks issued under the title Problems of American Society. Some of the books appropriate for student use are: *The Negro in the City, The City as a Community, City Government, Slums, The Traffic Jam, Air and Water Pollution,* and *The People of the City.* These are published especially for secondary schools with editorial assistance by the Curriculum Committee of the Trenton, New Jersey, public schools.

28. The Library of Urban Affairs, Front and Brown Street, Riverside, New Jersey 08075, is a book club that specializes in books dealing with urban affairs—planning, design, environment, economics, and government as well as history. The Library offers a chance to purchase books of general interest and importance at a reduced rate. Recommended for the teacher who wishes to build his personal library and for the institution which wants to build a small, select library in the subject area.

Films

This section contains a number of films which can be purchased or rented and which are appropriate for class use.

1. *Population Ecology* (Encyclopedia Britannica Films, 1963). This film is peripheral to the study of the city, but it does consider natural balance and the population explosion—problems which are exaggerated in the city.

2. *Portrait of the Inner City* (McGraw-Hill Textfilms, 1965). Part of the Teaching the Disadvantaged Child series, this film discusses growing up in the slums and portrays both the strengths and weaknesses that this experience provides.

3. *What Is a City?* (Bailey Films, 1959). A very elementary film which shows how cities meet the needs of people, what work cities perform, and how they grow and develop.

4. *The Living City* (Encyclopedia Britannica Films, 1953). The object of this film is to explain urban renewal and to stress the need for proper land use. The film does advocate urban redevelopment in a more simple fashion than more recent ones do.

5. *Megalopolis—Cradle of the Future* (Encyclopedia Britannica Films, 1963). This film shows life and problems in the urbanized Northeast seaboard from Boston to Washington, D.C., and makes a plea for a better planning and organization of American cities.

6. *Metropolis* (Encyclopedia Britannica Films, 1963). The film discusses ways of organizing city government and was part of the television course "The Structure and Function of American Government," presented on NBC. Suitable for advanced classes.

7. *The Restless City Speaks* (Wayne State University, 1958). This film tries to show the causes and effects of complex living in a vast urban area. Suitable for less advanced students.

8. America's Crises series (Indiana University, 1966). These films were shown on National Educational Television and are fairly sophisticated but extremely well done.

a. *The Rise of New Towns.* This film describes the development of totally planned communities, such as Foster City and Irvine, California. Planners, government officials, and others discuss the implications of the New Towns movement.

b. *Crime in the Streets.* This film portrays the difficulties of the police and the problems of rehabilitating the criminal.

c. *The Cities and the Poor.* (2 parts). This film studies the problem of the urban poor, the attempt by governmental and private agencies to help, and the rise of militant groups.

9. Lewis Mumford on the City series (Sterling Education Films, 1963). The leading American thinker on the city offers his ideas on a variety of topics. This is a must for students, though only the more perceptive will fully understand and appreciate Mumford.

a. *The City and Its Region.* Mumford here examines the relation between city and countryside and explains how balance can be maintained.

b. *The City and the Future.* Mumford offers a choice between low-grade urban sprawl and new regional cities, and suggests ways to achieve the latter, which he says is the focus of man's highest achievement.

c. *The City—Cars or People?* Mumford suggests how cities can be made livable and yet allow people to get from place to place easier.

d. *The City—Heaven and Hell.* Mumford's theme in this film is the historical background of cities. His theories of city growth and development are presented and explained.

e. *The City as Man's Home.* Mumford takes on the social problems created by slums, high-rise housing complexes, and suburbia. He indicates how lower standards of living can be improved through design and planning.

f. *The Heart of the City.* Mumford describes the sterility and dullness of the central city and suggests ways and means of improving it.

10. *Town Planning* (International Film Bureau, 1959). This older film shows what properly zoned business, industrial, and residential areas should look like, and indicates how a city may be replanned in a nontechnical fashion.

11. *A Community Project* (Av-Ed Educational Films, no date). This film deals with the need for cooperation in the community in order to obtain better services and living conditions. It can be used for primary as well as junior and senior high schools.

12. *It Takes Everybody to Build This Land* (Encyclopedia Britannica Films, 1952). Like the preceding film, this one emphasizes the interdependent nature of the city.

13. *Don't Crowd Me* (International Communication Films, 1969). This short film is concerned with the impact of population pressures in the city on the creation of stress and anxiety. It is useful in that the problem of crowding has become an ecological concern at the present time. Suitable for the average student.

14. *Overlord in the Cities* (International Communication Films, 1969). A short, simple film which concentrates on urban decay and the strategies of urban leaders. Useful to introduce a discussion of contemporary problems.

15. *1877–Today: Freedom Movement* (McGraw-Hill Textfilms, no date). Third in a series entitled A History of the Negro in America, the film gives a quick overview of the civil rights movement and looks at urban problems as well. It tries to cover too much in too little a time and thus tends to oversimplify. But it is good as an introduction to the whole problem of the black man in the cities, particularly for average students.

16. *Felicia* (University of California, Berkeley, Educational Media Center, 1965). The life of a black girl in Watts is shown in a documentary to illustrate the problem of a segregated community. The technique should involve the student and help him understand the difficulty of slum life.

17. *The Future and the Negro* (Indiana University, 1965). This is part of the History of the Negro People series done by National Educational Television. Ossie Davis is the narrator, and the main body of the film is taken up with a panel discussion. Excellent, but too long (75 minutes) to fit the usual class pattern.

18. *The House of Man—Our Changing Environment* (Encyclopedia Britannica Films, 1965). The ecological emphasis is obvious here in the portrayal of wasted resources in cities and country. Water and air pollution are discussed. Suitable for the average student.

19. *Challenge of Urban Renewal* (Encyclopedia Britannica Films, 1966). This was originally an NBC film called *America the Beautiful*. Like the preceding film, this one castigates urban decay and suburban sprawl. It also contains a plan for rebuilding American cities. Simple enough for the average student.

20. *The New Age of Architecture* (Fortune Magazine Films Department, 1958). Architects, city planners, and builders discuss the aesthetic, moral, and economic implications of architectural design on urban and suburban development. This film is more suited to design-oriented students who have some background in the area, but it can be used as informational and introductory material for the general student.

21. *Population Patterns in the United States* (Coronet Films, 1961). This film discusses the patterns of settlement which were obvious at the beginning of the decade of the sixties, including data on life span, infant mortality rates, immigration trends, as well as movements to the city and from East to West. Basic for the average student.

22. *Balkanization of Urban Life* (Encyclopedia Britannica Films, 1963). Arthur Naftalin, mayor of Minneapolis at that time, discussed the problem of effective government in the city where competing and overlapping governmental units make simple problems difficult. One of the NBC series in Structure and Function of American Government. Aimed at the college level, but suitable for upper-level high school students.

23. *The Changing City* (Coronet Films, 1963). Essentially a look at how cities grow and what effect this growth has on their inhabitants, including the implications of land use and urban renewal. Usable for all high school students.

24. *Crime in the Cities* (Encyclopedia Britannica Films, 1966). This film examines the connection between prejudice, segregation, and crime as well as the distinctions between crimes against persons and property. Timely and useful in current problems classes.

25. *Bert* (New York University, 1965). Bert is a New York City taxi driver who discusses his life, problems, and hopes. The film gives a personal view of the city as seen by a worker in it and ought to appeal to those from urban areas for whom the taxi is a familiar sight.

26. *Delineating the Area* (Iowa State University, 1962). This film discusses the problem of competing units attempting to obtain industries for their towns. Instead of piecemeal competition,

the film argues for a development concept based on a unit con-
sisting of a central city, its satellite towns, and surrounding rural
areas. This is particularly appropriate for those students in rural
or small-town areas which are struggling to survive and grow.

27. *The First Mile Up* (McGraw-Hill Textfilms, 1963).
The first mile up is polluted, and the extent of pollution as well
as possible cures for it are the topics of this film which is suitable
for the average student.

28. *How to Look at a City* (Indiana University, 1964). Eugene
Raskin, noted architect and author, discusses the standards used
by architects and city planners to judge the quality of city neighborhoods. These standards include human scale, density, and
variety. The film is a production of National Educational Television and is part of their The Metropolis—Creator or Destroyer
series. Not an easy film, but essential to courses on the city.

29. *The Persistent Seed* (Hank Newenhouse, 1963). A poetic
treatment of how nature persists despite man's attempts to alter
and shape it. The camera views shrubs and grass growing in very
unlikely places, and in so doing comments on the values of modern
society. The optimism here may be a useful antidote to the pessimism found in most films on air pollution. Also useful in suggesting images of the city, the major one being the country in
the city.

30. *Smalltown USA* (Encyclopedia Britannica Films, 1965).
This film looks at four representative small towns which are
vanishing because of changing industrial patterns, migration to
larger urban areas, and automation. Useful for students who live
in cities or small towns, because it shows alternative ways of life.

31. *The Troubled Cities* (Indiana University, 1966). One in
the National Educational Television series on America's Crises.
The emphasis is on urban problems.

32. *Kazin: The Writer and the City* (Chelsea House, 1969).
This film examines the city as an aesthetic force in literature from
Whitman and Melville to Norman Mailer. For the more sophisti-
cated student, but well worth the effort for any student. It is par-

ticularly good for an approach which attempts to combine literature and history; it offers much on images of the city.

33. *John Kenneth Galbraith: The Idea of a City* (Chelsea
House, 1969). Galbraith, the noted economist, traces the historic
transition from the pre-industrial to the industrial city in terms
of economic efficiency. He tends to take an organic view of the
city, but this does not detract from an essentially stimulating effort.
Suitable for sophisticated and advanced students.

34. *The Newcomers* (Methodist Board of Missions, 1963).
This film concerns the immigration of a rural family to the city
and the problems it encounters in the move. Since it was produced
by a church group, it naturally emphasizes how the church as an
institution can help in the situation. An accompanying discussion
guide outlines a program designed to aid newcomers. Suitable for
junior and senior high school students, and useful for inner-city
children who may have had the same experience.

35. *Metroplex Assembly* series (Washington University, 1963).
This series is based upon the experience of migrants to St. Louis
and the impact of the city on the migrants and vice versa. Five
films:

a. *The New Immigrants.* The background of the immigrant
is explored and related to the backgrounds of earlier ones.

b. *The First Hurdle: Jobs.* The primary economic problem
of employment is the topic of this film. The disadvantages of
the rural migrant in training and experience are shown.

c. *A Place to Live.* The housing available to the migrant is
likely to be in the decaying central city.

d. *Learning for a Purpose.* The film deals with the kind of
education necessary to help the immigrant fit into the city.

e. *In Whose Steps?* This is primarily about the Negro immigrant and his special problems.

f. *The Balance Sheet.* The concluding film sums up the
assets and liabilities and indicates what the future may bring.

36. *The Black Eye* (New Detroit, Inc., 1968). The producers
of the film are black nonprofessionals who look at Detroit through

the eyes of natives. Suitable for black and white students alike, though it may be more eye-opening for whites.

37. *The Green City* (Stuart Finley, 1963). The International Film Festival awarded this film first prize in 1963. It describes the destruction of green spaces by city development. An excellent film, and aesthetically pleasing. Good for the student who is interested in films.

38. *Superfluous People* (U.S. Department of Health, Education and Welfare, 1962). This CBS documentary touches on the lives of people who cannot or have not adjusted to the city. Depressing, but perhaps necessary.

39. *Form, Design, and the City* (American Institute of Architects, 1961). This film shows how planning has affected the growth of Philadelphia from the seventeenth century to 1960. Sophisticated, but suitable for senior high school students.

40. *One Dimension . . . Two Dimension . . . Three Dimension . . . Four!* (Modern Talking Picture Service, 1967). Rod Serling narrates this film produced for the Department of Housing and Urban Development. The subject is the need for planning in American cities, illustrated by the planning experiences of Chicago and Norfolk. In addition, the film suggests the shape of the future. Sophisticated, but useful.

41. *America's Crisis: The Community* (Indiana University, no date). This film examines two communities, Provincetown, Massachusetts, and San Jose, California. Provincetown wishes to keep its tradition in the face of an influx of tourists on Cape Cod, while San Jose wants to build a tradition in an area where most residents are strangers.

Filmstrips

These are sometimes more suitable than films as they can be used more flexibly.

1. *City and State* (New York Times Sound Filmstrip). The subject is the press of problems on local and state governments. Aimed at junior and senior high school students.

2. *Problems of Cities* (New York Times Sound Filmstrip). The problems treated are urban renewal, transportation tie-ups, educational defects, high tax rates, and high crime rates. Suited to junior and senior high school students.

3. *Ghettos of America* (Warren Schloat Productions, Inc.). The packet consists of four color filmstrips and four LP records. The two areas studied are Harlem and Watts. The multi-media approach is effective here, and the level is simple enough even for slow students.

4. *Landforms and Man* (McGraw-Hill). This is one of eight in a World Geography series. The emphasis is on man's response to natural conditions—his ability to adapt himself and his tools. Appropriate for junior and senior high school students.

5. *Village, Town, and City* (McGraw-Hill). Another in the World Geography series, this filmstrip concentrates on dwelling in groups. Understandable for the average student.

6. *Ecology and Man* (McGraw-Hill). There are three filmstrips in this set. The first defines ecosystems; the second shows five ecosystems and their structures; and the third shows applied ecology. The last is most appropriate to urban history, though the other two are excellent. High school and adult level.

7. *The Changing City* (Churchill Films). The subject in this filmstrip is the advantage of city living for economic, social, and cultural benefits. It also portrays city growth from the nineteenth century to the present day, looking at planning, the suburbs, and the central city. For the average student.

8. *Community Planning* (Sendak for the University of Georgia). A Carnegie grant helped develop this filmstrip which considers the planning of cities in the Northeast, Mid-Atlantic, South, Midwest, and West. The filmstrip covers the entire span of American history from the seventeenth century to the 1960's. A useful supplement to Reps's book, it should help dispel the notion that planning is only a modern invention.

9. *New York State* series (McGraw-Hill). This set has three filmstrips suitable for a course emphasizing urban history. These

three are *Colonial New York, New York's Communities,* and *New York City: Fabulous Metropolis.* While New York is not a typical state nor New York City a typical city, they are important examples.

The U.S. Department of Housing and Urban Development has developed a bibliography on films, filmstrips, slides, and audiotapes. The title of the bibliography is *Urban Outlook.* Available from the Superintendent of Documents, U.S. Government Printing Office, Washington, D.C. It includes sixteen subject categories:

a. Architecture and Design
b. Citizen Participation and Community Action
c. Building Codes and Standards
d. Concept of the City
e. Fair Housing and the Concept of Race
f. Homebuilding and Ownership
g. New Towns
h. Open Space and Beautification
i. Pollution
j. Public Housing and Housing for the Elderly
k. Research and Engineering
l. Sanitation and Pest Control
m. Social Problems of Poverty
n. Transportation
o. Urban Planning and Land Use
p. Urban Renewal and Rehabilitation

The most useful sections are a, d, e, g, h, i, o, and p. The materials listed are low cost or free.

Games

The production and sale of "serious" games has increased tremendously. Those listed below touch in some way on the community and its problems.

1. "City I" (Urban Systems Simulation, Washington Center for Metropolitan Studies, 1717 Massachusetts Ave., N.W., Washington, D.C. 20036). The game of "City I" involves the social,

economic, and political relationships of an urban center and its three suburbs. Sophisticated, and recommended for senior high students and adults.

2. "Disaster" (Academic Games Project, Center for Study of Social Organization of Schools, Johns Hopkins University, 3505 N. Charles St., Baltimore, Md. 21218). A natural disaster hits a local community. The simulation shows how a community can cope with the problems engendered by such a disaster. This game is simpler than "City I" and can be used on the junior high school level.

3. "Economic Decision Games" (Science Research Associates, 259 E. Erie St., Chicago, Ill. 60611). There are eight games in the set, two of which can be used in a course on urban development. These are *The Community* and *Scarcity and Allocation.* All of the games are good for developing economic concepts, however, and are suited to senior high students.

4. "Plans" (Project SIMILE, Western Behavioral Science Institute, 1150 Silverado, La Jolla, Calif. 92037). Participants take the roles of various interest groups. The object is to secure maximum advantage for your own group. While this game can be used at lower levels, it is most appropriate for senior high school students.

5. "Poor People's Choice" (Academic Games Project, Center for the Study of Social Organization of Schools, Johns Hopkins University, 3505 N. Charles St., Baltimore, Md. 21218). This simulation, originally entitled "Ghetto," puts the players in the position of residents in an inner-city slum. The object is to attain economic and social mobility despite the handicaps of the environment. The game can be used in classes from the junior high level on up.

6. "Region" (Urban Systems Simulation, Washington Center for Metropolitan Studies, 1717 Massachusetts Ave., N.W., Washington, D.C. 20036). In a growing urban area, the players are confronted with the need to make economic and political choices to solve the problems of the present and to assure future growth. For senior high school students.

7. "Sunshine" (Interact, P.O. Box 262, Lakeside, Calif. 92040). The players assume the role of various racial groups in an imaginary city and work out problems. This game is more simple than the others and can be used on the elementary level. It is useful for teaching problems of minorities as well as urban development.

8. R. S. Meier's "Game Procedure in the Simulation of Cities," in J. L. Duhl, ed., *The Urban Condition* (New York: Basic Books, 1963), discusses the why and hows of setting up an urban game. An imaginative and innovative teacher could use Meier's suggestions.

9. A. G. Feldt's "The Cornell Land Use Game" (Miscellaneous Paper No. 3, mimeographed, Center for Housing and Environmental Studies, Division of Urban Studies, Cornell University, 1964), sets out a rather complex game which might be suited to the advanced student.

10. John L. Taylor and Richard N. Maddison, in "A Land Use Gaming Simulation," *Urban Affairs Quarterly,* III (June 1968), 37–51, have created a game which, while sophisticated and British, could be adapted for advanced students.

11. "City II" (Urban Systems Simulation, Washington Center for Metropolitan Studies, 1717 Massachusetts Ave., N.W., Washington, D.C. 20036). A revised version of "City I," which was based on Feldt's "Cornell Land Use Game." "City II" attempts to engender a social conscience in the player and adds a construction industry and an adequate transportation system to the economic sector. It also has additional political jurisdictions. The University of Maryland has a contract from the U.S. Office of Education to develop a version of "City II" for high school use. The program was tested in selected high schools in the Washington, D.C., area beginning in the fall of 1969 and should soon be available for general use.

12. "Inner City Planning" (Creative Studies, for Macmillan, 866 Third Ave., New York, New York 10022). This simulation game, available in pocket form, is designed to help conceptualize

the problem of a blighted area—"James Park" in "Port City." Specially concerned with urban renewal, the game can be played by twenty to forty players who form six groups with a stake in urban renewal in "Port City." The data are taken from experiences in Boston. Suitable for high school students as well as adults.

The Foreign Policy Association, 345 East 46th Street, New York, New York 10017, has a *New Dimensions* booklet on "Simulation Games for the Social Studies Classroom." *Social Education* for February 1969 has a list of games and organizations developing games, which was abstracted from the above booklet. Two newsletters are also available. The "Gaming Newsletter," published by the National Gaming Council and available from the Washington Center for Metropolitan Studies, 1717 Massachusetts Avenue, N.W., Washington, D.C. 20036, costs $4.50 per year for four to six issues. The Western Behavioral Sciences Institute, 1150 Silverado, La Jolla, California 92037, publishes an "Occasional Newsletter" which costs $5.00 per year.

Chapter IV

TEACHING GOALS AND METHODS

In including urban themes in American history courses, the teacher can use these goals as guideposts to direct himself and his students:

1. To show that the city has always been part of the American experience and scene.

2. To show that Americans, because they have always lived in cities, have thought about what they want these cities to be, that there has always been an image of the city or a plan of the city.

3. To show that what we regard as urban problems now share much in common with urban problems in the past, that living in cities always creates certain demands for necessary services.

    a. The city has always had a problem of crime and police.

    b. The city has always had difficulties securing water, sewage, and utilities.

c. The city has always had problems with transportation.

d. The city has always had problems with public health.

e. The city has always had problems with heterogeneous populations.

4. To show how the city has been a vital force in the life of the larger American society, and how the drive for reform and improvement has originated in the city.

a. The city was the area where opposition to the British colonial system was most apparent.

b. The city was the area where political institutions such as the party originated.

c. The city was the area where the Progressive movement first became involved in reform.

d. The city was the area where civil rights groups—the NAACP, the Urban League, and others—originated.

e. The city has been the area where significant educational programs have been developed.

f. The city was the area from which came the capital, labor, and economic knowhow to develop America's industrial might.

g. The city has been the area from which significant cultural achievement has come. It has been the home of the poet, the artist, and the writer.

5. To show how the city has been a normal part of the American experience—not an abnormal part, that living in cities is not against the American tradition, that farmers are not necessarily God's chosen people.

a. The frontier was not settled first by farmers who then built cities; often cities preceded farmers to an area.

b. The settlement of the continent was made by persons who believed that the best way of life was in communities, not as individuals scattered over the landscape.

c. The developers of the United States not only thought of it as a nation with agricultural bounty but as a nation of cities. (For example, Benjamin Franklin and his views of Philadelphia.)

d. Even sections of the country thought of as primarily agricultural had spokesmen who talked in terms of regional cities. (William Gilpin in the West [Kansas City], and George Fitzhugh in the South.)

e. Those spokesmen who opposed cities in America opposed them often for specific reasons peculiar to their own times. Jefferson was anti-city in part because of the real health hazards of the eighteenth-century city. Persons who opposed the city in the latter part of the nineteenth century did so because of anti-immigrant feeling.

f. The significant migration within the United States has been from farm to city, and the normal expectation of many farm boys has been city life. As Fred Shannon has said, for every person who moved to the frontier, twenty moved to the city.

6. To show that the city has been called upon as the place where the pressing problems of American society have had to be solved.

a. The city was the place where the majority of immigrants from Europe were to be fitted into American society. It was here that the immigrant either became Americanized or came to live in a pluralistic society. The city is where the solutions of a heterogeneous society had to be found.

b. The city was the place where the racial problems of America were conspicuous and where they had to be faced. The problem of achieving equality for the black man became serious for most white Americans only when the black man was concentrated in cities and developed a significant political base from which to operate.

c. The city was the place where poverty could most readily be seen and where the problem could not be ignored. The relative isolation of farms served to hide rural poverty, as Michael Harrington has shown.

7. To help the student understand that urban life can be satisfying and that the future of the city can be good by introduc-

ing him to the advantages and possibilities of urban life, past and present.

    a. Contrast the quality of rural and urban life. Why does Franklin choose to live in Philadelphia or Jefferson in Paris? What is the average man doing in the city and in the country?

    b. Demonstrate that wealthy persons who have had the means to choose have had country estates but have also lived in cities. This has been true from the time of the aristocracy of South Carolina to Nelson Rockefeller today.

  8. To interrelate the social sciences by emphasizing the insights of economics, political science, and sociology in the understanding of urban life.

  9. To increase appreciation of the way of life of people throughout the world by showing the similarities of problems in cities outside the United States, as well as by showing how these cities have coped with their problems, some even more successfully than in this country.

Daily Planning: Some Specific Examples

There are several ways of introducing urban history materials into the curriculum. In some schools an urban history course may be offered as an elective along with other social studies courses. This ideal situation is unlikely to be found in many schools, particularly since the pressures to include more and more diverse material seem to be increasing. Another alternative —though not so satisfactory—is the use of an urban history week or month, similar to a Negro history week or month, during which urban history is emphasized. Special projects, illustrative materials, student discussions, research assignments, and other techniques would center on urban themes. If the teacher has an advanced class or one which employs independent study, he can suggest the possibility that urban study may have escaped the student's notice.

Under ordinary circumstances, the teacher is not likely to be fortunate enough to have the kinds of opportunities suggested above, and will probably have to weave urban materials into the American history course. In this case the teacher can use his own ingenuity and that of his students to emphasize at different eras in history the development of cities and of varying life styles in cities. In all cases, the consideration of urban life ought to enrich the courses that already exist or are formed.

While there are no special techniques which are appropriate to urban history, some methods can be used with particular effectiveness. Methods that have already been used, such as discussions, developmental lessons, committee work, dramatization, and audiovisual materials, lend themselves nicely to urban history. Several other methods may also be used. One is class preparation of visual materials about urban forms. Students can do a variety of things, such as finding out about the original plans of their own city, town, or neighborhood. These plans then can be produced for visual display by the student or teacher, either on cardboard for bulletin boards or on transparencies for overhead projectors. The original plans can be compared with the city, town, or section as it has developed. Students who have an interest in photography might well prepare a photographic essay on the local community. These pictures can then be analyzed to determine which elements of the community are old, which are new, and to determine the kind of visual image the city presents. Older histories of the community can be used to compare past pictures with present ones. Finally, the local community offers rich possibilities in the area of research. Local history is intimately tied to urban development, and in many areas local history has not been written. Students can gain a sense of discovery in delving into their community's past, especially since many historical resources are still available.

To illustrate how urban history can be integrated into an American history course, let us take a hypothetical American community in the Midwest and suggest some possibilities. The community can be studied in its own terms. When was it founded and why? Was it developed by railroad or by trading entrepreneurs? Was it a commercial center based upon local trade or a transportation center based upon certain natural advantages?

Why did this town prosper when other similar ones failed? (One of the most profitable areas of local history is the study of those communities that didn't make it. This helps to dispel the notion that physical advantage or some other kind of natural determinism is the only crucial factor in city development.) When did the city provide police and fire services on an organized, nonvolunteer basis? When did the city provide water, sewage, and other services? How does the provision of these services compare in time with other cities? Who controlled the cities, and how and why did this control shift from party to party and elite to elite? How does this compare with other cities? When did the city begin to develop modern planning and why? When did the city begin to zone and restrict land usage?

Outside of itself, the community can also be involved in the study of national events. Taking the hypothetical community as an example again, the teacher might add this community to the subject under consideration. As examples:

1. *Political involvement before the Civil War.* Was this community Democratic or Whig? Why? What local features helped to shape its political tradition? The answers to these questions will hinge in part on the character of the settlers, the early commercial interests of the area, the desire for internal improvements at federal expense. Did the community change its political orientation as it developed? Why did this happen? The possibilities here extend to an analysis of precinct and ward returns and research based upon a study of voter behavior. The use of insights from political science will be helpful.

2. *Community opinion on slavery, abolitionism, and the black man.* Recent research has shown that in many Midwest cities, most whites were anti-slavery but also anti-abolitionist and anti-black. In a number of communities the people supported the ending of slavery in the belief that the black man would return to a more naturally hospitable climate in the South. By examining newspapers and other media, the students may be able to shed some light on the extent of racism in their own community in the past.

3. *The impact of the Civil War on the urban area.* What social changes are evident? What economic trends can be detected? Here a study could be made of rising prices and expansion or contraction of the city's growth. A comparison with other cities will reveal how these cities reacted to the problems created by the war, and which cities were most successful in finding solutions to the problems. Certain cities might be evaluated in terms of their own characteristics. A student might want to compare his city with Washington, D.C. He could look at Constance McLaughlin Green's *Washington: Village and Capital* (Princeton: Princeton University Press, 1962) and *Washington: Capital City* (Princeton: Princeton University Press, 1963), for the impact of the war there. He could then look at Bessie S. Pierce's *A History of Chicago* (3 vols., New York: Alfred A. Knopf, 1937–1957) and A. Theodore Brown's *Frontier Community: A History of Kansas City to 1870* (Columbia: University of Missouri Press, 1964) for a look at what were to become two major Midwestern cities.

4. *The community reaction to Reconstruction and the black man freed.* This is quite similar to No. 2 and might be handled in much the same manner. The positions held by local congressmen and senators on Reconstruction measures, coupled with their attitude on the role of the black man in a free society, ought to shed light on racial attitudes in the area during the time.

5. *Industrialization, immigration, and urban growth.* As the student looks at these factors in the larger society, he can examine the impact of such features in his own area. He can read Sam Bass Warner, Jr.'s *Streetcar Suburbs: The Process of Growth in Boston* (Cambridge, Mass.: Harvard University Press, 1962) to see if his city's suburban growth paralleled that of Boston's. He might examine Washington, Chicago, and Kansas City using the books listed in No. 3. He could read Robert Ernst's book, *Immigrant Life in New York City* (New York: King's Crown Press, 1949), or Oscar Handlin's *Boston Immigrants* (Cambridge, Mass.: Harvard University Press, 1959) or Moses Rischin's *The Promised City: New York's Jews* (Cambridge, Mass.: Harvard Univer-

sity Press, 1962). He can also look at a model city attempt in Stanley Buder's *Pullman: An Experiment in Industrial Order and Community Planning, 1880–1930* (New York: Oxford University Press, 1967).

6. *Reform movements in the city.* Here the Progressive movement in the cities can be examined. What municipal reforms took place in our hypothetical community? How does this compare with cities in the area and the nation? The student can look at the problem of municipal corruption in New York in Seymour Mandelbaum's *Boss Tweed's New York* (New York: John Wiley, 1965) or in Alexander B. Callow, Jr.'s *The Tweed Ring* (New York: Oxford University Press, 1966). If he is interested in the Midwest, he can find accounts of corruption and reform in three of the books in the Oxford University Press series on Urban Life in America: Lyle W. Dorset's *The Pendergast Machine* (New York, 1968), Zane L. Miller's *Boss Cox's Cincinnati: Urban Politics in the Progressive Era* (New York, 1968), and Melvin G. Holli's *Reform in Detroit: Hazen S. Pingree and Urban Politics* (New York, 1969). The complexities of city government and the development of viable city management can be seen in these books. The comparison can provoke questions about local government. The whole sweep of the Progressive movement is better understood with a firm grip of the basic underpinnings.

7. *Social mobility in all periods.* Here is perhaps the greatest opportunity for research on the local level and the one most often ignored. It is time consuming but wonderfully rewarding for those willing to invest the time. The research can be as sophisticated as the teacher wants to make it; much that has been done requires only simple mathematical manipulation, such as counting numbers of persons in various occupations, easy enough for the average high school student. A model study which contains within it certain strategies for research is Stephan Thernstrom's *Poverty and Progress: Social Mobility in a Nineteenth-Century City* (Cambridge, Mass.: Harvard University Press, 1963), and the book he edited with Richard Sennett, *Nineteenth-Century Cities: Essays*

in the New Urban History (New Haven: Yale University Press, 1969).

8. *Urban problems.* The possibilities here are almost unlimited. The students can compare the development of racial difficulties, housing patterns, pollution, transportation snarls, and so on. Each city has had somewhat different experiences in the process of development, and these differences can be contrasted.

Speakers and Other Class Enrichments

The federal requirement that some kind of planning be done by professional planners before cities are eligible for urban development funds provides opportunities for the alert teacher who wishes to emphasize urban history. Trips to the planning office to visit and to study the work of planners can be used as a basis for further involvement of students in this very necessary work. Further, the planners may be used as guest experts who have surveyed the local community for certain facts and who can offer observations on local problems.

The development of planning as a profession and the urgent need for professionals can be used in conjunction with the school's career days or with the vocational guidance personnel. Many students are unaware of the need for planning or the extent to which it has become a function of American urban life. One of the values of introducing material on urban history into the curriculum is to emphasize the role planning has had in American city growth. Even if no students ever become planners, the acquaintance with the means and goals of planning is essential in modern America.

Just as planners provide a rich resource for urban history, so do architects and developers. The aims of these persons in manipulating the environment need to be explained. Their visions of the city ought to be exposed to public attention, particularly if they have not previously articulated their visions. And the vocational possibilities in both of these fields may surprise and engage some students.

Other possibilities may occur to the teacher, depending upon the kind of community in which he finds himself. He may also become involved in controversy, for city planning is inevitably characterized by disagreement, and the procedure of zoning and its enforcement invariably stirs up opposition. The instructor may wish to bring in individuals who have opposed zoning or have sought variances from it. These individuals are likely to stimulate discussion and to raise questions about the relationship of social control to individual enterprise in a free society.

Field Trips

Perhaps no other area of study lends itself to field trips so well as urban history. The history of the city remains in those areas untouched by urban redevelopment. Chambers of Commerce and local historical societies often have printed materials available for the asking. Within a few hundred miles of most communities are cities which have played important roles in American history. Restorations like Sturbridge or Colonial Williamsburg or Underground Atlanta or Old Town in Chicago, while commercial in certain respects, also give the flavor of the past.

In viewing these cities the student and teacher would be well advised to master the conceptual devices suggested in Kevin Lynch's *Image of the City*. Using the examples of how inhabitants have a visual map of their environs, the students can attempt to see how their city or the city they are visiting exists in the perceptual apparatus of its citizens.

An idea of a city's past and its design ought to lend more meaning to the characteristic junior or senior trip, which can otherwise be little more than a mad rush to see department stores and X-rated movies, and spend sleepless nights in noisy hotels.

Research in Local History

Teachers College Press, Teachers College, Columbia University, 525 W. 120th St., New York, N. Y. 10027, has an excellent series of books in local history. Unfortunately, it has not been too suc-

cessful as a commercial enterprise and has not been expanding
as rapidly as it might. The series is called Localized History and
is available in inexpensive paperbacks. The first volume in the
series is *Teaching History with Community Resources* by Clifford
L. Lord (1964). It is designed primarily for teachers and suggests
research topics, techniques, curriculum, and methods appropriate
to local history. It has valuable suggestions about community resources and means of fostering students' insights. The remaining
volumes are shorter, 32 to 50 pages, and are designed for student
use. The titles are as follows:

STATES:

Arizona, Madeline F. Pare (1968).

California, Andrew Rolle (1965).

Colorado, Carl Ubbelohde (1965).

Delaware, John A. Munroe (1965).

Georgia, James C. Bonner (1965).

Hawaii, Gerril P. Judd (1966).

Idaho, Merle W. Wells (1965).

Illinois, Olive S. Foster (1968).

Kansas, Nyle H. Miller (1965).

Kentucky, Thomas D. Clark (1965).

Louisiana, Joe Gray Taylor (1966).

Maryland, Harold Manokee (1968).

Massachusetts, William J. Reid (1965).

Minnesota, Russell W. Fridley (1966).

Mississippi, John H. Moore (1968).

New Hampshire, James D. Squires (1966).

New Jersey, Richard P. McCormick (1965).

New York, Marvin Rapp (1968).

North Carolina, William S. Powell (1965).

Ohio, Francis P. Weisenburger (1965).

Oklahoma, A. A. Gibson (1965).

Pennsylvania, S. K. Stevens (1965).

Rhode Island, Clifford P. Monahan (1965).

Tennessee, William T. Alderson (1965).
Utah, Everett L. Cooley (1968).
Wisconsin, Doris H. Platt (1965).
Wyoming, Lola M. Homsher (1966).

CITIES:

Cincinnati, Louis L. Tucker (1968).
Houston, Joe B. Frantz (1968).
Los Angeles, Andrew Rolle (1965).
New York City, Bayrd Still (1965).
Raleigh–Durham–Chapel Hill, William S. Powell (1968).
Boston, Walter Muir Whitehill (1969).
Denver, John D. Mitchell (1969).
Miami, Frank Sessa (1969).
Milwaukee, Charles N. Glaab (1969).
San Francisco, Moses and Ruth S. Richin (1969).
Chicago, Clement M. Silvestro (1969).

WATERSHEDS:

The Upper Mississippi Valley, Walter W. Havighurst (1966).
The Ohio Valley, R. E. Banta (1967).
The Sacramento Valley, Joseph McGowan (1968).
The Potomac, Walter Sonderlin (1968).
The Wisconsin, August Derleth (1968).

PEOPLES:

The Star of Hope: The Finns in America, John I. Kolehmainen (1968).
The Germans in America, Carl Wittke (1967).
The Greeks in America, Theodore Saloutos (1967).
The Irish in America, Carl Wittke (1968).
The Mexicans in America, Carey McWilliams (1968).
The Norwegians in America, Elinor Haugen (1967).

While those books devoted to individual cities are the most valuable for urban study, the others are also pertinent. They necessarily treat of urban development, whether it be in a state or a watershed or in the growth of an immigrant group.

Finally, there are many centers and institutes springing up around the country to do research in urban affairs. They have varying kinds of materials available for student use.

Journals for Research and Further Study

This is an abbreviated list of journals on urban affairs which may be of use and interest to students and teachers.

The American City
Buttenheim Public Corporation
Berkshire Common
Pittsfield, Mass. 01201

American Institute of Planners Journal
American Institute of Planners
917 15th St., N.W.
Washington, D.C. 20005

City: A Bi-Monthly Review of Urban America
Urban America, Inc.
1717 Massachusetts Ave., N.W.
Washington, D. C. 20036

Education and Urban Society
Sage Publications, Inc.
275 Beverly Dr.
Beverly Hills, Calif. 90212

Journal of Human Resources
University of Wisconsin Press
P.O. Box 1379
Madison, Wisc. 53701

Land-Use Controls: *A Quarterly Review*
American Society of Planning Officials
1313 E. 60th St.
Chicago, Ill. 60637

Metropolitan
Hitchcock Publishing Company
Hitchcock Building
Wheaton, Ill. 60188

National Civic Review
National Municipal League
47 E. 68th St.
New York, N. Y. 10021

Nation's Cities
National League of Cities
1612 K St., N.W.
Washington, D.C. 20006

Public Interest
404 Park Ave. S.
New York, N. Y. 10018

Trans-Action
Rutgers University
New Brunswick, N. J. 08903

Urban Affairs Quarterly
Sage Publications, Inc.
275 S. Beverly Dr.
Beverly Hills, Calif. 90212

Urban and Social Change Review
Institute of Human Sciences
Boston College
Chestnut Hill, Mass. 02167

Urban Data Service
International City Management Association
1140 Connecticut Ave., N.W.
Washington, D.C. 20036

Urban Education
University of Buffalo Foundation, Inc.
3435 Main St.
Buffalo, N. Y. 14214

Urban Review
Center for Urban Education
105 Madison Ave.
New York, N. Y. 10016

Urban West
593 Market St.
San Francisco, Calif. 94104

Western City
League of California Cities
702 Statler Center
Los Angeles, Calif. 90017

There are three available bibliographies of urban journals which can be obtained at nominal cost. These are:

Periodicals Received in the Housing and Urban Development Library. This periodical is published twice a year by the U. S. Department of Housing and Urban Development, Washington, D.C. 20410.

Current Information Sources for Community Planning: Periodicals and Serials by Leah Aronoff. This is Exchange Bibliography No. 35, published in 1967 by the Council of Planning Librarians, P.O. Box 229, Monticello, Ill. 61856.

Descriptions of Selected, Urban-Related Periodicals. This was published in 1969 by the Institute of Human Sciences, Boston College, Chestnut Hill, Mass. 02167.

Chapter V

UNITS IN AMERICAN URBAN HISTORY

The units which follow are patterned after those used in high school history courses. Along with the bibliographies of books and audio-visual materials, they are planned to show how urban history may be included in the year's curriculum. These units can be used as a guide to further reading. They are not complete, nor should they serve as the basis for an extensive research project. Each unit is composed of a short discussion of the significant factors in urban history at a particular point in time or on a particular topic. The discussion is designed as a skeletal unit, to suggest pertinent questions and themes around which to orient the unit.

The bibliography at the end of each unit includes books, movies, other audio-visual materials, and games when appropriate and available. The bibliography is annotated and is designed to stimulate the teacher and the student to do further work. Some books recommended are difficult and suitable only for the teacher; others are quite simple. The films tend to be less sophisticated. Teachers should be able to use the units selectively.

Cities and Country:
The Place of Cities in the Human Scheme

This introductory unit is a theoretical one. It revolves around two rather basic questions: Why and how do cities develop? What do cities have in common?

The first question has been answered in a number of ways. Geographers have emphasized natural factors, site features, and locational factors. Indeed, the High School Geography Project of the Association of American Geographers, with the support of the National Science Foundation, concentrates upon the settlement theme in its units. Its first unit of Geography in an Urban Age is *Geography of Cities* (1968). The unit contains a Teacher's Guide, a Student Manual, and a Student Resources booklet, all paperback. It consists of eight sections which can occupy up to thirty-five class sessions. The following sections are particularly useful for a course in urban history:

In Part I, "City Location and Growth," students study settlement sites using hypothetical diagrams. They are then asked to study drainage maps of the American Midwest and predict where settlements might develop. Their predictions are then checked with historical reality.

Part II, "New Orleans," treats the pattern of settlement in New Orleans as it exists today. It looks at three residential neighborhoods and attempts some generalizations about urban relations. This section does not contain much in the way of historical information, but it can be added to the unit to help explain the present design of New Orleans.

Part III, "Models of City Form," uses Chicago as a basis and generalizes from the data it offers. The Burgess "concentric ring" model and the Hoyt "sector" model are explained. Neither is very new nor very sophisticated, but the maps provided for students do give an impression of Chicago's city growth from 1875 to 1955.

Part IV, "Portsville," portrays the growth of Seattle. Using the abundant photographs and narrative material, students are supposed to figure out how the city should develop. This section is very useful in urban history in tracing the development of a port city in the Far West.

Part VIII, "Cities with Special Functions," considers cities outside the United States—Rotterdam, Holland; Karlovy Vary, Czechoslovakia; Monaco; Brasilia, Brazil; Lhasa, Tibet; Chuquicamata, Chile; Kitimal, Canada—as well as the American cities of Seattle, Salinas, Boulder, Grand Junction, Akron, Hartford, Port Arthur, and Sparrow's Point.

Two of the related optional activities in *Geography of Cities* are pertinent to urban history. These are a "Tale of Three Cities" and "Bruges." The "Tale of Three Cities" is an historical treatment of the growth of three American cities—Boston, New York, and Philadelphia, from their founding down to 1860. The treatment is necessarily simplistic and short. "Bruges" is the history of the rise and fall of that Belgian city from its founding in the

Aerial view of the ruins of Persepolis, the Persian capital under Darius I
(COURTESY ERICH F. SCHMIDT, THE ORIENTAL INSTITUTE)

ninth century down to the present. The example is an interesting one and does illuminate aspects of city development in the commercial, industrial area of the low countries.

The Geography in an Urban Age series fits nicely into an urban history program. The material is well researched and neatly packaged, the data is available in one place. The materials are extensive enough, in fact, to occupy more time than a history teacher would like to take. Ideally, a student should take the course in urban geography before the course in urban history. Since few teachers can expect to be that lucky, they can use the geography materials from time to time in their history course. If the teacher were to begin with city development, the appropriate units of the geography project would be most helpful.

The development of cities in other parts of the world also illustrates how culture-bound our views of the city are. And one can trace city development in various cultures.

The cities of Mesopotamia are a good place to start. These cities date from 3500 B.C. and include Erech, Eridu, Ur, Lagash, and Larsa in Sumer. Each city had a king, a similar language, a religion, a social organization, and material development. They had social classes, including priests who used writing to keep records. They were walled cities, made of mud brick, with religious centers. They dominated the geographical area in which they were located and commanded an agricultural area.

The cities of the Nile Valley also provide a clue to the origin of cities. These cities apparently were developing at the same time as cities in the Mesopotamian area. They were walled communities which had division of labor, social classes, advanced technology, priestly bureaucracies, religious deities native to the city, and rulers who partook of Divinity themselves. Some of the early cities were Memphis, This, Heliopolis, and Nekheb; later cities include Thebes and Akhetaten. These Egyptian cities are somewhat harder to trace because the Nile has buried them under silt, and because the Egyptians were used to changing their capital site with each new pharaoh.

The cities of the Indus Valley are somewhat later than those of the Nile but are useful in comparing the basic elements of city development. Two cities here are significant—Harappa in the Punjab and Mohenjo-daro in the valley of the Indus. Both of these West Pakistani cities have been excavated, and both seem to have been capitals of empires that emerged about 2500 B.C. and were destroyed along with the native civilization around 1500 B.C. by Aryan invaders. Harappa and Mohenjo-daro resemble the Nile and Mesopotamian cities in their close connection with an agricultural system and in their stimulation of technological advance. They vary in that they cannot definitely be said to have been dominated by temples or religious forces. Indeed, the cities seem not to have been primarily religious centers. Nor is it at all certain that they were walled as in the other areas.

The Chinese cities which first developed in the Yellow River valley are later in point of time. Two cities which have been excavated are City Chang, near Anyang, and Chengchow. These seem to have been built no earlier than 1500 B.C., about the time of the fall of the Indus valley cities. Their written records indicate that, like the other cities, they were characterized by specialization and labor division. Their rulers and bureaucracies enjoyed an exalted status. The cities were walled but were not characterized as religious centers.

The cities of meso-America are later still. Agricultural communities precede true cities, and the beginning of a population gathered around a temple-pyramid square seems to have occurred between 1200 and 400 B.C. Cities of this period include San Lorenzo, Monte Albán, and Tikal. Later Teotihuacan, Chichén Itza, and Mitla were developed. The earliest cities in Mexico were largely ceremonial centers with dominating temples, but there was no permanent population with the possible exception of temple attendants. A class structure was headed by an elite of royalty and priests. Only later did the cities in the area gain large populations. In the Mayan area—the second area of urbanization in meso-America—there never were the same large number of people.

Nor were the cities of meso-America walled. Areas inside the
city might be walled, and some Peruvian cities had citadels, but
the Incan cities in general were not fortified. The beginnings and
characteristics of meso-American cities are largely still open to
question.

The cities of Africa—particularly West Africa—have become
matters of considerable interest and ought to be studied in terms
of the origin of cities. Again, the investigation is just beginning
and the data are under constant revision. The earliest West African
state that has been located in written accounts is the empire of
Ghana. Its capital was Kumbi-Kumbi and is dated from about
400 A.D., thus making it contemporary with a number of meso-
American cities. Kumbi-Kumbi, as the name implied, was a double
city, at least from Muslim times on. One city, where the king lived,
was fortified and pagan; the other was not, and here the Muslims
lived. The arrangement allowed two competing religions to live
side by side. It also reflected an interesting division of functions
between city, military, ceremonial, and bureaucratic. Three other
noted cities of West Africa are Timbuktu and Gao of the Songhai
Empire, and Kano of the Hausa states. Gao was the capital of
the Songhai Empire; Timbuktu was a subsidiary capital. According to Arabic accounts, the cities were founded by Tuaregs about
1200 A.D. They became commercial centers and had social divisions within the towns. Their mud walls were low and not very
useful for defense. When the cities became Islamic, mosques were
built. Timbuktu developed a university, the University of Sankore.
Kano was quite similar to Timbuktu and Gao, except that it was
originally a settlement of iron workers. In all probability the Islamic Arabs found cities which already existed and took them over.

Other cities must also be taken into account in any general discussion of world cities—not original cities which arose in separate
parts of the world, but rather cities of second- and third-genera-
tional development. These include the cities of the Near East—
Tyre, Sidon, Beirut, Jericho, Damascus, Ephesus, Sardis, Ankara,
Smyrna, Babylon, and Persepolis—and the Greek and Roman

cities—Alexandria, Antioch, Sparta, Corinth, Byzantium, Athens, Pisa, Perugia, Siena, Rome, and Naples.

As we have seen, there are certain similarities about the earliest cities—social stratification, bureaucracy, division of labor, and aspects of advanced technology, particularly in the area of agriculture. Some of the cities were walled, apparently for purposes of defense; others were closely related to religious institutions. The student and teacher can at this point make generalizations about these features. The next step is to test them. Here the problem becomes more difficult.

For example, one of the frequent generalizations is that cities are the end product of a kind of cultural evolution, that agricultural societies develop food surpluses which are then divided to provide the basis for city life. This generalization is common in textbooks and appears as a cliché in everyday life. The farms support the city and come first; if the cities are destroyed, the nation remains, but if the farms are destroyed, the nation is gone. William Jennings Bryan said as much in 1896. But Jane Jacobs argues in *The Economy of Cities* that cities predate and help *create* agricultural societies. She places the development of cities before the development of agricultural societies and argues that these agricultural societies spring up to meet the demand generated by city people. This controversial thesis is one that might serve as a point of discussion, as a hypothesis which needs testing, or as the basis of a student research project.

Another generalization frequently associated with city development is one left over from nineteenth-century geography. Alexander von Humboldt, the German geographer, argued that the great cities of the world would be found on major rivers, and that these great cities were on an "Isothermal Zodiac" in the northern hemisphere. This Zodiac roughly corresponded to 40° north latitude. Von Humboldt in his *Cosmos* argued that nature therefore determined the pattern of man's settlement, and that mankind moved ever west. Implicit in this geopolitical assumption was the idea that civilizations were inevitably characterized by great cities where people lived, another social evolutionary assumption.

Since the nineteenth-century Western geographers were most familiar with cities on major rivers, and since their historical knowledge was limited to Western civilization, the generalization seemed correct. But archaeological evidence from meso-America and Africa refutes von Humboldt's idea. The major cities of West Africa were not oriented to rivers which ran to the Atlantic and to oceanic trade; they looked instead northward, across the Sahara, to trade with the Arabic world. The same is true of the cities in meso-America which were developed apparently with little regard to rivers or even to natural accessibility. The location of these cities can only be explained by cultural factors.

An interesting and revealing project is the location of cities in the world in their original position and the explanation of why these were located where they were. The student could be encouraged to test von Humboldt's theory in the nineteenth century and to develop alternate hypotheses as to the development of cities at other times.

Another facile assumption is that cities were developed in order to provide places for people to live, and that civilization depends upon urban life. This is the antithesis of the theory that cities are parasites on the country. It can be challenged again with data from meso-America. The Mayans evidently had an advanced civilization complete with cities, technology, bureaucracy, political centralization—but they appear not to have lived in their cities. The Mayan cities were ceremonial and not primarily residential centers. This circumstance challenges the idea that civilization depends upon population concentrated into cities, and that the function of cities is to facilitate a division of labor. Accounting for the peculiar role of cities in Mayan culture might stimulate insightful thinking about cities.

Another generalization that needs testing is one concerning religion and cities. Why do cities in the Near East and meso-America share an emphasis upon religious buildings as the center of the city? Why are these influences absent in India and China? To test this the student might well check to see if there are, in his immediate area or in the United States, cities which are oriented around a religious function. (An obvious one is Salt Lake City, Utah.)

These are just a few of the possible topics in an overview of the growth and development of cities. The teacher and student may wish to explore many other possibilities. Indeed, an entire semester's course could easily be devoted to the theme.

Bibliography

1. *Geography in an Urban Age,* Unit I: *Geography of Cities* (High School Geography Project, Association of American Geographers: Boulder, Colo., 1968). Discussed in detail in the text of this unit. A highly useful tool for conceptualization despite some of its more facile generalizations.

2. *Geography in an Urban Age,* Unit III: *The Geography of Cultural Change* (High School Geography Project, Association of American Geographers: Boulder, Colo., 1968). Useful in the discussion of similarities between cities. Activity 7 of the unit consists of readings in the Student Resources and worksheets in the Student Manual to accompany a set of slides which were provided to the High School Geography Project by the National Geographic Society. These slides include nine traditional-style city buildings—from Bangkok, Thailand; Bruges, Belgium; Toledo, Spain; a city in Chad; York, England; San'aa, Yemen; St. Louis, United States; Kano, Nigeria; Yakutsk, USSR—and seven slides of downtown sections of modern cities—Tokyo, Japan; Sao Paulo, Brazil; Ulan Bator, Mongolia; Boston, United States; Kinshasa, Congo; Cairo, Egypt; and a suburb of London. These slides are particularly useful in the comparison of cities throughout the world, despite the lack of historical change, and they fit very well into the conceptual scheme of this unit.

3. *Fourteen Metropolitan Areas* (Twin Cities Metropolitan Planning Commission, Minneapolis–St. Paul, Minn., 1964). This

set of slides shows primarily Western cities, some of them as projected in the year 2000. The cities include Baltimore, Boston, Stockholm, Copenhagen, Chicago, San Francisco, Washington, D.C., Kyoto, Rome, and Minneapolis–St. Paul. Useful in projecting future growth and may enable the student to see how cities are developing.

4. *Cities of Europe* (Encyclopedia Britannica Filmstrip, 1958). There are six European cities in this set: *Granada and the Alhambra; London; Madrid; Paris; Rome*: *The City; Toledo*: *Fortress City of Spain;* and *Vienna.* Suitable for junior and senior high school students, who should be able to see how these cities have developed in relation to their separate heritages as well as their points of similarity.

5. *Exploring the Ancient Civilizations* (Imperial Film, 321 S. Florida Ave., Lakeland, Fla.). There are six areas shown in this set of filmstrips: *Exploring Rome and Pompeii, Exploring Ancient Athens, Exploring Ba'albeck and Jeiash, Exploring Ancient Egypt, Exploring Ancient Mexico*: *Pre-Aztec,* and *Exploring Ancient Mexico*: *The Mayas.* Not highly sophisticated, so they may be used for varying grades. While they concentrate primarily upon civilizations, they also show the cities of the past and indicate urban form.

6. *Man—Builder of Cities* (Encyclopedia Britannica Filmstrips, 1954). The cities of Athens, Rome, Ch'ang-an, Venice, and Florence are viewed as old cities, while modern ones include New York, Paris, and Chicago. Useful for elementary through high school grades. The emphasis is mainly on cities in the Western tradition.

7. *Ancient Baalbek and Palmyra, Ancient Petra* (Encyclopedia Britannica Films, 1953). These films show the ruins of these cities as well as the impact of various civilizations upon them. Best suited for high school students.

8. *Angkor—The Lost City* (Contemporary Films, 1965). The film studies the ancient capital of the Khimers, the ancestors of

the Cambodians, and shows how an Eastern city was planned and formed. It illustrates the grandeur and frailty of this civilization. Suitable for all grades.

9. *The Miracle Builders* (Classroom Film Distributors, 1954). The theme of this film is the architectural and engineering genius that went into the building of Baalbek in Lebanon, the church of San Sophia in Istanbul, and the fortress of Sacsahuamán in the Peruvian Andes. A valuable film for its cross-cultural comparisons. Probably best for senior high school students, but useful in lower grades as well.

10. *Peruvian Archeology* (International Film Bureau, 1954). Five periods of Peruvian history are illustrated with examples of architecture, textiles, coverings, the arts, and aesthetic designs. The Inca Temple of the Sun is featured, as is Machu Picchu. Interdisciplinary in nature, and suitable for junior and senior high school students.

11. "The Sumerian Game" (Board of Cooperative Educational Services of Westchester County, N.Y., in cooperation with IBM). The basic economic principles at the time of the neolithic revolution in Mesopotamia are demonstrated in this game. The player assumes the role of Ludriga I, priest-ruler of Lagash in 3500 B.C., and tries to make the most productive decisions about the storage and distribution of grain, the development of crafts, the facilitation of trade, and other problems of economic life. While the game is aimed at the sixth-grade level, it could also be of use as an urban history introduction to higher grades.

12. Collins, George R., ed., *Planning and Cities* (New York: George Braziller, 1968), paperback. This series is invaluable for students and teachers. The books are written by historians who are interested in city planning and architecture. One of the most appealing features of the books (made possible by their being printed in the Netherlands) is the lavish use of visual materials. Fully half of each book is composed of maps, photographs, drawings, and plans. The text of the books may be too difficult for

the average student, nonetheless the books are necessary for room or school libraries if some emphasis upon planning is intended. The titles are:

    a. Douglas Fraser, *Village Planning in the Primitive World.*

    b. Paul Lampl, *Cities and Planning in the Ancient Near East.*

    c. Jorge Hardoy, *Urban Planning in Pre-Columbian America.*

    d. Howard Soalman, *Medieval Cities.*

    e. J. Ward-Perkins, *The Cities of Ancient Greece and Italy.*

    f. Giulio Argan, *The Renaissance City.*

    g. Françoise Choay, *The Modern City: Planning in the 19th Century.*

    h. George R. Collins, *The Modern City in the 20th Century.*

    i. Horst de la Croix, *Military Considerations in City Planning.*

    j. Bronko Maksimovitch, *Socialist Planning in the Cities of Eastern Europe.*

13. Jacobs, Jane, *The Economy of Cities* (New York: Random House, 1969), paperback. Here the controversial writer on urban affairs lays claim for primacy in civilization to the city. The book contains many references to historical cities and, while well written, may be somewhat difficult for students. Mrs. Jacobs' ideas, however, are challenging and should be introduced to the class.

14. Sjoberg, Gideon, *The Preindustrial City*: *Past and Present* (New York: Free Press, 1960), paperback. A difficult but essential book. Sjoberg is a sociologist who attempts to describe pre-industrial cities in terms of social class, marriage and the family, and economic, political, and religious structures. He assumes two forms of the city life, the industrial and the pre-industrial. His book is provocative and useful for deriving generalizations, but is not for any but the sophisticated reader.

15. Davidson, Basil, *The Lost Cities of Africa* (Boston: Little, Brown, 1959), paperback. Particularly useful in discussing the achievements of urban development in Africa. Suitable for senior high school students.

16. Adams, Robert McC., *The Evolution of Urban Society: Early Mesopotamia and Pre-Hispanic Mexico* (Chicago: Aldine, 1966). Adams' book is a comparison of city development in Mesopotamia and middle America. It is advanced and probably would serve best as a reference work for student projects.

17. Wolf, Eric, *Sons of the Shaking Earth* (Chicago: University of Chicago Press, 1959), paperback. A cultural history of the people of Mexico and Guatemala, well written and suitable for senior high school students. It has many illustrations and several chapters on urban life and form.

18. Bushnell, G. H. S., *Peru* (New York: Frederick A. Praeger, 1957), paperback. Part of the Ancient Peoples and Places series. Written in a rather formidable style, profusely illustrated, and useful for reference.

19. Vaillant, George, *The Aztecs of Mexico,* revised by Suzannah B. Vaillant (New York: Doubleday, 1962), Pelican paperback. A comprehensive history of the Aztecs with a number of illustrations. The first few chapters are the most useful on the development of cities in Mexico. Not for the average student, but an excellent reference source.

20. Childe, Gordon, *What Happened in History?* (Baltimore: Penguin Books, 1957), paperback. This book includes the classic statement of the evolution of Mesopotamian cities from rural surplus. Childe also treats Indian and Egyptian civilizations. Good for most senior high school students.

21. Childe, Gordon, *Man Makes Himself* (New York: Mentor Books, 1951), paperback. Quite similar to Childe's other book. Here he again chronicles the growth of urban civilization after neolithic revolutions. He calls urbanization a revolution also, and presents a theory for city growth. Not an easy book but rewarding.

22. Cottrell, Leonard, *Lost Cities* (New York: Rinehart, 1957), Universal paperback. The cities examined by this British author are Nimrud, Nineveh, Ur, Babylon, and Nippur. Good for senior high school students.

23. Silverberg, Robert, *Lost Cities and Vanished Civilizations* (New York: Bantam Books, 1962), paperback. Silverberg includes a number of cities in the world from the Near East to Chichén Itza. Useful for senior high school students.

24. Swann, Winn, *Lost Cities of Asia: Ceylon, Dagan, Angkor* (New York: Putnam, 1966). An account of the cities that have died in Asia. Popularly written and suitable for upper-level high school students.

25. Wheeler, Mortimer, *The Indus Civilization* (Cambridge: Cambridge University Press, 1953), paperback. The standard work on the cities of the Indus valley. Useful as a reference tool for those who wish to do research on urban development in that area, but not a book for general class use.

26. Creel, H. G., *The Birth of China* (New York: Frederick Ungar, 1954), paperback. The book contains references to the cities of the Yellow River. Mainly for reference use.

27. Mumford, Lewis, *Technics and Civilization* (New York: Harcourt, Brace, 1934), paperback. In this excellent book Mumford discusses the paleotechnic and neotechnic eras of city development. For advanced students.

28. Mumford, Lewis, *The Culture of Cities* (New York: Harcourt, Brace, 1938). Similar to the preceding book, but it concentrates more on cities.

29. Hall, Peter, *The World Cities* (New York: McGraw-Hill, 1966), paperback. Hall's book may be used with the Geography Project or by itself. Many illustrations, some of which are in color. The cities compared are modern and include London, Paris, Randstad, Holland, Rhine-Ruhr, Moscow, New York, and Tokyo. Hall concludes with a look at future cities. For senior high school students.

Colonial Towns,
1630–1732

Two basic points should be made about the settlement of towns in Colonial America. One is that the towns were totally planned; there was no freedom for private development. As planned communities, Colonial towns shared the assumptions of the medieval town on which they were based. The second point is that those entrepreneurs who established colonies, whether they were proprietors, joint-stock company shareholders, or royalty, believed that the good life was one which was to be lived in cities, either part or all of the time. These two characteristics were virtually turned around in the nineteenth century, and only in our time are we returning to conceptions of total planning and urbanism as desired ends. Students may be encouraged to speculate on what factors changed these American attitudes toward the city.

The towns of the Colonial period reflected the social values of the larger society. They tried to enforce social stability and regarded themselves as agents of social discipline. Faced with the dual problems of a frontier to defend and the removal of royal institutions and an intervening church structure (no American bishop ever having been appointed), towns had to be developed as autonomous and self-sufficient. There were several models of settlement from which to draw. Englishmen came to the New World with several town patterns in mind—the open-field manorial village, the incorporated borough, and the enclosed-form village of East Anglia. Those who came to the New World from the continent had even more possibilities from which to choose. From the start, then, despite the emphasis upon total planning and restriction, towns took shapes that their founders did not anticipate.

The basic town plans in the Colonies did have common features. Differences in social status were reflected in streets which were to be developed as residences for the better classes. The development of public projects was considered the responsibility of the whole community, and able-bodied male residents were required to devote time to these projects. The towns were structured so as to make possible economic regulation. The mercantile controls of the day were reflected in the town areas assigned for commercial development.

Despite similar assumptions, towns in the New World took on different shapes. In New England—and we know more about New England than other Colonial areas—there were contrasting town plans. Those patterned on closed fields were loosely organized with scattered farms and little sense of community. The open-field villages were tightly knit on the manorial pattern, with a strong sense of community and a pattern of living closely together. The towns based on the incorporated borough took a kind of middle ground.

The pattern of settlement varied, but quite often a group from a particular area would accompany a popular minister or significant lay person to begin a town elsewhere. A hundred people

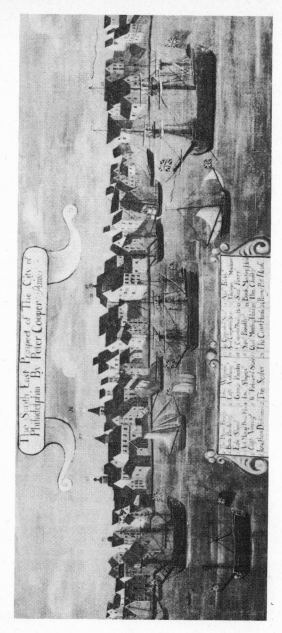

"South East Prospect of the City of Philadelphia," detail of a painting by Peter Cooper showing the city from the Delaware River in 1720 (THE LIBRARY COMPANY OF PHILADELPHIA)

came from Groton, Winthrop's home in England, in 1630 to settle in or near Boston. Thirty families settled Dedham, Massachusetts, in 1636. When Ann Hutchinson came to Massachusetts
Bay Colony it was to follow after John Cotton. When she left the
colony because of the antinomian crisis, she took followers with
her. Regardless of the pattern of settlement, towns took specific
forms because of custom or statute. Massachusetts Bay required
all settlers to build their houses within a half-mile of the meeting
house, which served as a focal point in the community. It was
used for secular functions during the week, for church on Sunday,
and for other special occasions.

Boston became the largest city in New England and in the
Colonies by 1640. The city had certain natural advantages: it was
located on a reliable supply of good water—the Charles River—
and it had suitable harbor facilities and natural barriers against
the Indians. Other prospective cities shared the same qualities,
but because Boston had become the hub of the Puritan commonwealth it outgrew the others. It became the center of Puritan government and church. Other cities in New England tried to emulate
the Boston experience.

The Middle Colonies developed two of the three major cities
in Colonial America. These were New York and Philadelphia.
New York, which began as New Amsterdam, was originally occupied by the Dutch in 1615. The original settlement was on the
southern part of Manhattan Island and became important because of its position as a political capital and official port. It grew
slowly at first because of relative lack of population along the
Hudson Valley and because of lack of goods to export. But the
location of New York is unique in that it is one of two of the
world's major cities which occupies an island. The other is Hong
Kong. The island location made possible excellent port facilities
and directed the growth of the city into a triangular area. The
physical forces at work in New York seem to have shaped this
city more than Dutch city planning.

Philadelphia, on the other hand, is the best example of a city which was carefully planned at its beginning. William Penn laid out the basic plan of Philadelphia in 1682. In choosing a site, Penn had three criteria: (1) the site must be on high ground, (2) it must be suitable for port facilities, and (3) the soil nearby must be fertile. The city laid out near the junction of the Schuylkill and Delaware rivers is often blamed for the uninteresting gridiron pattern of American city development. Penn did use a gridiron pattern, but he also provided for five parks to remain areas of natural beauty. Streets were named after trees, and a main street, Market, went the length of the city from the Delaware River.

By 1720, Boston, New York, and Philadelphia were the three largest cities in Colonial America. Boston was first with twelve thousand inhabitants, Philadelphia was second with ten thousand, and New York was third with seven thousand. The growth of New York was slow despite the fur and flour trade, and Boston's growth rate did not equal that of Philadelphia which became a center for immigrant entry into the South. The growth of Philadelphia was such that it became the largest city in the Colonies by 1750.

City development in the Southern Colonies was slow in the seventeenth century. Although Charleston was settled in 1670, it became the major urban center in the South only in the eighteenth century. For fifty years the town grew quite slowly; with the establishment of Georgia and the development of rice in 1732, Charleston began a period of rapid growth. It became the cultural center of the South and was distinguished by a genuine urban atmosphere. Charleston had a good natural location at the junction of the Ashley and Cooper rivers. It became the fashionable place to live for rice and indigo planters, and as a result large houses were built to accommodate these planters and slave quarters were developed. By the time of the Revolution, Charleston had a population of approximately twelve thousand, half of them black. The development of Charleston was significantly different from the development of cities further north.

Charleston's only real competitor in the Low Country was Savannah. Planned like Philadelphia, Savannah was the product of the talent of James Oglethorpe, one of the proprietors of the colony of Georgia. Savannah was laid out in a rectangular pattern with lots grouped in square wards of forty. These were divided by streets based on a gridiron design. The intersection of main streets provided the location of churches and public buildings. Savannah was probably the second best-planned community in Colonial America. Although it was laid out only in 1732, by the time of the Revolution it had three thousand inhabitants.

The Chesapeake Society, which encompassed Maryland, Virginia, and the upper part of North Carolina, was the section of the Colonies which experienced the least urban development in the early period. (Here a kind of dilemma arises. How can one explain the number of political and intellectual leaders who arise from Virginia? How does this square with the urban explanation for the development of culture?) Williamsburg, the capital of Virginia colony, never evolved a sizable population despite its political status and its service as a cultural center. Two cities in the area which grew in the eighteenth century, Norfolk and Baltimore, were planned cities, though they were planned for different reasons.

Norfolk was founded in the 1720's as a port town to be used for the shipping of tar, pitch, and turpentine from North Carolina and Virginia. The impetus for the organization of the town lay with the English mercantile policy of specifying certain towns to handle commercial activity. Norfolk was thus set up under royal direction to be the export center for lower Chesapeake Bay. Two factors aided the development of this planned town: the harbor facilities of Norfolk were superior to most of those off the coast of North Carolina, so that migrants and goods destined for that colony were easier sent to Norfolk; the city developed a lucrative trade in foodstuffs with the West Indies. It became the Southern center for supplying English planters with necessities for the slave society. By the time of the Revolution the port town of Norfolk had six thousand people.

Baltimore was chartered as a town in 1729 by a group of entrepreneurs who wanted to develop a town on land owned by the Carroll family. The original purpose of the town was commercial —to act as a port for the shipment of tobacco from the upper Chesapeake area, Maryland and Virginia. The competition of other ports and of plantations with their own facilities prevented Baltimore from growing: by 1750 the population was insignificant, numbering only around one hundred people. When flour became an important product, Baltimore led in the development of the flour exporting trade. The town helped to develop the nearby farming area and in so doing expanded rapidly. By the census of 1790 Baltimore had thirteen thousand people, rivaling Charleston as the urban center of the South.

The towns of Colonial America grew for a variety of reasons. New York had excellent natural features but its significance derived primarily from its status as capital of the colony. Williamsburg was a political center with fewer natural advantages, and it never grew. Philadelphia and Savannah were planned by the proprietors of Pennsylvania and Georgia to serve as the centers for their colonies. They did not grow spontaneously but were closely supervised. Norfolk owed its existence to superior natural facilities but also to a political decision by the crown which had economic consequences. Baltimore had little in the way of natural advantage over other areas at its start, but the skill of local entrepreneurs in finding a cash crop that was exportable made the city what it was.

A useful tool for discussing this unit is the inquiry method. Students can be encouraged to formulate what they think are the most significant reasons for the development of the Colonial towns. They can construct hypotheses and test them. Further, a kind of comparison can be made between towns in the New World and those in the Old. Which features were retained and which were discarded? What was American about American cities? Comparisons can also be made between cities in point of time. What features of Colonial cities are apparent in cities of the nineteenth and twentieth centuries?

Bibliography

1. *Geography in an Urban Age,* Unit I: *Geography of Cities* (High School Geography Project, Association of American Geographers: Boulder, Colo., 1968). The portion useful here is the one called "A Tale of Three Cities," which details the growth of New York, Philadelphia, and Boston from their founding to 1860. While the emphasis is on the natural features and economic reasons for city growth, the authors admit that the question of city growth is a very complex one.

2. *Freedom Trail in Boston* (International Film Bureau, 1965). A panoramic view of Boston, concentrating upon the elements which played a significant role during the Revolution. The student can see Boston Common, the Old North Church, Faneuil Hall, the Old State House, and other landmarks. Mostly for junior high school classes, but senior high students can discern the careful planning of Boston which took into account natural features.

3. *Life in a New England Town* (Curriculum Films, 1950). This filmstrip attempts to present a kind of social history of the New England town. Simple, and appropriate for primary through high school grades.

4. *Life in New Netherlands* (Curriculum Films, 1950). A companion film to the preceding one, this looks at New Netherlands. For primary through high school classes.

5. *Colonial New York* (McGraw-Hill Filmstrips, n.d.). Part of the New York State series, this filmstrip has views of New York City. For junior and senior high school classes.

6. *Portsmouth—American Mosaic* (Dan Stiles Associates, 1966). This film traces the history of Portsmouth, New Hampshire, from its inception. The factors contributing to the growth of the

town—in particular the maritime ones—are explored. Useful for junior or senior high school students.

7. *Influence of Geography and History on the Port of New York* (International Geography Pictures, 1950). This older film uses animated maps to show how New York City was a gateway to western settlement. The geographic features are perhaps over-emphasized, but the film is strong in its interdisciplinary emphasis. Aimed at junior high school students.

8. *Historic Plymouth* (International Film Bureau, 1965). This film re-enacts the establishment of Plymouth and then visits present-day historic sites. Suitable for elementary through high school classes.

9. *Eighteenth-Century Life in Colonial Williamsburg* (McGraw-Hill Textfilms, 1957). The social stratification of Williamsburg as well as the architecture of the area appears in the film. It nicely catches the urban-rural flavor of Williamsburg. The film can be used in classes from the primary level through senior high school.

10. *William Penn and the Quakers—The Pennsylvania Colony* (Coronet Films, 1959). While this film concentrates mainly on the issue of religious freedom, it also discusses Philadelphia. It can be used in junior and senior high school classes.

11. *The Jamestown Colony, 1607–1620* (Coronet Films, 1957). The Jamestown festival of 1957, which celebrated the 350th anniversary of the founding of the colony, is pictured in the film. Jamestown was reconstructed for the festival and the film explains the design of the village and the materials used, both of which reflected European rather than American experience.

12. *Colonial Philadelphia* (Barnwood Productions, n.d.). This film shows the historic landmarks of Philadelphia and can be used to show the plan of the city. Useful for all grades.

13. Reps, John William, *The Making of Urban America: A History of City Planning in the United States* (Princeton: Princeton University Press, 1965). Reps's book contains city plans of European cities at the time the New World was being settled, as

well as the plans of Colonial cities. This very essential book ought to be in the reference library.

14. Reps, John William, *Town Planning in Frontier America* (Princeton: Princeton University Press, 1969). An abridgement of Reps's larger book and more specifically oriented to American city origins.

15. Andrews, Wayne, *Architecture, Ambition and Americans* (New York: Harper, 1955), Free Press paperback. The first two chapters discuss architecture in the Northern and Southern Colonies. Useful as a reference for design-oriented students.

16. Scully, Vincent, *American Architecture and Urbanism* (New York: Frederick A. Praeger, 1969). The early beginnings of American city architecture can be found in Scully. This provocative book ties architecture and urbanism together quite well. For advanced students and teachers as a reference tool.

17. Glaab, Charles N., and A. Theodore Brown, *A History of Urban America* (New York: Macmillan, 1967), paperback. Chapter I is an excellent summary of the factors involved in city development in the Colonial era. For advanced students.

18. Callow, Alexander B., Jr., ed., *American Urban History* (New York: Oxford University Press, 1969), paperback. The section entitled "The City in Colonial America" contains three thoughtful essays on colonial cities. This book is an excellent reference for ideas about the city, but is usable primarily by senior students and teachers.

19. Smith, Page, *As a City upon a Hill* (New York: Alfred A. Knopf, 1966). The first chapter sets out Smith's theme, that New England towns provided a "covenanted community" as a model for small-town America. This community represented a sense of unity and emphasized conformity. It affected small-town growth throughout the United States as New England model towns spread to the west. These towns, according to Smith, exercised a pernicious effect upon democratic attitudes and were strongholds of conservatism. The ideas in this book lend themselves to inquiry and can be used for senior high school students.

20. Bridenbaugh, Carl, *Cities in the Wilderness* (New York: Alfred A. Knopf, 1966), Capricorn paperback. Bridenbaugh has been a pioneer in the development of urban history, and this book helped to establish his reputation. It concentrates upon five cities —Boston, New York, Newport, Philadelphia, and Charleston— taking them from their inception to the Revolution. Useful for advanced students' projects and for teacher information.

21. Haller, William, *The Puritan Frontier: Town Planning in New England Colonial Development, 1630–1660* (New York: Columbia University Press, 1951). Puritan views of town development are presented in this sophisticated book. Probably for research projects only.

22. Wertenbaker, Thomas J., *Norfolk: Historic Southern Port,* revised edition by Marvin W. Schlegel (Durham: Duke University Press, 1962). This history of Norfolk can be used as a .research resource for its treatment of the beginning of the city. Its assignment is probably not justified for general use.

23. Powell, Sumner Chilton, *Puritan Village: The Formation of a New England Town* (Garden City: Doubleday, 1965), paperback. A painstaking work which traces the founding of Sudbury, Massachusetts. It contains a number of maps, charts, drawings, and photographs. Powell looks to the English background as the source of the ideas about the town, but he also notes the American circumstances which changed the plans. The book is full of detailed facts and microscopic research, so it is suitable only for the best students and for the teacher.

24. Garvan, Anthony N. B., *Architecture and Town Planning in Colonial Connecticut* (New Haven: Yale University Press, 1951). This specialized study looks to Connecticut and sees English and American influences at work there. A reference work for teachers or students.

25. Rutman, Darrett, *Husbandmen of Plymouth: Farms and Villages in the Old Colony, 1620–1692* (Boston: Beacon Press, 1967). Rutman's book studies the process of town formation in the Plymouth area in great detail. The author is interested in

social history and traces life styles in rural and village life. Useful for further readings and study.

26. Rutman, Darrett, *Winthrop's Boston*: *Portrait of a Puritan Town, 1630–1649* (Chapel Hill: University of North Carolina Press, 1965), paperback. A study of the forces that shaped Boston. Rutman, as one of the new social historians, sees a number of factors but discounts Puritan ideology. Like the preceding book, this one is difficult but rewarding.

27. Lockridge, Kenneth A., *A New England Town*: *The First Hundred Years* (New York: Norton, 1970), paperback. This is the history of Dedham, Massachusetts, from 1636 to 1736. Lockridge claims Dedham tried to emulate an English village and duplicated the old as much as possible. Another book with possibilities for research.

28. Winslow, Ola Elizabeth, *Meetinghouse Hill, 1630–1783* (New York: Macmillan, 1952). Winslow has written a social history of the churches in New England down to the successful termination of the Revolution. For the design student's special project.

29. Petry, Ann, *Tituba of Salem Village* (New York: Crowell, 1964). The witch trial of Salem is seen through this biography of a Negro woman who was closely involved. For the junior high school level.

30. Fishwick, Marshall W., *Jamestown*: *First English Colony* (New York: Harper and Row, 1965). This volume in the American Heritage Junior Library is amply illustrated and treats the settlement in such a manner that the book can be used in junior high school classes.

31. "The Game of Empire" (Education Development Center, 15 Mifflin Place, Cambridge, Mass. 02138). While this game is designed for an understanding of mercantilism, the development of the port of Norfolk can be illustrated through the mercantile concepts. For the junior high school student.

The City:
Growth and Revolution, 1740–1783

Carl Bridenbaugh has identified five cities which he considers to be important in the American Revolution. These cities are New York, Boston, Newport, Philadelphia, and Charleston. Bridenbaugh says these cities share certain characteristics which make them more alike than different and which make them instrumental in helping to bring on the Revolution.

By 1740 these five cities had evolved from small towns into genuine urban areas with problems and advantages not unlike our own. They held their own in a period when America was becoming increasingly rural. Charles N. Glaab has estimated that by 1690 between 9 and 10 per cent of Americans lived in urban areas, but that by 1790 only 5 per cent lived in such areas. Thus the eighteenth-century American city and town grew more slowly

than the corresponding rural area, and it was not until 1830
that the percentage of urban dwellers equaled that of 1690.

Counter to this trend, these five American cities thrived for
a variety of reasons. They were all seaports and important commercial centers which soon began to challenge English pre-
eminence in the West Indian trade. Boston entrepreneurs sent
provisions to the Sugar Islands while Newport merchants built
ships and engaged in the slave trade. New York exported flour
and furs; Philadelphia sent out wheat, meat, and lumber; Charleston became important for rice and indigo. All of the cities had
a solid economic base upon which to build.

Further, all five cities showed the results of commercial wealth
in their social systems. The rich who had gained their wealth in
trade lived separately and affected a different life style. They
provided the capital and clientele for plays, dances, clubs, and
the other cultural advantages of the city. To the extent that an
intellectual life was characteristic of the cities, these people subsidized it. Below the rich were the middle-class persons who provided services and goods to each other and to the other classes.
The growth of the professions—medicine and law—was most
obvious in the city, as was the increase in the number of furniture
makers, barbers, tanners, and so forth. Below the middle class,
the lower class of free laborers performed menial tasks; below
them were the bottom strata of Indian and Negro slaves. The
beginnings of urban poverty can be found in the eighteenth-century
city; and the social stratification of our own time is more complex
but little different in kind.

The use of cooperative effort to provide municipal services
characterized these cities as much as our own. The problems of
planning for essentials was not entirely left in private hands. Each
city made some provision for streets, fire protection, police protection, poor relief, and public health. While the cities varied in
their approaches, each recognized the need for planning and attempted to meet it.

The Boston Massacre, March 5, 1770, as depicted in an engraving by Paul Revere (THE GRANGER COLLECTION)

Cities directed the location of streets, though private individuals could build streets dedicated to public use in return for tax exemption or special favors. In all of the cities maintenance of the streets fell upon the community, which either required labor from able-bodied residents or taxed the citizens to employ laborers. Municipal regulations limited the size and weight of vehicles using the streets, prevented too much garbage from being dumped on them, and placed some responsibility upon the citizens to keep the streets open and reasonably clean. The wharf facilities in the port cities were often a combination of public and private efforts, like the streets, but again public regulation was an essential part of these commercial developments.

Fire often consumed the cities of the day, hence all of these five cities made provisions to prevent fires and to limit them when they occurred. Each city regulated at least one of the following: the kinds of building materials, the state of chimneys, the closeness of houses to each other, and the use of double-wall construction to prevent fires from spreading from building to building. Despite private fire companies which were dedicated to the aid of subscribers, the burden of fire-fighting fell mainly on the shoulders of publicly organized and supported firemen.

The problem of law and public order appeared as great in Colonial towns as in our own. Once again public regulation was essential. The policing of towns took place largely at night, when watchmen patrolled areas to protect property and to detect persons who appeared suspicious. These watchmen were not uniformed and were often citizens voluntarily serving required times. In the more affluent cities, watchmen were paid from city funds which were collected from property owners. Constables served as day police and were relatively inefficient. The constables tried to solve crimes, but quite often citizens had to recover stolen articles through their own efforts or the efforts of privately hired persons. Those criminals who were caught were often turned in by informers. In many cities the areas of high crime were avoided by citizens and constables alike. Persons who were accused of crimes were confined in jails which each city had to provide. These jails were not usually used for long-term confinement, save in the case of debt, but as a safe place until trials could be held. Criminals were still corporally and capitally punished, reflecting both penury and a simpler concept of crime.

While American cities seemed to have less problems with the urban poor than comparable cities in Europe at the same time, adjustment to the problem was recognized as a necessity in all of the cities. Two methods of poor relief were in vogue in the eighteenth century—indoor and outdoor relief. Outdoor relief provided for payments to paupers in their own homes, while indoor relief restricted help to institutions where the paupers had to go for relief. In New York and Charleston, outdoor relief was used; Philadelphia, Boston, and Newport ran workhouses or almshouses. Legislation designed to prevent urban poverty was passed in the various cities. These laws tried to prevent strangers or European immigrants from entering if they seemed to lack means of support or if they seemed likely to become a public burden. In addition, poor children were forced into apprenticeships to prevent them from becoming public charges, and public stores of food were set aside for periods of want. Private charities also existed for the diminution of poverty, but these, like the private fire companies, only supplemented the public source.

Finally, all of the cities showed some concern for public health. Despite the primitive nature of public health knowledge at the time, cities enacted quarantine regulations and established hospitals for the treatment of some of the more infectious diseases. Those facilities which caused the most noxious problems—privies, slaughterhouses, dumps, tanneries, and refuse heaps—were subject to municipal regulation which specified their location and the terms of their use. These regulations, combined with building regulations, were the forerunner of modern zoning ordinances.

From this description, several significant questions become obvious. Students should explore the minimal services a city may provide. How far should municipal services go in caring for the lives of citizens? A further question is, How much progress has occurred in America since the eighteenth century? Many small towns in present-day America have not advanced any further in their conceptions of municipal services than had eighteenth-century Boston. This realization might give the student some historical humility.

The American city's part in the Revolution has not been given full credit. The existence of the city made possible the organization of revolutionary groups and provided the necessary facilities for creating, printing, and distributing the propaganda which led to public support for the rebel cause.

The Sons of Liberty, a New York City organization, were of urban origin and are an interesting example. Founded in the fall of 1765 as a secret organization, the Sons of Liberty became a public body with meetings announced in newspapers. The group encouraged the formation of like chapters throughout the colony through the use of committees of correspondence. In 1766, Sons of Liberty appeared in Albany, Oyster Bay, White Plains, and other New York towns. In addition to communicating with other groups in the New York colony, the Sons of Liberty also kept in touch with organizations in such other Colonial towns as Boston, Baltimore, and Newport. The Sons of Liberty armed themselves and became a paramilitary group ready to resist British encroachments. The group also provided an organizing function, marshaling two thousand people in October 1765 to prevent the landing of stamps to be used for tax purposes. They were unsuccessful in preventing the landing, but by demonstrations and harassments they were able to coerce the Lieutenant Governor into turning the stamps over to be burned. The Sons of Liberty in New York City also threatened stamp agents and merchants, either driving them out of the colony or forcing them to disown the sale and use of stamps.

After the success of their action against stamps, the Sons of Liberty disappeared from the New York scene until the fall of 1773, although individual activities by former members continued. The occasion for the re-emergence of the group was to resist the

Tea Act. The Sons of Liberty even formed a group known as "Mohawks" to prevent the landing of tea. This group, similar to the one in Boston, did not dump tea in New York harbor—but only because an irate crowd beat them to it in 1774. The Sons of Liberty propagandized for the war, supported Boston, and continued their radical ways. They helped select delegates to the First Continental Congress and, when hostilities began at Lexington and Concord, seized arms from an arsenal in New York City and fought the British.

The actions of the New York Sons of Liberty were typical of the groups in other cities. The organization in Boston was even more active. The significant point is that only the towns and cities provided the ingredients for a revolutionary group—population for mass demonstrations, meeting places, direct access to incoming boycotted goods at the port areas, and newspaper and printing facilities for propaganda purposes.

Just as the Sons of Liberty were located in the significant cities of the Revolution, so were the major newspapers of the period which did so much to raise revolutionary fervor. At the beginning of the Revolution there were thirty-six newspapers in the Colonies. These newspapers were uniformly located in the major cities, with New York having three and Philadelphia seven. The newspapers were typically issued two or three times a week, but their issuance was staggered enough that an interested reader could find a paper every weekday. The newspapers were printed in English and in other languages suitable to the immigrant population. In 1762, Henry Miller, a German, started *Der Wöchentliche Philadelphische Stoatsbote,* designed to meet the needs of those who came from that area of Europe. The *Stoatsbote,* like the other Philadelphia and New York newspapers, had wide circulation outside of the city and the colony. New Jersey had no newspaper, so New York and Philadelphia papers shared the area. Philadelphia newspapers were read as far away as Canada and the West Indies.

Magazines and books also were published in the New World. Franklin began his *General Magazine* in 1741. Another well-known figure in the Revolution, Thomas Paine, was editor of the

short-lived *Pennsylvania Magazine,* or *American Monthly Museum,*
which began in January 1775 and expired in July 1776. The
availability of newspapers and magazines in taverns and books
in libraries meant that the people were able to be informed of
the issues of the day.

This is not to say that Colonial newspapers were uniformly in
favor of the revolutionary cause. Like the citizens of the colonies,
they were divided politically. New York furnishes the best example. Of the three newspaper editors there, one was pro-Revolu-
tion, one was Tory, and the other wavered between the two sides
until pressure caused him to take a loyalist position. While such
an even split of opinion was not found in other cities, newspapers
representing patriot views did exist. In Boston the Tory *Massachusetts Gazette* was balanced by the patriot *Boston Gazette.* The
patriot side could also be found in the other newspapers of the
period.

Two points have been emphasized in this unit. First is the
essential role of cities in the American Revolution. Two examples
of the contributions made by cities were the patriotic organization
Sons of Liberty and the Colonial newspaper. In providing the
necessary population concentration for group action and a market
for newspapers, and in providing the division of labor and the
skills necessary for publishing, the social system of the city advanced the cause of the Revolution. These two examples do not
exhaust the possibilities; others may come as readily to mind.
The second point is the elements of similarity in American cities
by the time of the Revolution. Both points lend themselves to the
inquiry approach and to generalizations about the past and present
growth of cities, and past and present possibilities of revolutions
with or without cities.

Bibliography

1. *Geography in an Urban Age,* Unit I: *Geography of Cities*
(High School Geography Project, Association of American

Geographers: Boulder, Colo., 1968). The section "A Tale of Three Cities," which details the growth of Boston, New York, and Philadelphia to 1860, contains about a page on the growth of the cities from 1760 to 1800. The major point is that New York was gaining on Philadelphia and had surpassed Boston, but the reasons are not fully explained. There is no discussion of how the cities helped to bring on the Revolution.

2. *Freedom Trail in Boston* (International Film Bureau, 1965). A panoramic view of Boston, concentrating upon those features— the Old North Church, Faneuil Hall, and the Old State House— which were prominent in the Revolution. This film can be used in junior and senior high school classes.

3. *Portsmouth—American Mosaic* (Dan Stiles Associates, 1966). The section of the film on the growth of the port of Portsmouth is valuable in looking at the development of the city and the impact of the Revolution. For junior and senior high school classes.

4. *Eighteenth-Century Life in Colonial Williamsburg* (McGraw-Hill Textfilms, 1957). The Colonial newspaper and the social role of the tavern as a place for the dissemination of news appear in this film. The social stratification of Williamsburg and the apprentice system also fit into the unit's discussion. For primary through senior high school.

5. Reps, John William, *The Making of Urban America: A History of City Planning in the United States* (Princeton: Princeton University Press, 1965). The section of Reps's book devoted to eighteenth-century American cities is important for looking at urban problems.

6. Andrews, Wayne, *Architecture, Ambition and Americans* (New York: Harper, 1955), Free Press paperback. The first two chapters on architecture in North and South to 1790 are useful for considering the design ideas of the time.

7. Scully, Vincent, *American Architecture and Urbanism* (New York: Frederick A. Praeger, 1969). This sophisticated book is strong on features of American city architecture and can be used

for advanced students' research into the connection between an urban attitude and urban design.

8. Tunnard, Christopher, and Henry H. Reed, *American Skyline* (Boston: Houghton Mifflin, 1955), Mentor paperback. A survey of urban design. The first period is called the era of the Colonial city. Not a difficult book, suitable for senior high school students.

9. Burchard, John, and Albert Bush-Brown, *The Architecture of America* (Boston: Little, Brown, 1961), paperback. The authorized history of American architecture. The first chapter takes American architecture from its inception to 1860. An authoritative reference for research papers.

10. Burchard, John, and Albert Bush-Brown, *The Modern American City* (New York: Van Nostrand, 1968), paperback. Readings and commentary. The first chapter is a good simple introduction.

11. Glaab, Charles N., and A. Theodore Brown, *A History of Urban America* (New York: Macmillan, 1967), paperback. This survey history does not say much about the role of the city in the Revolution, but it does treat city development. For the teacher's library and for advanced students.

12. Green, Constance McLaughlin, *The Rise of Urban America* (New York: Harper and Row, 1965), paperback. Another survey of urban history. The first two chapters outline city development and the impact of cities on the Revolution. A basic book which ought not to be too difficult for senior high school students as either a supplementary text or reference work.

13. Callow, Alexander B., Jr., ed., *American Urban History* (New York: Oxford University Press, 1969), paperback. A collection of readings. The section "The City in Colonial America" has two excerpts from the books of Carl Bridenbaugh which are the standard ones for the period. For advanced students and teachers.

14. Bridenbaugh, Carl, *Cities in the Wilderness* (New York: Alfred A. Knopf, 1955), Capricorn paperback. The development

of five colonial cities—Boston, New York, Newport, Philadelphia, and Charleston—is the theme of this standard work. For reference.

15. Bridenbaugh, Carl, *Cities in Revolt* (New York: Alfred A. Knopf, 1966), Capricorn paperback. The succeeding volume to *Cities in the Wilderness* discusses the role of the cities in the Revolution. It is the authoritative work on this theme. Primarily for reference.

16. Bridenbaugh, Carl, *Seat of Empire: The Political Role of Eighteenth-Century Williamsburg* (Williamsburg: Institute of Early American History and Culture, 1950), paperback. The discussion of the part played by Williamsburg in the Revolution can be assigned to students who are interested in how the Revolution caught hold in the South, which was lacking in cities.

17. Bridenbaugh, Carl, and Jessica Bridenbaugh, *Rebels and Gentlemen: Philadelphia in the Age of Franklin* (New York: Oxford University Press, 1962), paperback. The most comprehensive look at urban life in the leading city of the Colonies at the time of the Revolution. Best used for better students or for reference purposes.

18. Tolles, Frederick B., *Meeting House and Counting House: The Quaker Merchants of Colonial Philadelphia, 1682–1763* (New York: Norton, 1963), paperback. The growth of Philadelphia depended largely upon the energy and enterprise of the Quakers in that city. Tolles' book shows why Philadelphia grew to become the second largest city in the British Empire by the time of the Revolution. Useful for reference for teacher and student.

19. Tolles, Frederick B., *James Logan and the Culture of Provincial America* (Boston: Little, Brown, 1957). Logan was secretary to the Proprietor of Pennsylvania; Tolles' account of his life casts much light upon the development of the colony and the city. Useful for reference.

20. Conner, Paul A., *Poor Richard's Politicks: Benjamin Franklin and His New American Order* (New York: Oxford University Press, 1965), paperback. The author attempts to sort out Franklin's ideas about the desired shape of the American

future. Conner says Franklin's praise of rural life was a disguised attack on shopkeeper ethics. For the advanced student or teacher.

21. Donovan, Frank R., *The Many Worlds of Benjamin Franklin* (New York: Harper and Row, 1964). One of the American Heritage Junior Library series, well illustrated and well written. The level of comprehension here is the fifth grade, hence it might be helpful for slow students. Attention is paid to Franklin's urban contribution.

22. Warner, Sam Bass, Jr., *The Private City: Philadelphia in Three Periods of Its Growth* (Philadelphia: University of Pennsylvania Press, 1968). One of the most significant books in American urban history today. Warner examines Philadelphia in three periods: 1770–1780, 1830–1860, and 1920–1930. He proposes a thesis to explain how Philadelphia, and hence other American cities, grew. This book is only for the most advanced students.

23. Heaps, Willard A., *Riots U.S.A., 1765–1965* (New York: Seabury Press, 1966). The book uses a legal definition of riots from a New York court decision in 1848, from Le Bon, and from the dictionary. The section on the Stamp Act Riots is good, and the whole book is useful in showing that urban violence has long been part of the American experience. For reference purposes.

24. Zobel, Hiller B., *The Boston Massacre* (New York: Norton, 1970). Zobel is a lawyer who is anti-rebel and who takes a dim view of the behavior of Boston citizens during the Revolution. He claims that the Boston mob ran the city by force and terror and that Sam Adams and Richard Dana were real villains. Zobel's position is interesting in that it is conservative both in the past and today. The book does show how we romanticize violence in the past if it accomplishes what are considered desirable ends. For student research and teacher information.

25. Wertenbaker, Thomas J., *The Golden Age of Colonial Culture* (Ithaca: Cornell University Press, 1942), paperback. Wertenbaker puts together his vast knowledge of Colonial social history in this book, which has some material on urban history. A good reference work.

26. Pomerantz, Sidney I., *New York: An American City, 1783–1803* (New York: Ira J. Friedman, 1965). While the time span of this book is somewhat later than that covered in this unit, the development of New York by the end of the Revolution is the starting point. A specialized study for research purposes.

27. Dobler, Lavinia, and Edgar A. Toppin, *Pioneers and Patriots* (New York: Doubleday, 1965), paperback. Contains pictures and essays on Peter Salem and Benjamin Banneker, black figures of the Revolutionary era. The level is junior high.

28. "The Game of Empire" (Education Development Center, 15 Mifflin Place, Cambridge, Mass. 02138). The function of American seaports in the mercantile scheme is obvious in this game designed for the junior high school student.

Anti-City Attitudes,
1790–1860

The period from the Revolutionary War to the Civil War is often described as one during which anti-city attitudes shaped the American mind. The leading thinkers of the era, from Thomas Jefferson to Ralph Waldo Emerson, proclaimed the virtues of a rural way of life, and an entire section, the South, supposedly built a political and economic theory upon an agricultural system. The American view of the city taken from the intellectuals of the day, then, is that the city was evil.

Certainly a case can be made that members of the generation of the Founding Fathers wrote of the perils of city life and that the Transcendentalists echoed that theme. Benjamin Franklin, perhaps the most urbane member of the Republican generation, did not share this affinity for the virtues of the country. Indeed,

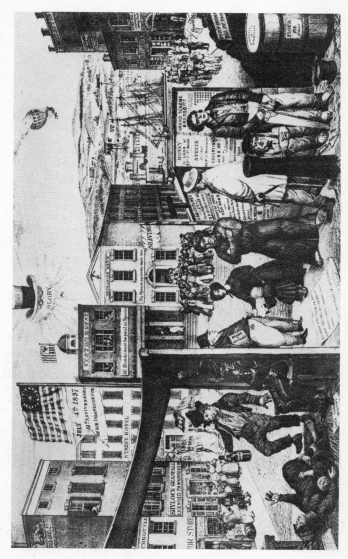

"The Times," lithograph by Edward W. Clay depicting the evils of city life in 1837 (J. CLARENCE DAVIES COLLECTION, MUSEUM OF THE CITY OF NEW YORK)

quite often he championed the city. But there were effective spokesmen for the anti-urban position, and the most eloquent was to be found in the rural South, more particularly in Virginia, in the person of Thomas Jefferson.

Jefferson's thoughts about the city which are most often quoted appear in his *Notes on Virginia* in 1784. Here he contrasts Europe to America, to the detriment of the former. America is virtuous while Europe is immoral. Part of the reason for European immorality is that European societies are old and have almost completed the organic cycle. The symbol of European decadence is its cities. Americans, to forestall their own eventual decay, should stay with the land. All Americans should be farmers, including those who service farmers—carpenters, masons, and smiths. None should engage in manufacture. As Jefferson said in the *Notes on Virginia*:

> For the general operations of manufacture let our workshops remain in Europe. It is better to carry provisions and materials to workmen there, than bring them to the provisions and materials, and with them their manners and principles. The loss by the transportation of commodities across the Atlantic will be made up in happiness and permanence of government. The mobs of great cities add just so much to the support of pure government as sores do to the strength of the human body. It is the manners and spirit of a people which preserve a republic in vigour.

Jefferson also wrote to Benjamin Rush in 1800 during an outbreak of yellow fever in Philadelphia:

> When great evils happen, I am in the habit of looking out for what good may arise from them as consolation to us, and Providence has in fact so established the order of things, as that most evils are the means of producing some good. The yellow fever will discourage the growth of great cities in our nation and I view great cities as pestilential to the morals, the health and the liberties of man. True, they nourish some of the elegant arts, but the useful ones can thrive elsewhere, and less perfection in the others, with more health, virtue and freedom, would be my choice.

It is such statements as these that historians use to show that the first generation of Americans was determined to keep the nation rural. But even in the case of Jefferson some qualifications about his position must be made. His views of the city reflected other assumptions about man's physical and social nature. He believed that men collectively acted worse than men separately, and that the best society was achieved when men lived apart from each other. This prevented their innate selfishness from being multiplied. Jefferson was pessimistic about the final outcome of the American experiment. Americans will become old and degenerate also; the only hope we have is in postponing the day. Further, given the better moral position of Americans, their cities did not equal those of Europe in their evil. Americans might be corrupted by city life, but for the present American urbanites were of a different quality than their European counterparts.

In addition, Jefferson shared the medical notions of the time which regarded the city as a noxious environment. The miasmic theory of disease was still respectable. This held that one of the factors contributing to disease was the quality of the air, that swamps and cities had bad air and hence more disease. The view could be upheld empirically since fevers—especially those spread by mosquitoes—were more likely to occur near swamps and in cities. Given the uncertain water and sewer facilities and inadequate public health practices, the cities were places where people lived shorter lives and where epidemics and plagues were more likely. In passing, one may speculate that the miasmic theory of disease has returned under the guise of air pollution, and that Ralph Nader might not have been given a bad reception in nineteenth-century Philadelphia. An interesting class project might be to compare the evils attributed to miasmas in the early nineteenth century with those attributed to air pollution in the twentieth.

Despite his social thought which by its very nature condemned cities, Jefferson was able to compromise. When Louisiana became part of the United States, Jefferson proposed that cities be developed in such a way as to limit their physical hazards. His solution was a checkerboard with alternating blocks of houses and open country. The introduction of nature into the city would purify the air and reduce disease. Two cities were in fact planned to follow this suggestion: Jeffersonville, Indiana, and Jackson, Mississippi. Neither persisted in the plan because of the pressure to sell off the blocks of open country. But the nineteenth-century movement to provide for parks in cities owed something to Jefferson and to others who regarded natural areas in the city as "lungs" which expelled bad air.

Finally, after the War of 1812, Jefferson reluctantly concluded that the United States must become a manufacturing nation and thus a nation with cities. The war with England changed his views. While he did not abandon his ideas about the difficulty of city life, he accepted the necessity of it. Jefferson was always the pragmatist; his views of the city, like his views on strict construction of the Constitution, had to give way to what he considered political reality. If manufacturing or Louisiana were essential to American interests, they must be obtained despite the contradictions of previous theory. If America had cities, they must be habitable, with safeguards to counteract the physical and social difficulties inherent in urban life.

Jeffersonian anti-urbanism became a part of the Southern defense of its way of life. From Jefferson there is a direct line to John Taylor of Caroline, who in his *Orator* (1813) argued that governmental poverty went hand in hand with public virtue. Taylor was opposed to political power, to the growth of money, to monopoly capitalism—which he defined as achieving wealth unmixed with labor by use of monopolies and government aid. Farmers by definition could not be given government aid and hence farming would not lead to the vices Taylor saw in American society in his own day. Only manufacturing required special dispensation from government, and this subsidy encouraged the growth of monopoly capitalism. But Taylor was pessimistic; he carried Jefferson to his logical extreme. As Loren Baritz has put it, "America, for Taylor, had meant rural simplicity and had degenerated into civilization."

The third Virginian, who spoke for the South in the 1850's, was less opposed to cities than his predecessors. George Fitzhugh's *Sociology for the South* (1854) and *Cannibals All* (1857) attacked Northern capitalism as strongly as had Taylor and went beyond both Jefferson and Taylor in the most thoroughgoing of all defenses of the slave system. Fitzhugh, however, did not attack Southern manufacturing or Southern cities. While he was conservative to the degree of admiring feudal society and holding that changes since the seventeenth century had mainly been pernicious, Fitzhugh was not the convinced argarian that his predecessors were. He typifies the problem of anti-city sentiment in the era, in that his thoughts on the place of the city are not central but only peripheral elements in a larger critique of the nature and function of American society. Anti-city sentiment in Southern thought is not simple nor necessarily constant.

The same may be said for the anti-city views of the greatest American Transcendentalist, Ralph Waldo Emerson. Emerson wrote:

> The city delights the understanding. It is made up of finites: short, sharp, mathematical lines, all calculable. It is full of varieties, of successions, of contrivances. The country, on the contrary, offers an unbroken horizon, the monotony of an endless road, of vast uniform plains, of distant mountains, the melancholy of uniform and infinite vegetation; the objects on the road are few and worthless, the eye is invited ever to the horizon and the clouds. It is the school of Reason.

Emerson disliked the city because it was artificial and because it prevented men from becoming self-reliant. He did not equate cities with civilization; instead he held that the virtue of the citizens was the test of civilization and that cities were of dubious moral virtue. Emerson had mixed feelings about cities, for he recognized that urbanity and learning could be concentrated in the cities.

These were important aims for Emerson, but their connection with mass life was enough to put him off.

Emerson's anti-city position, like Jefferson's, was an offshoot of his social theory. He was really more pro-nature and pro-individualism than he was anti-city. Like Jefferson, Emerson altered his position as he grew older and as events overtook him. The Civil War caused him to rethink his position and to lean toward exalting American nationalism as expressed in the collective common man. This nationalism, combined with a faith in the American future, turned to the West where better cities could be found. Here the American could forge a better city, a city of the West. Emerson celebrated not only the city of the future but America the industrial and America the hope of the immigrant. At the end of his career, Emerson dreamed of the coming American mission in modern, urban terms. As Loren Baritz notes, "That the rhapsodic worshipper at the shrine of the Aeolian harp ended his prayer in a boiler factory is proof of how completely he had marched in time with his nation."

What is found in Emerson can also be found in Hawthorne, Poe, Melville, and Thoreau. They all viewed the city with varying amounts of distrust, skepticism, and even horror. Their view of the city is echoed in the popular literature of the time with more explicit suggestion as to the nature of urban evil—crime, seduction, slums, extremes of wealth and poverty. The cheap literature of the period painted livid pictures of the dangers lurking for virtuous farm boys in the city. These works, however, like the more rarified thoughts of Emerson and Jefferson, were not unambiguously anti-city. Charles Glaab and A. Theodore Brown have quoted one of the popular exposé writers of the mid-nineteenth century, George G. Foster of the *New York Tribune,* as saying in his *New York in Slices by an Experienced Carver:*

> A great city is the highest result of human civilization. Here the Soul, that most perfect and godlike of all created things, the essence and spirit of the visible world, has put forth all its most wonderful energies. . . . Yes—man in isolation, or thinly

gathered in feeble neighborhoods and scattered villages, is powerless to accomplish great works or to fulfill the mission of his race. It is only in a large city, where some hundreds of thousands combine their various powers, that the human mind can efficiently stamp itself on everything by which it is surrounded—can transmute the unsensible earth to a fit temple and dwelling place for immortal spirits.

While popular writers attacked the sinful city, one noted American author celebrated it:

> I, chanter of Adamic songs,
> Through the new garden the West,
>   the great cities calling.

So said Walt Whitman, who was able to see mystic good in nature but also in man's creation, the city, who found subject matter for his works in the Brooklyn ferry and the hospitals of Washington. Whitman accepted man in his many roles, including man the sensual as well as man the moral. For Whitman, the spontaneous life could as easily be lived in the city as out. Yet, despite his lack of fear of the city, or perhaps because of it, Whitman is not often mentioned by those who were concerned with anti-city thought.

In American thought during the first seventy years of the Republic, the city did not fare well. From Jefferson to Emerson there was a questioning of the role of cities and a belief that cities were places of physical danger and moral evil. Yet the other side of this belief saw that the march of progress would require cities, that American cities would be different, that Americans might shape and develop the city so as to minimize the dangers inherent in it. It is to this often ignored belief that we must look in order to understand why the American city grew so rapidly after 1830. Daniel Boorstin says that those who find anti-city ideas in the nineteenth century are looking in the wrong place, that they are looking at a literature that appealed to the sensibilities of a cultured few. To find out how the majority of Americans felt, Boorstin says, the student should look at the promotional literature of the time which was aimed at the mass market. In the booster tracts of the time the city is portrayed as the place to live the good life, as a place of refinement and culture combined with material comforts. The common man's vision of the city has yet to be fully defined.

This unit lends itself very nicely to a core approach. It is a difficult unit, one that ought to be limited to superior students, but one which may be expanded to considerable length. The teacher may find it interesting to combine history and literature courses, concentrating upon the view of the city which American writers had in the pre–Civil War period. The views of the city held by promoters and entrepreneurs and by writers of popular works are harder to find, but an attempt to mine local sources such as newspapers, early developers' prospectuses, railway announcements, and so forth, might prove fruitful. Students can also be encouraged to detect anti-city attitudes in contemporary writing and to compare these attitudes with those of the past.

Bibliography

1. *Walt Whitman's World* (Coronet Films, 1966). This film uses Whitman's manuscripts and hospital notes in juxtaposition with pictures of the scenes he was describing. Part of the Cultural History series and a good portrayal of the cities in Whitman's experience. Suitable for senior high school students primarily, but the film can be shown to lower grades.

2. *Walt Whitman's Western Journey* (Francis R. Line Productions, 1965). Whitman took a western trip in 1879, going as far as the Rockies. In this re-creation of his trip can be found Whitman's attitudes toward the town and country alike. Suitable for junior and senior high school students.

3. *Washington Irving's World* (Coronet Films, 1966). As part of the Cultural History series, this film uses the same techniques as in *Walt Whitman's World*. Some paintings and prints also appear. Irving is less consciously anti-urban than his contemporaries. For junior and senior high school students.

4. *American Literature—The Westward Movement* (Coronet Films, 1954). The authors whose views are explored in this film are Washington Irving, Mark Twain, Joaquin Miller, Bess Streeter Aldrich, and Emerson Hough. While not commenting specifically upon city and country, the authors do reveal their feelings on the nature of the West and the possibility of cities there. For both junior and senior high school students.

5. *Kazin: The Writer and the City* (Chelsea House, 1969). This excellent film examines through the noted literary critic Alfred Kazin the city as an aesthetic force and inspiration in literature from Whitman and Melville to Mailer. Highly recommended for better students.

6. *Mark Twain's America* (McGraw-Hill Textfilms, 1960). Originally a Project 20 production, this film uses photographs, prints, and engravings to portray Twain's view of America. The time span goes beyond the one in this unit, but the movie helps to focus on the literary imagination. For junior and senior high school students.

7. Reps, John William, *The Making of Urban America: A History of City Planning in the United States* (Princeton: Princeton University Press, 1965). Reps's book contains the plans for Jeffersonville, Indiana, as well as for other cities that utilized parks, graveyards, and other natural breaks.

8. Andrews, Wayne, *Architecture, Ambition and Americans* (New York: Harper, 1955), Free Press paperback. Those interested in architectural design should read Chapter 4, "The Romantic Era, 1820–1860." Not for the average student.

9. Burchard, John, and Albert Bush-Brown, *The Architecture of America* (Boston: Little, Brown, 1961), paperback. The first chapter indicates the aesthetic preferences of a number of literary figures—Cooper and Emerson among them—as applied to architecture. Useful for reference purposes.

10. Tunnard, Christopher, *The Modern American City* (New York: Van Nostrand, 1968), paperback. Chapter 2, "A City

Built Foursquare," covers the gridiron plan which Tunnard attributes primarily to Jefferson. The chapter includes a plan of Sparta, Wisconsin. While Tunnard tends to overemphasize the grid, the chapter is easy to understand. He also includes a section of readings by Harriet Beecher Stowe and Edgar Allan Poe. For senior high school students.

11. Rudofsky, Bernard, *Streets for People: A Primer for Americans* (Garden City: Doubleday, 1969). Rudofsky attacks the grid, which he sees as typical of the American city plan and which he claims was set in 1811. He feels the grid reflects a belief that people are secondary to the city and, hence, a kind of anti-urbanism. For possible ways to make streets usable for people he uses illustrations from Perugia, Osaka, Milan, Alcudia, and other cities. A good reference work for comparing city layouts; the ideas may be used for discussion material.

12. Glaab, Charles N., and A. Theodore Brown, *A History of Urban America* (New York: Macmillan, 1967), paperback. Chapter 3 is an excellent summary of thoughts on the city and is highly recommended as the best short essay on the topic. A sophisticated book, useful only for advanced students.

13. Callow, Alexander B., Jr., ed., *American Urban History* (New York: Oxford University Press, 1969), paperback. This collection contains, in the section on "The City in the American Mind," five good articles on the topic. Most of the articles, however, are on the modern period. For advanced students.

14. White, Morton, and Lucia White, *The Intellectual versus the City: From Thomas Jefferson to Frank Lloyd Wright* (New York: New American Library, 1964), paperback. An excellent review of anti-city sentiment. It is difficult, as might be expected coming from a social philosopher, but ought to be required reading for better students and for teachers.

15. Boorstin, Daniel J., *The Americans: The National Experience* (New York: Random House, 1965), paperback. The section on Boosterism is a good antidote to the anti-urban thought found

in *The Intellectual versus the City.* While Boorstin's book is sophisticated, better students can profit from it.

16. Handlin, Oscar, and John Burchard, eds., *The Historian and the City* (Cambridge, Mass.: MIT Press and Harvard University Press, 1963), paperback. Frank Freidel's chapter "Boosters, Intellectuals, and the American City" suggests that most nonintellectuals and even some intellectuals were pro-city. Freidel points to Benjamin Franklin as an example of an intellectual who supported cities. For advanced students and teachers.

17. Strauss, Anselm, *Images of the American City* (Glencoe: Free Press, 1961). Strauss discusses the many images of the city which have appeared in novels and in booster and travel literature. Useful for reference work and for ideas for student discussions.

18. Dunlap, George A., *The City in the American Novel, 1789–1900* (New York: Russell and Russell, 1965). Dunlap's book contains much information on the novelist's view of the city when America was still a rural society. An excellent reference source, it can be used by students who are interested in beginning projects of this sort.

19. Gelfant, Blanche H., *The American City Novel* (Norman: University of Oklahoma Press, 1954). A general overview of the novel about the city. It attempts to cover the span of American history and has more material on twentieth-century novels than does Dunlap's book. For a standard work on the topic, the teacher should turn to Gelfant.

20. Fein, Albert, ed., *Landscape into Cityscape: Frederick Law Olmsted's Plans for a Greater New York City* (Ithaca: Cornell University Press, 1967). Olmsted was a journalist, social critic, and landscape architect who helped plan parks in New York and Chicago as well as design estates for the rich. His views of what New York should be are presented here. For design students' reference.

21. *The American Fiction Series, 1774–1860* (New York: Garret Press, 1969–). Garret Press is reprinting forty-seven

novels which were popular before the Civil War. A number of
these give interesting insights into fictional views of the city.
Typical is George Leppard's *The Quaker City, Or the Monks of
Monk Hall: A Romance of Philadelphia Life,* which appeared in
1844 and is considered a forerunner to the naturalism and muck-
raking of the post–Civil War era. These books are inexpensive
and provide a primary resource for independent study.

22. Cowan, Michael H., *City of the West: Emerson, America,
and Urban Metaphor* (New Haven: Yale University Press, 1967).
Cowan's book depicts Emerson as less anti-city than the Whites
say he was. The book is particularly good for the urban aspect
of Emerson's thought and his ideas about the ideal community.
For teachers and sophisticated students only.

23. Strauss, Anselm, ed., *The American City: A Sourcebook
of Urban Imagery* (Chicago: Aldine, 1968). This collection of
readings parallels Strauss's other book.

24. Weimer, David R., ed., *City and Country in America* (New
York: Appleton-Century-Crofts, 1962), paperback. Another collection of readings which shows how theorizers of the city have
often tried to bring elements of the country into it. For the thoughtful student.

The Urban Frontier,
1790–1861

The influence of Frederick Jackson Turner on Americans' historical imagination is still great. The connection he made between the frontier and the American character, while severely attacked for at least thirty years, remains part of conventional knowledge. His framework for studying frontier settlement has been even more persistent and is still orthodoxy in most textbooks, high school and college. This framework posited a series of frontiers—the hunter's and trapper's frontier, the miner's frontier, and the farmer's frontier—each of which seemed to represent a step in a process of civilization. The theme of America's frontier story, then, was how a wilderness was tamed in successive stages and how this wilderness changed those who tamed it. Despite Turner's own complexity and ambiguities, his disciples and popularizers have made the frontier experience into an evolutionary, progressive phenomenon capable of lineal expression. Teachers in elementary schools start with pioneers who live in log cabins and lead solitary lives and then go on to lead their students to farmsteads on the prairie. Little is said about cities until after the Civil War.

This stage-by-stage conception, however, distorts historical reality. It is here that Jane Jacobs' argument, that the city precedes the country, can be demonstrated. Richard C. Wade, one of our leading urban historians, states flatly that "the towns were the spearheads of the American frontier. . . . Whether as part of French and Spanish activity from New Orleans or part of Anglo-American operations from the Atlantic seaboard, the establishment of towns preceded the breaking of soil in the transmontane West." Wade goes on to say that before 1800 the sites of every large city that was to develop in the Old Northwest, except Chicago, Milwaukee, and Indianapolis, had been established and work commenced on settlement. These cities included St. Louis, founded in 1764; Pittsburgh, founded in the same year; Louisville and Cincinnati, founded in 1778; and Lexington founded in 1779. Between 1780 and 1800, Detroit, Buffalo, and Cleveland became towns. All of the cities preceded much settlement in the area; indeed, most of them were established before the land nearby was even available for settlement, either because of hostile Indians or because of the pressures of war.

Why is Wade's contention not found in textbooks? The reason is that in their writing few historians have bothered to look at how towns and cities in the new Republic were founded and developed. They have assumed that after an area became peaceable because of the removal of the Indians, and after farmers had settled to create a market, cities sprang up. Yet, if the history of American cities is studied, the picture is something quite different. Three examples of Western cities ought to suffice.

The first is Fort Wayne, Indiana, a medium-sized metropolis of over 200,000 population in 1960. Fort Wayne began as a French trading post in 1717 as Fort St. Philippe. The Miamis

The Cincinnati waterfront at Front and Main Streets, from an 1835 painting by John Casper Wild (CINCINNATI HISTORICAL SOCIETY)

called the center Miamitown or Kekionga. The town became Fort
Wayne in 1792, named after "Mad" Anthony Wayne. The development of the town was financed in part by fur traders who used
the capital gained from exchange with the Indians to lay out the
town and provide building lots as well as commercial centers.
In other words, the trading post of Fort Wayne existed from the
beginning of the French fur trade and became an American town
before farmers ever arrived on the scene. Typically, the same
persons who became rich in the fur trade also tried to add to
their wealth by promoting the city. They built banks and hotels,
as well as saloons, and speculated in city and farm property.

The second example is Cincinnati, the "Queen City," which
was born in December 1788. Cincinnati was the second town to
be formed in Ohio out of the purchase of a man named Symmes,
a New Jersey speculator. Symmes sold part of his purchase, which
he pushed through Congress in 1788, in the same year to Matthias
Denman. Denman proposed the city as an outlet to Kentucky
through a ferry system he hoped to establish. In order to develop
the town, Denman took two partners, Robert Peterson and John
Filson, who had been town developers in Kentucky. Filson disappeared and was replaced by Israel Ludlow, who did the actual
laying out of the town, using a gridiron plan based upon Philadelphia. Cincinnati's first name was Losantiville—a name that was
to be perpetuated in southern Indiana—but the town was re-
named after the Society of the Cincinnati in the 1790's. Cincinnati,
then, began contemporary with the settlement of Ohio by Americans in an organized way. It was typical of a number of such cities
which were developed by speculators who hoped to make money
off a growing city either because of a natural or political advantage.

Cincinnati was a successful town, and its success was as much
a product of political developments as of natural advantage. While
the city was fortunate to be located on the Ohio River, its location
was not entirely advantageous because of susceptibility to flooding.
But the problem with the Miami Indians proved to be an unfore-
seen advantage. Fort Washington became part of Cincinnati in

1792 in order to defend against the Indians, and the port thrived in its role as the main supply center for the army in its expeditions to the North. After the Indians lost at Fallen Timbers in 1794, Cincinnati continued to grow as a center for the shipping of produce from Ohio to New Orleans. Farm settlement in the area grew with the city as it provided an outlet for the grain surplus. Soon Cincinnati was to become the packing center of the new West.

The third and last example is St. Louis, the farthest city west and the most isolated from a farming frontier. St. Louis preceded farming in its area by a longer time than that of any other Western city. St. Louis was a French city, deliberately planned after the French and Indian War because of the peace treaty which provided that the Kaskaskia and Cahokia posts had to be given to the English. In order to replace the posts, the French looked for another good natural site. This they did through the offices of Pierre Laclede Lignest, who, with a company of men, located the site in the fall of 1763. Laclede laid out the town in 1764 on a gridiron pattern with a public plaza after the plan of New Orleans. St. Louis became a center for the fur trade as well as the capital of Upper Louisiana. Under Spanish and American rule, the role of the town remained about the same. The fur trade expanded greatly for Americans only after the explorations of Lewis and Clark. The city also profited from nearby lead mines and from the army trade in the War of 1812. By the end of this war, St. Louis was the gateway to the West. Farmers were selling their produce there for transhipment down the Mississippi and, along with the fur traders, were buying goods from commercial establishments in the growing city.

In each of these three cities a different plan of development appears. Fort Wayne had a long history as a French trading post and Indian settlement before becoming an American city. Cincinnati was the product of town promotion by American settlers just as Ohio was opened to land development. St. Louis was a French post which replaced the loss of other posts to the

British after the French and Indian War. But each of these cities originated *before* farming interests made them necessary. They were intimately connected to the Indian frontier, either as part of the fur trade or as army depots for subduing the Indians. Profits from the fur trade, from the sale of supplies to the army, or from government grants to the Indians aided in town growth. Each of these cities, then, became a center for the sale or shipping of farm products. In this sense the cities helped create the farms and were spearheads of the frontier.

Another of the relations between town and frontier which is often neglected is the urban aspiration of many frontiersmen. The names of town promoters in the Old Northwest often were the names of the Indian traders and fighters of the same area. Even those who did not found towns often had urban aspirations. This relation has been best developed by William H. Goetzmann in his study of the Mountain Man as Jacksonian Man. Goetzmann points out that the Mountain Man, who is often regarded as a typical hero, did not expect to remain a fur trapper forever, nor did he enter the trade for romantic reasons. Goetzmann claims this man was primarily a capitalist whose purpose, like most Americans, was to make as much money as quickly as possible. The Mountain Men did not want primitiveness; they wanted to return to St. Louis to live in a fine house, or to build a city like Denver, or to develop the land. As Goetzmann says:

> They may have dreamed of "Arcadia," but when they turned to the task of settling the West as fast as possible, the former Mountain Men and perhaps others like them brought with them all the aspects of an "industrial," mercantile, and quasi-urban society. The opera house went up almost simultaneously with the ranch, and the Bank of Missouri was secured before the land was properly put into hay.

Goetzmann has done a statistical study of 446 Mountain Men who were in the fur trade from 1805 to 1845. This constitutes, according to his reckoning, about 45 per cent of the total. Of this number, 182 were killed in the fur trade, 110 had later occupations which he could not determine, 117 entered other occupations, 32 probably had other occupations, and only five stayed on as trappers. The occupations taken on by the ex-Mountain Men ranged from farmer to saloonkeeper. One became a superintendent of schools, while another was an opera house impresario. A number became famous in political and economic roles. Three helped found Denver, and several helped begin the wine industry in California.

The urban aspect of pioneer life as seen in the careers of the Mountain Men can be found in the lives of others engaged in different pioneering occupations. The cowboy Deadwood Dick ends his days as a porter on the railroad. The Indian fighter becomes a street commissioner. The failure to put these pioneers in their proper perspective is in part the result of a romanticizing process and in part the failure to realize the short duration of the pioneer activity which caused men to abandon other careers and to regard the activity as transitory. We have done a disservice to our students by leaving the impression that the frontier was the antithesis of the city, and that those who were solitary isolates for a short time preferred that life to one lived in a community. The city and the frontier were not mutually exclusive, nor were frontiersmen necessarily anti-urban.

This unit ought to suggest possibilities for further local history studies. The founding of cities in the Midwest and West during the era might be analyzed, particularly by those students living in urban areas in the region. Class projects could include the writing of the biography of an important frontiersman to trace his beginnings and ending. A study of the occupations of local founding fathers is almost certain to reveal connections with frontier activities. Another feasible and useful study is to compare the dates of the founding of towns with the admission of the states in which they are located, and with the population statistics of the surrounding area. This would relate the towns to the economic developments of the time.

Bibliography

1. *Geography in an Urban Age,* Unit I: *Geography of Cities* (High School Geography Project, Association of American Geographers: Boulder, Colo., 1968). Activity 1, "City Location and Growth," in the teacher's manual contains material on site selection in the Ohio Valley–Great Lakes region in 1800, 1830, 1860, 1890, and 1910. It also includes some population data which make possible comparisons between cities. Activity 2, "New Orleans," looks at the city area by area and indirectly touches upon historical growth.

2. *Ghost Towns of the Great Divide* (Classroom Film Distributors, 1951). While this film of Leadville, Colorado, treats of a town that does not quite fit into the period suggested, it is good in showing the aspirations of the town as seen in its opera house and hotel. The furnishings and general decor ought to interest junior and senior high school students.

3. *Santa Fe and the Trail* (Encyclopedia Britannica Films, 1963). The impact of Spanish culture on the settlements of the Southwest is the theme. A good film in the sense that it shows alternate ways of looking at city planning. For junior and senior high school students.

4. *Mississippi River—Its Role in American History* (Bailey, 1964). This film contains maps, old prints, and scenes from along the Mississippi River. The ideas are plain enough so that the film may be used for elementary grades up.

5. *New Salem Story—Lincoln Legend* (Teaching Film Custodians, 1964). While the major interest in the film is Lincoln's life, the town of New Salem occupies much of the scene. Adapted from a 1953 Cavalcade of America series, the film can be shown in elementary grades as well as in high school.

6. *Emergence of a Nation, 1800–1817* (Graphic Curriculum, 1966). The film is part of the Story of America: Exploring series, and shows the main events of the period. There is some reference to cities, although the concentration is elsewhere. For elementary grades.

7. *Era of the Common Man—The Age of Jackson* (Graphic Curriculum, 1966). Another in the Story of America: Exploring series.

8. *Fur Trappers Westward* (Arthur Barr Productions, 1953). The main events in the life of the fur trappers included the exploration of California, trading with the Indians, and the rendezvous. The film is useful as an example of perpetuating the romantic myth. It can be used on several levels, elementary and advanced.

9. *Settlers of the Old Northwest* (Encyclopedia Britannica Films, 1962). A part of the Westward Movement series, the film also contains information on the backgrounds and destinations of settlers. While not oriented directly to cities, it does include them. For elementary as well as junior and senior high school students.

10. *Settlement of the Mississippi Valley* (Encyclopedia Britannica Films, 1962). Another film in the Westward Movement series, this one covers the next area west.

11. Reps, John William, *The Making of Urban America* (Princeton: Princeton University Press, 1965). Reps's book contains plans of the cities which were begun in the period. Useful for reference for the student interested in city planning.

12. Reps, John William, *Town Planning in Frontier America* (Princeton: Princeton University Press, 1969), paperback. Specifically tailored to the frontier, Reps's book shows what kind of thinking went into frontier development. Again, a reference tool for student projects.

13. Glaab, Charles N., and A. Theodore Brown, *A History of Urban America* (New York: Macmillan, 1967), paperback. Chapter 2 devotes space to America's Western cities. Advanced students will find this chapter a good place to begin.

14. Green, Constance McLaughlin, *The Rise of Urban America* (New York: Harper and Row, 1965), paperback. There is some pertinent material in Chapter 3, although most of the attention is given to seaboard cities.

15. Green, Constance McLaughlin, *American Cities in the Growth of the Nation* (New York: John De Graff, 1957), Harper paperback. These are Mrs. Green's Commonwealth Fund lectures in history at University College, London, in 1951. For the student interested in the biography of specific cities in the Midwest, this book is more valuable than her *The Rise of Urban America*. For student projects and teacher use.

16. Callow, Alexander B., Jr., ed., *American Urban History* (New York: Oxford University Press, 1969), paperback. Section 3, "The City in the Era of Manifest Destiny," contains two important articles, one by Richard C. Wade, and one by Bayrd Still, which are basic to an understanding of the development of Midwestern cities. Advanced senior students and teachers can handle the material.

17. Wade, Richard C., *The Urban Frontier: Pioneer Life in Early Pittsburgh, Cincinnati, Lexington, Louisville, and St. Louis* (Chicago: University of Chicago Press, 1964), paperback. Essential to the study of the symbiotic relation of the city to the frontier. The book contains much factual as well as interpretive material and can be understood by senior high school students.

18. Boorstin, Daniel J., *The Americans: The National Experience* (New York: Random House, 1965), paperback. In a section on the Western cities in the early nineteenth century, Boorstin coins a term, "upstart cities." These are cities which grew with no past to support them. Boorstin discusses the promotion of three cities—Chicago, Cincinnati, and Denver—by three boosters—Ogden, Drake, and Larimer. Boorstin is particularly good on the business aspect of city growth in the West. For senior high school students.

19. Smith, Page, *As a City upon a Hill* (New York: Alfred A. Knopf, 1966). Smith's book discusses the settlements in Ohio, Indiana, Illinois, Michigan, and North Dakota by New Englanders who set up covenanted communities. He calls these communities colonized towns and says they were more significant for frontier

development than were the stereotyped frontiersmen. The book is suitable for projects by senior high school students.

20. Goetzmann, William H., *Exploration and Empire* (New York: Alfred A. Knopf, 1966). This award-winning book on the West puts the Mountain Man in his proper historical perspective and is vital for the study of that phenomenon. Goetzmann's book ought to be a reference work for students and teachers.

21. Pierce, Bessie L., *A History of Chicago* (3 vols., New York: Alfred A. Knopf, 1937–1957). The standard history. Students interested in the history of the establishment of Chicago should look here first.

22. Bontemps, Arna, and Jack Conroy, *Anyplace But Here* (New York: Hill and Wang, 1966). The first chapter discusses the life and career of Du Sable, the black trader who first built his trading post on the Chicago River in 1779. The chapter is helpful because it not only suggests the varied activities of a trader but also because the trader was black. The second chapter recounts the hectic life of Jim Beckwourth, Indian fighter and trapper. Beckwourth started as a blacksmith's apprentice in St. Louis and had an adventurous life. He settled down for a time as a store operator in Denver. Suitable for junior and senior high school students.

23. Filton, Harold W., *Jim Beckwourth: Negro Mountain Man* (New York: Dodd, Mead, 1966). This biography of Beckwourth relies on his own autobiography. For junior high school students.

24. James, D. Clayton, *Antebellum Natchez* (Baton Rouge: Louisiana State University Press, 1968). This history of a pre–Civil War Southern city suggests comparisons with Northern cities. Recommended for projects only.

25. Wheeler, Kenneth W., *To Wear a City's Crown: The Beginnings of Urban Growth in Texas, 1836–1865* (Cambridge, Mass.: Harvard University Press, 1968). Wheeler considers four Texas cities—Galveston, Houston, Austin, and San Antonio—and concludes that these cities, the last urban frontier of the Old South,

served the same function in Texas that Cincinnati, Louisville, Lexington, and St. Louis did in the Midwest. For better students only.

26. Lord, Clifford L., *Teaching History with Community Resources* (New York: Columbia University Press). The pamphlets that are useful in this unit are:

> *Denver,* John D. Mitchell (1969).
> *Milwaukee,* Charles N. Glaab (1969).
> *Chicago,* Clement M. Silvestro (1969).
> *The Upper Mississippi Valley,* Walter W. Havighurst (1966).
> *The Ohio Valley,* R. E. Banta (1967).
> *The Wisconsin,* August Derleth (1968).

The City:
Promotion and Transportation, 1790–1860

From the beginning of the Republic to the Civil War, existing American cities competed with new cities for population and wealth. It was during this period of national growth that economic and political decisions meant success for certain towns and decline for others. The advent of canals, turnpikes, toll roads, and railroads challenged cities either to use these facilities to their advantage or to die. The location of these means of transportation in or near a community gave an instant advantage over the town that was bypassed. The fortunes of seagoing trade increased the potential of favored seaport towns, while others engaged in less timely efforts grew at a slower pace. The designation of towns as political centers, whether for local or state purposes, also meant life, and the removal of the political services often meant death.

This unit concentrates upon the reasons why certain cities grew, how they responded to the challenges of the times, and why others were less fortunate.

Among the older American cities, the classic case of urban rivalry was between New York, Boston, and Philadelphia. In 1790, according to the census of that year, Philadelphia was the leading city in the United States with a population of 42,000; New York had a population of 33,000, and Boston 18,000. By 1860, however, New York had become the major American seaport on the Atlantic and the major American city with a population of 805,000 (not including its near neighbor, Brooklyn, which had a population of about 200,000 but which was politically separate). Philadelphia had a population of 563,000 in 1860, still good enough to make it the nation's second largest city, but Boston's population of 178,000 was already surpassed by that of Baltimore which had 212,000. The first part of the nineteenth century belonged to New York City. As Charles N. Glaab and A. Theodore Brown have said, " . . . By mid-century, it is in a broad way accurate to say that with the [exception of New England], the entire country was the hinterland of New York City, with Philadelphia and Baltimore competing for that business which New York was simply not big enough to handle." How did this happen?

New York became successful for a number of reasons, some economic and others social. The economic reasons are connected with maritime activity, both inland and trans-oceanic. During the pre–Civil War period, American balance of payments ran a deficit —we imported more than we exported. There are years where exceptions can be found, particularly in the 1840's, but the overall pattern was deficit. New York City became the primary port of entry for several reasons. One was an historic accident: after the War of 1812 the British determined to win back their pre-war trade. This they hoped to accomplish by dumping goods. The port they chose was New York, and this helped establish the city as a good place to find bargains. In 1817 the Black Ball Line established packet service across the Atlantic. These were regularly

Junction of the Erie and Northern Canals, aquatint by J. Hill, about 1830
(THE NEW-YORK HISTORICAL SOCIETY)

scheduled sailings as opposed to the practice of sailing irregularly depending upon when the passengers filled the ship. This meant that the burgeoning immigrant business as well as material goods went to New York.

New York City also became a leader in the export trade by capturing the major export business of the era, the shipping of cotton to England. This was accomplished by aggressive solicitation of business in the South, by the provision of financial services which the cotton-poor South did not provide for itself, and by the failure of Southern ports to expand and respond to the opportunity. Norfolk and Charleston did not grow enough to take any significant business from New York, and while New Orleans had at one time equaled New York in the volume and the value of export trade, the spreading network of railroads from east to west successfully diminished the flow of goods down the Mississippi to New Orleans. New York became the major commercial city for the South, providing the necessary commercial services for the whole region, a fact which Southern nationalists recognized and used as a basis for their argument that secession would impoverish the North and enrich the South.

Finally, New York increased its export business because of the completion of the Erie Canal in 1825. The canal made possible the use of Midwestern products in trans-oceanic trade. In other ways the Erie Canal only accelerated a process that had already begun, but its visibility caused other cities to attribute the major success of New York City to the canal.

Philadelphians were particularly concerned about New York and its Western connections. The energy of the Quaker community was declining; religiously the Quakers were becoming quietists, nor were they as aggressive in business as they had once been. After much debate and public discussion in Philadelphia over whether to build a canal or railroad to the West, the decision was made to construct canals with connecting cable cars to cross the mountains. But the system failed as a challenge to the Erie Canal, and while

Philadelphia grew, its rate of growth failed to match that of New York.

Bostonians were less concerned with the Erie Canal because of several factors. One was that much of the capital generated in Boston went into factories and industrialization in the area. Another was that New England ports still traded and profited from the China trade. As a result there was little sense of urgency in Boston business circles, and much time elapsed before connecting rail lines to the interior were started.

Urban rivalry also characterized the newer cities of the interior, and their success often depended upon promotion and connection with the significant transport facilities. Two examples suffice— Chicago and Cleveland.

Chicago, which was not incorporated until 1833, had been occupied by Indians and traders before the territory became part of the Union. The fort located at Chicago took on strategic importance after the War of 1812 when the canal craze started. The digging of canals to connect Lake Michigan with the Illinois River would provide an all-water communications route from the east coast through the Great Lakes to New Orleans. John C. Calhoun advocated such a canal during his stay of office as Secretary of War. The town of Chicago was designated as one terminus of the canal in 1829, though the canal was not opened until 1848.

In 1832 Chicago had less than one hundred inhabitants. By 1850 it had approximately 30,000, and by 1860, 109,000. The phenomenal growth of Chicago was due in large measure to the drive and aggressiveness of city promoters who tried hard to develop connections to interior farmland and, in the other direction, to the seaports which could export Midwestern goods. While a canal was the major reason for the original location of Chicago, the city's success was due mainly to rapid railroad building in the 1850's. The Galena and Chicago Union Railroad, the first to connect Chicago with the lead mines of Galena and with the Mississippi River, began traffic operation in 1849. Connection with

the East was via the Pittsburgh, Ft. Wayne, and Chicago Railway
—later to become part of the Pennsylvania; connection to the
North was through the Chicago, St. Paul, and Fond-du-Lac Railroad—later to become part of the Chicago and Northwestern.
When Chicago became the second largest city in the United States
in 1890 with over one million inhabitants, a major reason was the
rail network which had Chicago at its center.

Cleveland owed much of its growth to favorable historical circumstance. As already noted, the town originated in 1796 on a
site chosen by representatives of a Connecticut land company.
Like many other small towns in Ohio, Cleveland had natural advantages—it was located at the mouth of the Cuyahoga River and
was also on Lake Erie. It grew where other towns failed because
of promotion and because of transportation links. After the War
of 1812 a road and later a canal connected it with the Ohio River,
and it naturally benefited from the completion of the Erie Canal.
Cleveland's first railroad connecting it with southern Ohio came
in 1851. As a result, Cleveland's population grew from 1,000 in
1830 to 17,000 in 1850. While its growth was not as spectacular
as Chicago, it was similar in that transportation links and industrialization helped to make this city successful.

Richard Wade has listed some of the cities of the West which
failed despite the fact that their original promise equaled that of
cities which became important. Edwardsville, Illinois, never grew
to rival St. Louis. Jeffersonville and New Albany, Indiana, never
matched Louisville. Pittsburgh overshadowed Steubenville, Ohio,
and Wheeling, West Virginia (then Wheeling, Virginia). The latter city believed after the War of 1812 that its time for greatness
had come, especially when it became the western terminus of the
National Road. But the technological base for road travel, consist-
ing as it did largely of ox carts and wagons, proved unequal to
the task of making Wheeling the important center on the Upper
Ohio.

Almost every area in the United States can boast of towns
which became important regional cities. Conversely, almost every

area has towns which once were thriving rivals to these regional cities, but which are now gradually dying. The study of city rivalry is a study of economic success and failure. Nowhere else does urban history and economic theory merge so significantly. This unit is an ideal one to apply to the study of a single town, by concentrating either upon success or failure, and attempting to find the significant variables that made for that success or failure. Moreover, such a case study shows the contradictory nature of history, the contrariness of men in making some cities succeed when circumstances favor others, and the frailty of human prediction.

Bibliography

1. *Geography in an Urban Age,* Unit I: *Geography of Cities* (High School Geography Project, Association of American Geographers: Boulder, Colo., 1968). The section in the Student Resources part entitled "A Tale of Three Cities" attempts to answer the question of city growth and decline. The cities considered here are Boston, Philadelphia, and New York; the era 1800–1860 occupies a large part of the unit. The presentation is generally accurate, though it overemphasizes geographic location and errs in suggesting that Boston made a "strenuous effort" to compete with New York and that neither Philadelphia nor Boston could successfully compete as long as canals and rivers were the main route to the West. The last statement fails to account for the canal which was built to the West by Philadelphia interests.

2. *Chicago: Midland Metropolis* (Encyclopedia Britannica Films, 1963). The physical and social characteristics of Chicago serve as the focus for this film, which attempts to show why Chicago became a major urban center and what problems it encountered in urban development. For junior and senior high school students.

3. *Industrial Lake Port—Buffalo, New York* (United World Films, 1949). An older film which uses a geographical explana-

tion for the growth of Buffalo. From The Earth and Its Peoples series, suitable for junior and senior high school classes.

4. *New Orleans Profile* (Wayne State University, 1959). This quick survey of the history, tradition, and economic importance of New Orleans suggests that transportation helped to accomplish growth. For junior and senior high school students.

5. *Era of Water Commerce* (McGraw-Hill Textfilms, 1960). Part of the American Adventure series, this film covers the period from 1750 to 1850. It shows the interaction between water commerce and economic growth, including city development. For junior and senior high school classes.

6. *Saga of the Erie Canal* (Coronet Films, 1966). One of Coronet's Cultural History series. It is a fine film which combines technical discussion—the building of canal locks—with the impact of the canal on the popular mind—songs about the canal. Highly recommended for junior and senior high school students.

7. Tunnard, Christopher, and Henry H. Reed, *American Skyline* (Boston: Houghton Mifflin, 1955), Mentor paperback. The section on the cities of the young Republic (1825–1850) argues that the city design of the period reflects contemporary values which centered on economic growth and progress. For the sophisticated student and teacher interested in city design.

8. Glaab, Charles N., and A. Theodore Brown, *A History of Urban America* (New York: Macmillan, 1967), paperback. Chapter 2 contains an excellent discussion of urban rivalry which could serve as a springboard for an in-depth study. For better high school students.

9. Callow, Alexander B., Jr., ed., *American Urban History* (New York: Oxford University Press, 1969), paperback. Part 3, "The City in the Era of Manifest Destiny," contains four articles which discuss the phenomenon of city growth and rivalry in the period. For advanced students and teachers.

10. Green, Constance McLaughlin, *The Rise of Urban America* (New York: Harper and Row, 1965), paperback. Chapter 3 offers a quick look at economic growth. The material can be handled by the average senior high school student.

11. Green, Constance McLaughlin, *American Cities in the Growth of the Nation* (New York: John De Graff, 1957), Harper paperback. This book is much better than Mrs. Green's *Rise of Urban America* in detailing the process of urban rivalry. She describes the growth of several cities here and attempts more in the way of generalizations. A good reference for student projects.

12. Boorstin, Daniel J., *The Americans: The National Experience* (New York: Random House, 1965), paperback. Boorstin, in developing his theme of boosterism, describes the impact of several city promoters—Ogden of Chicago, Larimer of Denver, and Drake of Cincinnati— and the economic tactics they used to promote city development. Better students can use Boorstin.

13. Wade, Richard C., *The Urban Frontier: Pioneer Life in Early Pittsburgh, Cincinnati, Lexington, Louisville, and St. Louis* (Chicago: University of Chicago Press, 1964), paperback. Wade's book is necessary for an understanding of the economic forces that helped cities to succeed, and for the intense urban rivalry in the Midwest along the river routes west and south. Not difficult for senior high school students.

14. Albion, Robert G., *Square Riggers on Schedule: The New York Sailing Packets to England, France, and the Cotton Ports* (Princeton: Princeton University Press, 1938). Albion's book discusses the beginnings of scheduled service out of New York City to Europe, and its economic impact. While this is an older book, it is interesting and ought to appeal to senior high school students who are interested in maritime development.

15. Pomerantz, Sidney I., *New York: An American City, 1783–1803* (New York: Ira J. Friedman, 1965). This short period study of New York shows that the elements of rapid growth were evident at the beginning of the nineteenth century. A specialized book which can be assigned for reference or projects.

16. Wertenbaker, Thomas J., *Norfolk: Historic Southern Port*, revised edition by Marvin W. Schlegel (Durham, N.C.: Duke University Press, 1962). The sections on the first half of the nineteenth century explain why Norfolk did not rival New York. Another good reference tool.

17. Morison, Samuel Eliot, *Maritime History of Massachusetts, 1783–1860* (Boston: Houghton Mifflin, 1921), paperback. Morison, one of the leading American historians, wrote this book fifty years ago, but it remains the classic statement on the sea trade of Massachusetts, especially of Boston. For projects only.

18. Taylor, George R., *The Transportation Revolution, 1815–1860* (New York: Rinehart, 1951), Harper paperback. This is Volume 4 of the Economic History of the United States and is most detailed on the aspects of transport-canal, rail, and turnpike. For reference only.

19. Pierce, Bessie L., *A History of Chicago* (3 vols., New York: Alfred A. Knopf, 1937–1957). This standard history of Chicago has much useful reference material on the impact of the railroads and other reasons for Chicago's successful growth.

20. Reed, Merl E., *New Orleans and the Railroads: The Struggle for Commercial Empire, 1830–1860* (Baton Rouge: Louisiana State University Press, 1966). Reed's book shows how a city tied to the Mississippi River failed to expand with enough vigor to meet the competition of Northern cities. As such, it clearly presents the case that too much reliance on past success means future failure. A useful reference tool.

21. Belcher, Wyatt W., *The Economic Rivalry Between St. Louis and Chicago, 1850–1880* (New York: Columbia University Press, 1947). The rivalry involved alternate methods of transportation as well as competition for industry and railroads. For teachers and reference only.

22. Livingood, James W., *The Philadelphia-Baltimore Trade Rivalry* (Harrisburg: Pennsylvania Historical and Museum Commission, 1947). During the first half of the nineteenth century, Baltimore grew faster than Philadelphia. This book suggests reasons why.

23. Rubin, Julius, *Canal or Railroad: Imitation and Innovation in Response to the Erie Canal in Philadelphia, Baltimore, and Boston* (Philadelphia: American Philosophical Society, 1961). This book is one of the most significant in the unit because it describes

how various urban communities reacted to the challenge of technological advance. For sophisticated students only.

24. Shaw, Ronald, *Erie Water West: A History of the Erie Canal, 1792–1854* (Lexington: University of Kentucky Press, 1966). The definitive work on the Erie Canal and the one which students should read first. For projects and teacher enrichment.

25. Miller, Nathan, *The Enterprise of a Free People: Aspects of Economic Development in New York State During the Canal Period, 1792–1838* (Ithaca: Cornell University Press, 1962). Miller's work is concerned with the growth of state bureaucracy as well as the impact on city development. Recommended for outside projects.

26. Scheiber, Harry N., *Ohio Canal Era: A Case Study of Government and the Economy, 1820–1861* (Athens: Ohio University Press, 1969). Scheiber's interest is in the interplay between government and business, but he also shows how economic growth in cities was dependent upon transport facilities. For research projects.

27. Mazlish, Bruce, ed., *The Railroad and the Space Program: An Exploration in Historical Analogy* (Cambridge, Mass.: MIT Press, 1965). A difficult but rewarding book. It is a collection of speculative essays which tries to draw an analogy between the extension of railroads and the space program insofar as each brought about economic and social change. For teachers and advanced students only.

28. Pred, Allan R., *The Spatial Dynamics of U.S. Urban-Industrial Growth, 1800–1914: Interpretive and Theoretical Essays* (Cambridge, Mass.: MIT Press, 1966). This is a volume in the Regional Scene Studies series and is quite sophisticated. Pred takes a design viewpoint. Valuable for a teacher with background in the area.

29. Lord, Clifford L., *Teaching History with Community Resources* (New York: Columbia University Press). The pamphlets that are of use in this unit for suggesting local research are:

Cincinnati, Louis L. Tucker (1968).
Milwaukee, Charles N. Glaab (1969).
Chicago, Clement M. Silvestro (1969).
The Upper Mississippi Valley, Walter W. Havighurst (1966).
The Ohio Valley, R. E. Banta (1967).

The Black Man in the City, 1775–1865

The history of the Negro in America is tied closely to the history of the city, but this fact is often unrecognized in surveys of United States history. It is true that most blacks in this country were urbanized only in the twentieth century, but before the Civil War the black man in the North was predominantly found in cities and towns. In the South the urban regions became havens for the free Negro. As Richard Wade has said, "Freemen constituted the most highly urbanized group in Dixie. By 1860 they outnumbered slaves ten to one in Baltimore and 9209 to 1774 in Washington. . . . Across the South nearly a third of the free blacks were found in the larger urban centers." Additionally, slavery in the city changed because of urban conditions into a system more closely resembling segregation than one of plantation servitude.

The study of the Negro in ante-bellum cities, then, sheds light on the beginnings of segregation as well as on the accomplishments of black men in creating a separate set of social institutions paralleling those of the white community. These institutions range from fraternal and abolitionist societies to churches and business enterprises.

The famous Negroes of the period 1775–1865 are all connected in some way with cities. Benjamin Banneker (1731–1806), although born in Maryland in a rural area—Ellicott's Lower Mills (now Ellicott City), a settlement on the Patapsco River near Baltimore—achieved most of his fame in such urban occupations as almanac writer and city surveyor. Banneker had his almanac published in Baltimore by Goddard and Angel through the help of James McHenry, a resident of Baltimore who later became Secretary of War. Banneker, again through the intervention of a friend, Andrew Ellicott, and with the approval of George Washington, helped to draw the plans for Washington, D.C., under the direction of the Frenchman Pierre Charles L'Enfant. When L'Enfant returned to France in a fit of pique, Banneker and Ellicott finished the plans. Banneker's fame as an astronomer, an almanac writer, and a city planner demonstrates that from the beginnings of the Republic black men served in significant urban roles.

Biographies of other prominent black men similarly reflect urban conditions and settings. In Boston, Prince Hall, an immigrant from Barbados in 1765, drew another career line. He became a Methodist minister and organized the first black Masonic lodge, which is counted the first black social structure in the United States outside of the black church. Hall first asked to join a Masonic lodge composed of native white Bostonians. He was refused and joined instead a lodge formed by a group of British soldiers on March 6, 1775, along with fourteen other black men. After Boston was evacuated, Hall led African Lodge No. 1, which was officially recognized after the Revolutionary War by the Grand Lodge of England. Hall helped to form other lodges in Boston, Philadelphia, and Providence. These fraternal orders, which

Frederick Douglass (LIBRARY OF CONGRESS)

emerged simultaneously with the Republic, served as a vehicle for black education, development, and solidarity.

The formation of black churches in America had its start in Philadelphia, under the guiding hand of Richard Allen. Allen was born a slave in Philadelphia, but was sold with his family to a plantation owner in Dover, Delaware. Allen bought his way out of slavery through money earned in his time off. He then became an itinerant minister in the Methodist Church, preaching to black and white members alike. In 1786 Allen returned to Philadelphia, and the following year, with Absalom Jones, began the Free African Society of Philadelphia. This organization was religious but nonsectarian and included a mutual-aid department—the forerunner of an insurance company. After Allen was refused a seat in the front of St. George's Methodist Episcopal Church, the Free African Society grew into two churches: the Free African Church of St. Thomas (Episcopal), and Bethel African Methodist Episcopal Church (Methodist) led by Richard Allen. The latter prospered, and by 1816 a national group, the African Methodist Episcopal Church, emerged. Allen became the second bishop of the A.M.E. Church while serving as pastor in Philadelphia. His career and the formation of black churches show how the black minister in early America could achieve social mobility and how the movement for collective action could be focused by religious organizations.

The black press in America had its beginnings in New York City as a result of the work done by two black men, Samuel E. Cornish and John B. Russwurm. Cornish came from Delaware and settled in New York City after a stay in Philadelphia. He developed the first black Presbyterian Church in Manhattan and in 1827 collaborated with Russwurm, a native of Jamaica who was the first black graduate of an American college—Bowdoin—in 1826, to publish *Freedom's Journal,* the first black newspaper in the United States. The newspaper's aim was to serve as the voice of the black community, to resist the slander of whites, and to attack slavery. Cornish served as editor for a few months but then relinquished that position to Russwurm. Russwurm became increasingly engaged in the African colonization movement and in 1829 openly supported the American Colonization Society. He was publicly attacked by other black leaders, resigned from the paper, and left for Liberia where he lived the rest of his life as a newspaper editor and superintendent of schools. Cornish returned to *Freedom's Journal* after Russwurm's departure, but the newspaper folded and Cornish started another, *The Rights of All.* The start of the black press in the largest city in America represented an attempt to improve the lot of black people, free and slave.

Black abolitionism and black newspapers were to be found together in the cities, as evidenced by the careers of Henry Highland Garnet and Frederick Douglass. Garnet was born a slave in Maryland but fled to New York City with his family when he was nine. He attended Free African schools there as well as Noyes Academy in Canaan, New Hampshire, and the Oneida Institute in Whitesboro, New York. He then taught school in Troy, New York, from 1840 to 1842, when he was ordained a Presbyterian minister and was assigned a church in the same town. Garnet became famous in the abolition movement in 1843 when he advocated a general strike of slaves at that year's convention of free Negroes. His position was regarded as extremely radical at the time, even by individuals such as Douglass, but later Garnet's ideas became more respectable. He helped found the Liberty party, one of the forerunners of the Republican party, and advocated the abolition of slavery and colonization in Africa. Garnet became the minister of Shiloh Presbyterian Church in New York City in 1855, a position he held until 1881, with time out during the Civil War to serve in the Fifteenth Street Presbyterian Church. Garnet died in Liberia as minister-resident of the United States, ending a long career as minister, abolitionist, and political figure.

Frederick Douglass, the most famous black abolitionist, lived in much the same areas as Garnet. His career is another example of how black resistance blossomed in America's cities. Douglass was born into slavery in Maryland but was sent to Baltimore where

he became a skilled caulker in the shipyards. He fled Baltimore
in 1838 to go to New York and thence to New Bedford, Massachusetts, where he found employment again in shipyards. In 1841
Douglass made an anti-slavery speech in Nantucket and was heard
by white abolitionists who recruited him to lecture for the Massachusetts Anti-Slavery Society. After lecturing in the United
States and the United Kingdom, Douglass began a paper in Rochester, New York—the *North Star,* first published in 1847. In it
he advocated integration, economic and school boycotts, political
action, and, only as a last resort, military means to attain freedom.
He broke with the white abolitionist leader William Lloyd Gar-
rison before the war and opposed back-to-Africa movements.
Douglass moved to Washington, D.C., and became Marshal of the
District of Columbia in 1877 and Minister to Haiti before his
death in 1895.

Recounting the careers of black leaders from the Revolution
to the Civil War ought to produce some profitable generalizations
about urban life and social structure. First, the student might well
consider what elements are necessary for protest movements and
whether such movements can have a rural population as a base.
Cities provide the necessary population and technical means for
organization. Second, the number of black leaders who were also
clergymen should suggest a theory about the role of the church in
the history of the black man in America. Has the church been the
most significant institution for generating leadership in the black
community? Third, the various strategies and tactics of black leaders before the Civil War show a remarkable similarity to those of
today. The question that becomes apparent here is why these
strategies and tactics failed to achieve equality in the past.

But the history of the free black man in the cities goes beyond
the development of black social structures. It reveals much about
white social structures and attitudes as well. It also reveals much
open and covert racism. Nearly all of the Northern states placed
restrictions upon black immigration from other states. Some required posting of bonds and certification of freedom, or refused

entry altogether. Most of the states prohibited the education of Negro children either directly or by refusing support for public schools for such children. Typical was the refusal to permit black men the right to vote or serve on juries, sometimes by the device of outright restriction, other times by the retention of property qualifications for black persons only. The legal position of the black man in the North was clearly inferior.

In the cities of the time, the black population was discriminated against by popular prejudice which was often extra-legal. Public transportation in the cities either systematically excluded Negroes or relegated them to special sections. The same pattern appeared in theaters and other places of public entertainment. Nor were black citizens usually permitted in hotels or restaurants. In churches they were led to sit in special pews and forced to wait until last to be served communion. As Leon F. Litwack says, ". . . They were often educated in segregated schools, punished in segregated prisons, nursed in segregated hospitals, and buried in segregated cemeteries."

In addition to being denied equal facilities in the cities, the black man was an object of derision and ridicule. On the street, in newspapers, on the stage, in shops and stores, stereotypes haunted him wherever he went. He was tormented and taunted by individuals and persecuted by groups; mobs intent on inflicting bodily harm on Negroes were to be found in almost every large Northern city. New York City's Draft Riot of 1863 seems most notorious, but this riot was not a singular occurrence: New York had several racial disturbances before 1863. Philadelphia had five major anti-Negro riots between 1832 and 1849. Cincinnati had a riot in 1829 which resulted in half the black population being driven out. In 1841 Cincinnati was the scene of another major racial disturbance. Contrary to our ahistorical beliefs, racial violence in the United States has not been confined to the South nor to the twentieth century.

The city was the arena, North and South, where the social arrangement of segregation was forged in the nineteenth century. The segregation of the North reflected an incipient racism in a free society, while the segregation of the South reflected the breakdown of slavery under urban conditions. Starting from different positions, the North and the South arrived at remarkably similar social solutions. Despite the Northern argument which portrayed the slave South as the basis for all racial evil, there is much evidence to show that the North was equally as guilty of institutional racism.

Urban history can shed light on the development of segregation out of slavery as well as on the question of why slavery could not be maintained in the cities. This provides a necessary antidote to the usual picture of plantation slavery which informs much of historical thinking on the period. By seeing the problems of slavery in the city, one can better understand the implicit conditions of geographic and social isolation which seemed vital to the institution.

The history of slavery in Southern cities from 1820 to 1860 is one of relative decline. In 1820 blacks comprised 37 per cent of all town dwellers in the South, but forty years later the proportion was 17 per cent. Richard Wade suggests that the reason for the decline was that "Discipline over those remaining proved difficult to sustain. The network of restraint so essential to bondage no longer seemed to control the blacks nor wholly govern the whites."

Slavery became segregation for a variety of reasons, but the major one seems to have been the inability of slave owners to prevent the gathering of slaves together with free black men at night, and a gradual corresponding growth in a feeling of independence. Black organizations in the city, or those white ones which catered to black trade, fostered a social atmosphere lacking in rural isolation. The ideas of the free Negro permeated the cities, and his freedom to own property and have a family became common knowledge in the black community. Further, the labor specialization required in the city bred a spirit of confidence which was lacking in the more basic skills essential to the plantation economy.

As a consequence of the freedom afforded the black slave in

the city, the Southern white who wished to retain slave discipline was forced to try three methods of control. One was the sale of young black men to the countryside. These men were the ones who were likely to be most aggressive and least susceptible to control. Another was to reduce the number of free Negroes in cities by making emancipation more difficult and freedom less attractive. Owners were either prevented or discouraged from manumitting their slaves, and black codes limited the physical mobility of those already freed. The third was the development of a system of segregation. As Wade puts it, "Increasingly public policy tried to separate the races whenever the surveillance of the master was likely to be missing. To do this, the distinction between slave and free Negro was erased; race became more important than legal status; and a pattern of segregation emerged inside the broader framework of the 'peculiar institution'."

Social segregation in the South thus became a matter of formal as well as informal fiat. The public facilities of the South became segregated. Certain streets, accommodations, and public houses were declared off limits. Necessary facilities—welfare and correctional—were separate. These included jails, cemeteries, hospitals, churches, and jobs. The slave and the free black man became more and more alike in the limits of their freedom; indeed, it was often difficult to determine which was which.

The study of the relation of black men to the city in ante-bellum America reveals much about the social structure of the black and white communities and the attitudes of each, as well as the impact of urban conditions on them. The growth of black institutions paralleling those of whites signifies the difficulty of integration at that time. The accomplishments of black men in the cities show the possibilities of mobility in certain social roles. Segregation and violence in urban areas illustrate the nature and extent of prejudice, North and South, in American society. Finally, the roots of a legally segregated society go back to the pre–Civil War American city, where the dominant white majority placed sanctions upon the black minority.

The interaction between the black man and the city provides an excellent basis for original research. The various federal censuses show nonwhite population, and the census of 1840 in particular was skewed to show a high incidence of insanity among free Negroes of the North. (Leon F. Litwack discusses this point in *North of Slavery*.) Students can obtain the census data for their own cities and can calculate the changing proportion of blacks in the area. They can also locate the changing residential patterns of the city and arrive at a theory of social and residential mobility.

Bibliography

1. *Slavery in a House Divided* (McGraw-Hill, 1965). This color filmstrip of drawings concentrates on slavery on the plantation, but offers a few insights into the nature of urban slavery.

2. *Adventures in Negro History,* Vol. II: *The Frederick Douglass Years* (Pepsi Cola, 1967). This filmstrip is a study of the life of Douglass from 1817 to 1895. It is accompanied by a long-playing record which recounts Douglass' life. Useful for the view of a black abolitionist and for the urban setting in which he worked. The barriers against which Douglass fought are well delineated.

3. *Washington, D. C.—Story of Our Capital* (Coronet Films, 1956). The original plans of L'Enfant for Washington are the basis for this film, which traces the growth of the city from its beginnings. The work of Banneker can be discussed in conjunction with the visual aspect of Washington.

4. *House on Cedar Hill* (Artisan Productions, 1953). Frederick Douglass' life is traced through the use of drawings, old photographs, and mementoes of his home in Washington, D. C. The film catches the flavor of nineteenth-century life, particularly as it was lived by this famous black abolitionist.

5. *History of the Negro in America,* Part I: *1619–1860: Out of Slavery* (McGraw-Hill Textfilms, 1965). This film traces the development of Negro history to the Civil War. It is somewhat superficial and tends to accept the orthodox views of slavery and the causes of the Civil War.

6. *History of the Negro in America,* Part II: *1861–1877: Civil War and Reconstruction* (McGraw-Hill Textfilms, 1965). This film traces the roles of the black man in the Civil War and in Reconstruction. Useful for junior and senior high school students as it contains the pictures of many of the leaders of the black community.

7. *The Negro in Civil War and Reconstruction* (McGraw-Hill, 1965). This color filmstrip covers the same era as the preceding film. Recommended for high school students.

8. *Slavery in a House Divided* (McGraw-Hill, 1965). This color filmstrip is a parallel piece to the McGraw-Hill movie and presents much the same data. The level of the filmstrip is the same as that of the movie.

9. Wesley, Charles H., *Richard Allen* (Washington, D.C.: Associated Publishers, 1935). Wesley's book is the standard biography of Allen, who was the outstanding pioneer of the Negro Methodist Church in America. His life reflects the problems of the urban black in Philadelphia and New York. For teacher reference and student projects.

10. Dobler, Lavinia, and Edgar A. Toppin, *Pioneers and Patriots* (New York: Doubleday, 1965), paperback. These profiles include such men as Benjamin Banneker. Illustrated, and simple enough for junior high school students.

11. Graham, Shirley, *Your Most Humble Servant* (New York: Julian Messner, 1949). A biography of Banneker aimed at a juvenile level. It recounts Banneker's efforts as an astronomer, almanac maker, and surveyor in Baltimore and Washington.

12. Hughes, Langston, and Milton Meltzer, *A Pictorial History of the Negro in America* (New York: Crown, 1963). A standard reference tool which contains pictures of individuals and their environments. It can be used to compare black living conditions from the Revolution to the present.

13. Bontemps, Arna, and Jack Conroy, *Anyplace But Here* (New York: Hill and Wang, 1966). The book was written in the 1930's; this edition has been updated. The theme of the book is

the urban migration of the black man in America. For the period under consideration, the sections on Du Sable and the founding of Chicago, William Still in Philadelphia, and John Jones in Chicago are most reflective of the interaction of the city and the Negro. For senior high school students.

14. Quarles, Benjamin, *Black Abolitionists* (New York: Oxford University Press, 1969), paperback. Quarles has written perhaps the best study of the black abolitionists, which takes into account the educational, organizational, and propaganda efforts of the movement and makes clear its urban setting. A useful reference tool.

15. Bennett, Lerone, Jr., *Pioneers in Protest* (Baltimore: Penguin Books, 1969), paperback. Benjamin Banneker, Prince Hall, Richard Allen, and Frederick Douglass are some of the black leaders to be found in this book. The essays are short and popularly written; the book is illustrated and ought to appeal to high school students.

16. Litwack, Leon F., *North of Slavery: The Negro in the Free States, 1709–1860* (Chicago: University of Chicago Press, 1961), paperback. Almost all of Litwack's book is concerned with the treatment of blacks in the North before the Civil War. Since significant numbers of blacks were in cities, Litwack's book is significant in showing the social arrangements in Northern cities and the discrimination visited upon blacks there. Highly recommended for senior high school students.

17. Forten, Charlotte, *The Journal of Charlotte L. Forten* (New York: Collier Books, 1961), paperback. Charlotte Forten was born in Philadelphia a free Negro. She went to school in Salem, Massachusetts, in 1854, then taught in Salem, but because of poor health returned to Philadelphia. During the Civil War she taught in Port Royal, South Carolina. Her journal ought to interest high school students as it provides an interesting insight into the mores of the day as well as the expectations of a black girl in a white society.

18. Douglass, Frederick, *Life and Times of Frederick Douglass* (New York: Collier Books, 1962), paperback. This is Douglass' final autobiography written in 1892. In it he views his long life as slave and free man. There is not as much concerning Douglass' city impressions as one might expect, still the book is a significant resource for research.

19. McPherson, James M., *The Negro's Civil War* (New York: Pantheon, 1965), Vintage paperback. This collection of documents shows how blacks reacted to the Civil War. It also reveals conditions in the cities of the time, particularly the draft riots of 1863. Suitable for special assignments for high school students.

20. Wade, Richard C., *Slavery in the Cities: The South, 1820–1860* (New York: Oxford University Press, 1964), paperback. Wade's book is the definitive statement on slavery in the cities. This much-neglected phenomenon, which seemed to be evolving from a system of slavery to one of segregation, had largely been ignored until Wade considered it. The book is particularly useful in that it details how urban environments can force changes in social institutions. Especially recommended for teachers and for better students.

21. Wade, Richard C., *The Urban Frontier* (Chicago: University of Chicago Press, 1964), paperback. This history of life in early Pittsburgh, Cincinnati, Lexington, Louisville, and St. Louis tells much of race relations in these cities of the West. The book can be used in conjunction with Litwack's by students on research projects.

22. Green, Constance McLaughlin, *The Secret City: A History of Race Relations in the Nation's Capital* (Princeton: Princeton University Press, 1967), paperback. This study of Negro Washington from 1791 to 1961 is a pioneer effort. It shows the growth of a community within a community over the span of the nation's history. The development of urban black institutions and the limits placed upon them by white power structures are themes in this book, which ought to be read by teachers and used by students for research.

23. Taeuber, Karl E., and Alma F. Taeuber, *Negroes in Cities* (Chicago: Aldine, 1965), Atheneum paperback. This is the definitive study of the distribution of Negroes in American cities by two reputable demographers. Their conclusions on urban black populations present a base from which to go back into the past to find out why development went as it did. Useful for research data.

24. Ottley, Roi, and William J. Weatherby, eds., *The Negro in New York: An Informal Social History* (New York: New York Public Library and Oceana Publications, 1967), Praeger paperback. This collection of writings includes essays, poems, and miscellaneous items. While it is best on later periods, it contains some material of the pre–Civil War era. For special studies only.

25. Headley, Joel Tyler, *The Great Riots of New York: 1712–1873* (Indianapolis: Bobbs-Merrill, 1969), paperback. This reprint of an 1870's book includes a section on the draft riots of 1863, which were aimed at New York Negroes. The book can be used as a source for anti-black feeling in the cities in student research units.

26. Meier, August, and Elliott Rudwick, *From Plantation to Ghetto* (New York: Hill and Wang, 1966), paperback. This interpretive history of the Negro in America is the best to date. Chapter 3 is an excellent summary of the black man in antebellum cities, North and South. Not too difficult for high school students.

The Development of Municipal Services, 1790–1860

One of the reasons for anti-urban attitudes among the first few generations of Americans was the considerably lower life expectancy in cities of the era. People seemed to live shorter lives in the cities. While this shortened longevity was wrongly attributed to an environmental cause of disease, rather than to the poor sanitary conditions and rudimentary public health facilities of the time, the end result was the same. Cities were unhealthy places in which to live in addition to being dangerous places where criminals lurked. Almost all of the problems associated with urban life today can be identified early in the Republic, and the attempts to cope with these problems are almost as old.

Dilapidated housing and slum areas were noted by observers in Boston and New York early in the nineteenth century; they became the habitat of the lower classes. But the amenities for others were not necessarily much better. By the beginning of the Civil War, few cities had many sewers, and streets were still often of dirt or unpaved. More than one-third of the persons living in cities relied on slop jars and outhouses for sanitary purposes, while in other cities sewage ran untreated into rivers which supplied drinking water. Such was the case in Philadelphia with the polluted Delaware River. As a consequence, cities suffered numerous outbreaks of diseases caused by contamination—typhoid, dysentery, cholera, and typhus. These diseases were often of crisis proportion. The filthiness of American cities was augmented by the use of horses as the principal means of conveyance and by the almost universal habit of using pigs to scavenge through the garbage thrown into the streets. In many sections the streets were a combination of mud and manure, adding to the danger of infection from simple cuts, and bands of pigs posed a physical threat to children and others. High on the list of municipal priorities were the paving of streets, provision for sewers, and the development of pure water facilities.

In addition to health hazards in the city, there were those created inevitably by the concentration of population in one area. The crowding of people into tenements and basements made the danger of fire that much worse. Given the wooden construction and the lack of building codes to prevent houses from crowding together, conflagrations became major disasters. Volunteer fire companies of an earlier era were obviously inadequate for the day. More organization and professionalization were needed, and supplementary services, such as adequate water supplies, also had to be developed. The city needed fire departments to secure the safety of its citizens.

Finally, the concentration of people in cities and the growth of slums and poverty as part of city living led to an increase in crime. By 1860 American cities had criminal districts and criminal gangs similar to those in European cities. There were areas in New York, Cincinnati, Philadelphia, and Baltimore where citizens

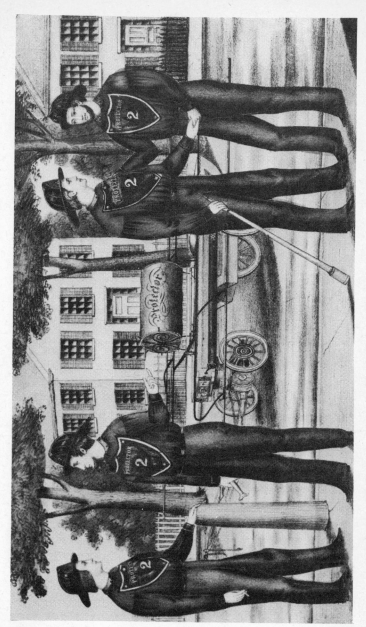

"Protector Engine No. 2," engraving of a fire department in the 1840's (SMITHSONIAN INSTITUTION)

would not go because street gangs preyed on strangers. These street gangs had picturesque names such as Buffaloes, Bowery Boys, Crawfish Boys, and Dead Rabbits. The police forces of the era were unorganized, untrained, and did not even wear uniforms. They were likely to be persons out of work who were hired by private or public subscription to patrol areas during the day or to watch establishments all night. They were not so much interested in solving crimes as in protecting property from thievery— and they were generally inadequate in doing that. The association of crime with the American city is an old one, and attempts to prevent crime with a professional police force is a product of the pre–Civil War era.

Proposed solutions to the problems of poor housing, poor sanitation, poor public health, and rising crime reflected the attitudes of the time. Prevailing laissez-faire economic ideas militated against public action, though in some areas the needs were so pressing that collective effort had to be taken.

The regulation of housing through building codes (with the exception of those forbidding wooden houses), zoning laws, and other direct governmental effort had to wait until the end of the nineteenth century. The crowding of persons into tenements caused alarm, but the answer to the overcrowding was not a direct one. Instead of regulating housing, the attempt was made to limit immigration and to help the pauper, either by direct relief or by putting him in an almshouse. Only in the latter case did the city government become involved. In the large cities on the eastern seaboard, almshouses became a part of the urban scene and were disproportionately full of foreign-born immigrants. Concern for paupers began early. Typical of the organizations of the time was the New York Society for the Prevention of Pauperism, begun in 1817. Others similar in scope were created after the Panic of 1819 had impoverished many persons and made the conditions of others more obvious. Needless to say, the decay of the city continued with inadequate housing and overcrowding becoming more and more a part of the urban scene.

The problem of public health was more pressing than that of housing, for disease struck rich and poor alike despite the claims of some rich persons that more of the lower classes were affected because of their bad habits and poor living conditions. American cities suffered from numerous outbreaks of disease, including consumption (tuberculosis)—the disease of overcrowded, poorly housed people—malaria, typhoid, typhus, dysentery, yellow fever, and cholera. The latter two, while not responsible for as many deaths as some of the others, were more feared because of their plague-like nature. Yellow fever, for example, killed four thousand people in Philadelphia in 1793, or 10 per cent of the population. In 1798 an epidemic of yellow fever hit Boston, New York, and Philadelphia with considerable force. Cities in the South in the nineteenth century were particularly susceptible to outbreaks of yellow fever. In 1852, New Orleans lost eight thousand people to the disease. Cholera was epidemic in the United States in three particularly severe years, 1832, 1849, and 1866. These years were a severe test of the ability of American cities to survive.

While the causes of the epidemic diseases were not known, the attempts to end them were partially successful. Cholera, dysentery, and typhoid fever, which are carried by contaminated water, and yellow fever and malaria, which are carried by mosquitoes, were controlled somewhat by measures taken in the belief that filthy conditions contribute to disease. Although the prevailing miasmic theory of disease—which held that bad air caused illness—was incorrect, the impetus this theory gave to improve sanitary conditions meant cleaner streets, more sewers, and better water supplies, all of which added to better public health. Further, the traumatic nature of the diseases led to collective attempts to deal with them. Cities established boards of health in the ante-bellum period, and these agencies increased their powers and responsibilities throughout the rest of the century. Generally these boards of health attempted to quarantine areas and control urban sanitation. The most successful of them was the Metropolitan Board of Health in New York, whose work in the cholera epidemic of 1866 gave impetus to the public health movement.

The Civil War added to the concern about public health. The United States Sanitary Commission, set up in 1861 as a private philanthropy, showed how a large and well-organized group could raise the level of health care in the army. The end of the war caused many ex-slaves to settle in nearby cities in the South, thus adding to the health hazards of the day. Both the war and Reconstruction called attention to the presence of and possible solutions for health problems—organization and sanitation.

Coincident with the drive to improve sanitary facilities was the movement toward better water systems. Originally, American towns relied upon wells. By the nineteenth century, however, such limited sources were becoming inadequate. The first publicly owned municipal water system was Centre Water Works in Philadelphia in 1801, designed by Benjamin Latrobe, a noted architect. In New York City a private firm, the Manhattan Company, began in 1799 to supply water. It was replaced by a public company in 1835. Other cities moved in the same direction, either relying upon private or public water systems and phasing out individual sources of water. With the collective effort, the overall quality of the water supply improved, though the contamination of a central system was still possible. Water sometimes was impure because of a lack of sewage facilities and the increasing use of common streams both for disposing of wastes and as a source of drinking water.

With an available source of water and with the growing danger of conflagration, more organized means of fighting fires emerged. The original fire-fighting groups in American cities were made up of volunteers whose equipment varied from city to city. These groups were often subsidized by governmental units or by fire insurance companies. Consequently the units often put out fires only in buildings with the correct fire mark, and neglected others. Often they were conservative in buying new equipment and reluctant to expand operations. Such was the case in Cincinnati, with the result that in 1853 the city established the first paid municipal fire department in the United States. This example proved successful and was emulated by other cities. The Cincinnati move was the result of a gradual evolution, however, with a number of intervening steps between a volunteer fire department and a fully professional one. As Richard Wade has said:

> Municipalities began to screen applicants [for volunteer fire companies], passed ordinances to establish discipline during emergencies, and supervised company finances. Moreover, councils took over almost the entire burden of furnishing the apparatus and keeping it in repair. In 1829 Cincinnati, going even further, paid its firemen a modest salary, symbolizing the growing competence of government in this field.

It was only with the advent of the steam pumper and the proliferation of fire dangers that cities assumed full responsibility for protection against fires.

Protection against crime followed much the same pattern. Originally, cities relied on private enforcement. Many citizens armed themselves as in the Old West. The next step might be to set up temporary patrols, especially at night. These patrols were composed of persons hired by the city, often of doubtful character and reputation, or of citizens who were required to serve a stint. Such was the case in Cincinnati in 1805; but when the emergency which helped create the watch passed, the city fathers did not institute another night patrol for twenty years. The night watch usually patrolled in districts, sometimes equipped with noisemakers—rattles and trumpet—to use as warnings or to call for assistance. Later the night watches were extended to cover Sundays and other daytime hours.

The watches grew into police forces and gradually supplanted the work of state officers such as sheriffs and constables. These officials, who were to be found in most cities, lost ground in numbers and in responsibilities. In Boston, for example, from 1840 to 1851 the watch increased in numbers from 150 to 190, while the constables decreased from 44 to 30. Those constables who remained in office became agents of the courts whose main function was the execution of civil writs. Those constables who left the office often became members of the police force.

The transformation of police in many cities occurred in the 1850's, the same year that firemen became city employees. New York City was first to establish a police force in 1844, but the system became efficient only in 1853 with the creation of a board of police commissioners. Philadelphia set up its single police system in 1850, Boston in 1854, and Baltimore in 1857. With the establishment of a police force came the drive for uniforms. As Charles Glaab has said, "The wearing of uniforms was successfully resisted for years by policemen, who argued that the uniform was a badge of European servitude. Since they were not identifiable, policemen often fled serious disturbances."

The systematic gathering and publishing of statistics on crime also waited for the establishment of single police units. It is therefore very difficult to estimate the extent of crime in American cities in the first half of the nineteenth century. The patrols did not seek out criminal activity and acted primarily on the basis of complaints. They were inadequate to handle any serious disturbance or even to enforce traffic laws, liquor laws, or laws against prostitution. The anti-Negro riot in Cincinnati in 1829 is a case in point. For three days Negroes were terrorized while the police forces—in this case the sheriff and constables—did nothing. Other cities experienced similar problems with urban riots which were often sparked by anti-slavery, anti-Catholic, or anti-Negro sentiments. No generalization concerning the extent of crime in the nineteenth century, consequently, is likely to be of much validity. The only one that holds much water is the one that denies the peaceful character of ante-bellum cities and likens them to our own.

Certain features of the city described in this unit ought to be brought home to the student. Municipal services grew largely because of pressing needs and such problems as epidemics of disease, crime, fires, slums, and poor sewage and water systems. Almost all of our present-day difficulties with our cities can be found in the past, but the average person is unaware of this and is under the impression that our urban past was idyllic. Water pollution today can hardly be compared with the intolerable conditions of the nineteenth-century city; the health problems of the poor today are pressing, but the general level of health for the urban population is much higher than it once was; the crime rate today is high, but that of the past, though difficult to judge, seems to have been equally high. Finally, few remember that when the automobile was introduced into city streets it was hailed as the harbinger of cleaner cities. The old city streets fouled with the manure and urine of thousands of horses would be gone, never to return.

Beyond this changed perspective toward urban problems is the rich opportunity for inquiry into such questions as: What alternatives are there to a police system? What can be done about urban disorder? What limits can be placed upon the rights of citizens in order to assure public health and safety? The first restrictions on private property in the United States were in the cities, according to W. Stull Holt, and these were caused by problems of public health and sanitation. Holt attributes the growth of the idea of the welfare state to the growth of cities. While the assumption may be simplistic, it does have the merit of stimulating discussion on this vital point.

Finally, the provision of municipal services can be an object of local study. Students can trace the history of their own city's action in providing pure water and adequate sewage disposal, and in setting up fire and police departments. They may be surprised to find that these services have been only recently acquired or, conversely, that they have been provided for many years. In any case, the comparison of a local community's past with that of other cities will be instructive. The forces that pushed for the reforms are also worthy of consideration. Who in the community wanted the municipal services and why? What kinds of political and economic pressures were brought to bear in order to effect change? Was the action the monopoly of any party? There is also an aesthetic dimension. The building of waterworks and police and fire stations reflects the attitudes of the age as well as the assumed function of the edifices. Are waterworks examples of the classic revival, and if so, why? Do police stations share the same architectural features as fire stations? Is there an "architecture of public buildings" which all share?

Bibliography

1. *Keeping the City Alive* (Encyclopedia Britannica Films, 1953). This filmstrip emphasizes the services necessary to hold a city together—police, fire protection, water, utilities. While it is not historically oriented, it is a useful introduction to the problem. For junior high school and below.

2. *Problems of the City* (Encyclopedia Britannica Films, 1953). This filmstrip in the same series as the above discusses the problems of the city in terms of traffic, poor housing, and overcrowding, as well as in terms of governmental difficulties. Like the preceding filmstrip, the problems are recent but serve as an introduction to the area, and the filmstrip is simple.

3. *Problems of Cities* (New York Times, 1968). The set consists of two records and a filmstrip. It is more advanced than the preceding ones, though it treats of the same area. The set can be used to indicate present difficulties and to project these difficulties back into the past.

4. *Crime in the Streets* (Indiana University, 1966). One in the National Educational Television America's Crises series, this film shows the operation of a police department, indicating the kinds of situations police encounter, as well as the treatment and rehabilitation of criminals. The level is senior high school.

5. *Our Immigrant Heritage* (McGraw-Hill Textfilms, 1966). While this film emphasizes the later immigration and the cultural values brought by immigrants, there is some treatment of the earlier immigration and the conditions in cities. For junior and senior high school.

6. *Functions of a City* (Progressive Pictures, 1951). The contrasting methods of providing water, light, fuel, and garbage disposal between early America and the present are portrayed in this film. Useful in connection with this unit despite its rather elementary approach.

7. Andrews, Wayne, *Architecture, Ambition and Americans* (New York: Harper, 1955), Free Press paperback. The third chapter contains several pages on Benjamin Latrobe, the architect and engineer who built the water system in Philadelphia. His influence on the Greek Revival is detailed. For reference use and for projects.

8. Burchard, John, and Albert Bush-Brown, *The Architecture of America* (Boston: Little, Brown, 1961), paperback. The first chapter says a little about balloon-framed houses and the Greek Revival efforts of Latrobe. It can be used as a reference work or as a resource for student projects.

9. Hamlin, Talbot, *Benjamin Henry Latrobe* (New York: Oxford University Press, 1955). Hamlin's biography is the definitive work on Latrobe and includes the work Latrobe did in rebuilding Washington, D.C., after the War of 1812. Ironically, Latrobe and his son, Henry, were both victims of yellow fever in New Orleans, where they were building a water system similar to Philadelphia's and designed to eliminate the disease. This biography might be assigned to students interested in architecure or early attempts at water systems.

10. Glaab, Charles N., and A. Theodore Brown, *A History of Urban America* (New York: Macmillan, 1967), paperback. Chapter 4, "The Urban Milieu," contains a useful summary of the development of urban services. Not difficult for better students.

11. Green, Constance McLaughlin, *The Rise of Urban America* (New York: Harper and Row, 1965), paperback. Chapter 3 devotes a section to the provision of municipal services. The material is a good summary, though not as detailed as Glaab and Brown. Simple enough to be understood by senior high school students.

12. Callow, Alexander B., Jr., ed., *American Urban History* (New York: Oxford University Press, 1969), paperback. The selections on municipal services in this reader are sparse. The articles by Richard C. Wade and Bayrd Still do apply and can be utilized as a point of departure. The book should be used as a reference tool.

13. Wakstein, Allen M., ed., *The Urbanization of America: An Historical Anthology* (Boston: Houghton Mifflin, 1970), paperback. This reader has an excellent section entitled "The Growth and Development of Urban Services" which includes selections on water supply, transportation, and police, as well as a full range of urban services in one city, Milwaukee. For senior high school students.

14. Mohl, Raymond A., and Neil Betten, eds., *Urban America in Historical Perspective* (New York: Weybright and Talley, 1970). Chapter 3 in this anthology has two sections on working-class and immigrant conditions in the city before the Civil War. For research projects.

15. Wade, Richard C. *The Urban Frontier: Pioneer Life in Early Pittsburgh, Cincinnati, Lexington, Louisville, and St. Louis* (Chicago: University of Chicago Press, 1969), paperback. This essential book contains valuable material on all of the municipal services provided down to about 1830. It can be assigned to high school students with profit.

16. Ernst, Robert, *Immigrant Life in New York City, 1825–1863* (New York: King's Crown Press, 1949). Ernst studies the social conditions which faced the immigrant Irish and Germans in New York City down to 1863. He is particularly good on the living conditions in tenements. For reference only.

17. Lane, Roger, *Policing the City: Boston, 1822–1885* (Cambridge, Mass.: Harvard University Press, 1967). While Lane's book covers more than the era under consideration, it does outline in detail the changes in one American city in the organization and function of the police department. Boston had peculiar problems—the mass immigration of the Irish is one—but it was

typical in its solution to the pressing dilemma of public order. The best book on the development of modern police for students with this interest.

18. Blake, John B., *Public Health in the Town of Boston, 1630–1822* (Cambridge, Mass.: Harvard University Press, 1959). The development of public health in Boston down to the beginnings of a modern system is the theme of this work. It is a significant effort and can be used to show the development of public concern and the displacement of private efforts. Supplementary reading for advanced students.

19. Duffy, John, *A History of Public Health in New York City, 1625–1866* (New York: Russell Sage Foundation, 1968). Duffy is the dean of historians of public health, and this is the most significant book on the evolution of public health. Students should turn to it first for information on public health.

20. Blake, Nelson M., *Water for the Cities: A History of the Urban Water Supply Problem in the United States* (Syracuse: Syracuse University Press, 1956). The definitive work on the development of water systems in the United States. Like Duffy's on public health, Blake's is the one with which to begin. A reference for teachers and students.

21. Handlin, Oscar, *Boston's Immigrants* (Cambridge, Mass.: Harvard University Press, 1959), Atheneum paperback. The period covered in the book is 1790 to 1865, and the subtitle, "A Study in Acculturation," reveals clearly what the book is about. Handlin is especially good on the factors which contributed to the creation of Irish slums in North End and Fort Hill. Recommended for projects and research.

22. Rosenberg, Charles, *The Cholera Years* (Chicago: University of Chicago Press, 1962), paperback. This is the authoritative book on the impact of cholera on American cities. Rosenberg shows how the social attitudes of the day shaped medical theory and practice, and how the cholera in the years 1832, 1849, and 1866 was treated differently and with increasing success. Useful for student projects.

23. Warner, Sam Bass, Jr., *The Private City: Philadelphia in Three Periods of Its Growth* (Philadelphia: University of Pennsylvania Press, 1968). The second of the three periods Warner uses is 1830–1860. It is at this time that Philadelphia's growth fails to keep pace with pressures generated by the drive for individual wealth and the housing of the poor becomes located in different areas. Highly recommended for teachers and better students.

24. Headley, Joel Tyler, *The Great Riots of New York, 1712–1873* (Indianapolis: Bobbs-Merrill, 1969), paperback. This reprint of a book issued in the 1870's shows how helpless police were to curb urban violence throughout the period. Recommended for work on police and civil disturbances.

25. Briggs, Asa, *Victorian Cities* (New York: Harper and Row, 1970), paperback. Briggs's classic work can be assigned to students to demonstrate that the problems of American cities were not unique. Briggs studies Leeds, Manchester, London, Melbourne, and other English cities.

26. Teeters, N. K., *The Cradle of the Penitentiary: The Walnut Street Jail in Philadelphia, 1773–1835* (Philadelphia: Pennsylvania Prison Society, 1955). This book examines the evolution of the main jail in Philadelphia. The conception of crime, police, and detention can all be found here. For research only.

27. Cole, Donald B., *Immigrant City* (Chapel Hill: University of North Carolina Press, 1963). Cole's book is about Lawrence, Massachusetts, a textile town which attracted many workers in the middle of the nineteenth century and which had more than its share of urban problems as a result. Useful for reference purposes.

28. Richardson, James, *New York Police: Colonial Times to 1901* (New York: Oxford University Press, 1970). The book traces the development of a professional police force in New York City from early beginnings down to the turn of the century, including the changing problems and conflicting jurisdictions of city and state governments. A volume in the Urban Life in America series, the book is an excellent one for special studies.

The City of the West,
1860–1920

Nowhere does the myth of the American as an individual struggling alone against the forces of nature appear stronger than in the West. In the role of cowboy, prospector, hard-rock miner, and rancher, the American conjures up visceral reactions of loneliness, scattered population, and rural isolation. While the myth, like many myths, contains elements of truth, it is overstated. As was the case with the Mountain Man, the cowboy rarely stayed a cowboy very long. Philip Ashton Rollins, in his book *The Cowboy,* estimated that the average man was able to have only seven years of active riding because of physical injury, generally a hernia from poorly broken horses, and then had the choice of becoming a cook or going into another occupation. As with the Mountain Man, the cowboy often ended his career somewhere in the city.

The life of Deadwood Dick is instructive. Born in 1854 in Tennessee, Nat Love began life as a slave. In 1869, at the age of fifteen, he applied for a position with a Texas ranch group which had driven cattle to Kansas. He stayed three years with them before going to another ranch on the Gila River in southern Arizona. There he became a brand reader and participated in drives into Mexico and to Northern railheads. On July 4, 1876, Love was in Deadwood, South Dakota, with a trail crew. In the Fourth of July celebration, Love won both first prizes in roping and shooting and was given the title "Deadwood Dick." Despite his fame as a cowboy, Love finally had to leave the range. In 1890 Deadwood Dick became a Pullman porter on the railroad and lived in town.

A look at the town marshal, another Western hero, also shows the urban nature of the West. Robert Dykstra's *The Cattle Towns,* a study of five Kansas towns which served at one time or another as collecting points for cattle driven from Texas, de-emphasizes the violent nature of the towns and suggests instead that they were relatively peaceful. In no Kansas cattle town did the marshal serve as the sole law-enforcer. Sheriffs and constables also were available. Nor did the marshals commit much mayhem. "Wild Bill" Hickok killed two men, one a fellow police officer shot in error. Wyatt Earp of Wichita claimed to have mortally wounded one person, who was also claimed by another police officer. In fifteen years (1870–1885) in the five cattle towns studied, forty-five homicides were recorded. This averages out to three a year, less than one per year per town. Dodge City, with the highest murder rate, had an average of only one homicide per year.

What, then, did the marshal do? His duties were specified by local ordinances and Kansas law as far as police work was concerned. In addition, the marshal usually participated in other town duties. "Wild Bill" Hickok was street commissioner in Abilene; Wyatt Earp repaired sidewalks and thoroughfares in Wichita. Marshals in other towns were charged with the chores of being fire marshals and inspecting chimney flues, or acting as sanitary inspectors concerned with water and food supplies.

Kansas Peace Commission of the 1870's, including, left to right, seated, Charles Bassett, Wyatt Earp, M. F. McClain, and Neal Brown; standing, W. H. Harris, Luke Short, Bat Masterson, and W. F. Petillon (KANSAS STATE HISTORICAL SOCIETY)

Nor were these views of the role of marshal out of keeping with the self-image of the towns. The cattle towns were promoted as much as were the towns further east; and the competition for railroads and drovers was as keen as that of Galena or Chicago. In the cattle towns rural interests often felt slighted by the allocation of tax moneys designed to improve the community's position for the cattle trade by overlooking closer agricultural needs. In 1872, in Ellsworth, Kansas, the business community raised $4,000 to build a hotel to encourage the cattle drovers, but a proposal to raise funds to build a steam mill to process local grain got nowhere. Dykstra posits a kind of continual conflict between a "rural ring" and a group loosely identified as representing business interests.

The cattle towns were not the only cities of the West, of course. The discovery of minerals—gold, silver, and copper—led to the building of many small towns which were dependent upon extraction for survival. These towns in California, Colorado, Utah, Arizona, New Mexico, Wyoming, and Montana quite often failed. The areas are full of ghost towns which did not make it, but these failures illustrate the ideas of the town fathers who built them and the economic base upon which they were built. The towns contained saloons, assay offices, and provisions for high and low culture—opera houses and houses of prostitution. Quite often the mining towns were regulated and owned by companies which were extracting the mineral resources of an area. They were abandoned when the companies pulled up stakes and left.

The mining towns of the West are not all ghost towns. Some survived and prospered because of railroads which, through luck, promotion, or accident, chose the route that made these towns rail centers. Among the cities which began as mining towns are Denver, Reno, El Paso, Albuquerque, and Santa Fe, which had been a trading center of significance under Spanish rule. There is no adequate generalization about why certain mining towns prospered and others failed. Natural location seemed to be the answer in some cases, but other towns with more natural advantages failed. The coming of railroads seemed to be the answer in other areas, but there were towns on the railroad that never developed and that remained only a name on an antique map.

Denver is a good example of a city that made itself. General William Larimer, the town promoter of Denver, came to the mining area along Cherry Creek in 1858 and helped found the city. Denver was originally bypassed in favor of Cheyenne, Wyoming, by the Union Pacific Railroad, but a local company built a connecting line to Cheyenne with its own resources, and service was initiated in 1870. Later, Denver was also connected to the East by the Kansas Pacific, and local leaders built south with the Denver and Rio Grande. These railway connections plus the location of a United States mint meant prosperity for Denver, but it was an earned prosperity.

The growth of cities in the mining and ranching West can be statistically demonstrated. Keeping pace with the urbanization of the rest of the United States, the states of the West when admitted to the Union had a relatively high urban population. One of every four persons living in these states lived in towns of between 5,000 and 25,000 population at the time of admission. Contrary to the usual assumption, Western states were not conspiciously more rural than those in the Midwest, and were more urban than Southern states. The Western states did not evolve from rural beginnings to city endings, as older states did, but had cities at the same time they had ranches and mines.

Beyond the mining and cattle frontiers lay the Pacific states which, though California and Oregon were admitted to the Union before the Civil War, shared the same characteristics of rapid urbanization with the states of the interior West. The motives for settlement were again commercial, but the locations on the coast substituted port facilities for railway connections. It was no accident that the significant cities of the west coast—Los Angeles, Portland, San Francisco, and Seattle—were seaports as well as being the western termini of transcontinental railroads. Each of these coastal cities, however, had characteristics of its own, based upon the nature of the settlers, the time of settlement, and factors influencing development. For examples, let us consider Los Angeles and Seattle.

Los Angeles, unlike San Francisco, did not become an important city until late in the nineteenth century. While it was the third largest city in California (though it had less than six thousand people) in 1860, its takeoff period began in 1885. Before this date, farms, ranches, vineyards, and other cultivated areas occupied much of the thirty-six square miles of the city. After 1885, with the advent of the electric railroad and the dispersion of business, the city began to fill up and spread out. Immigrants to Los Angeles were not Europeans who took what they could get in a strange new land, as they had in Chicago and New York City. Instead, they were native Americans who viewed the city as a residential suburb: they wanted to live in detached houses with gardens and no industrial plants nearby to clutter the view or the landscape. The advent of streetcars meant that suburban developments were feasible, and that subdivision would follow subdivision. When Mexicans, Japanese, and Negroes came into Los Angeles in numbers, they moved into the abandoned subdivisions and created ethnic areas which were of older suburban styles. Thus Watts was born as a ghetto of single family dwellings.

The growth of Los Angeles was due in part to transportation and industrialization. The Southern Pacific came to Los Angeles in 1876, and by 1887 the Atchison, Topeka, and Santa Fe also made connections. This accelerated the influx of immigrants to the city, which was being boomed widely at the time. Manufacturers also came and located in the many available sites that had rail connections but were not yet developed. A great deal of land was also available on the waterfront at Long Beach. All this contributed to urban sprawl and made Los Angeles a unique city without a very coherent downtown center and with miles of suburb development. It also led to Los Angeles becoming the second largest city west of the Rockies with the second highest rate of growth in the area in the latter part of the nineteenth century (San Francisco was the largest city, and Seattle the fastest growing).

Seattle's growth rivaled that of Los Angeles, but for different reasons and in a different way. It was founded in 1851 by settlers who wished to exploit the timber resources of the area. The timber was to be shipped south to San Francisco to support the building needs of the gold rush there. By 1852 a sawmill was built and Seattle continued to grow. Because of Indian problems and the Civil War, however, Seattle's growth in the late 1850's and early 1860's was stunted. By 1870 the town numbered only eleven thousand people, and in 1873 the Northern Pacific decided to place its western terminus at Tacoma, a site twenty-four miles south of Seattle on Commencement Bay. Tacoma was to be developed as a company-inspired town under the guidance of Frederick Law Olmsted. Seattle, although it lost a railroad at that time, did become part of an established steamship run with San Francisco. And local promoters built a railroad to the interior which was eventually bought out by Henry Villard, the new president of the Northern Pacific who had promised to build a line from Tacoma to Seattle. In 1891, because local people had proposed a connecting link to the Canadian Pacific, the Northern Pacific finally tied Seattle into its system, and in 1893 Seattle became the major terminus of the Great Northern. Increased trade with the orient, the burgeoning salmon canneries, and the Alaskan Gold Rush of 1898 made Seattle the fastest growing city on the west coast. Its excellent port facilities, including the best anchorages north of San Francisco, nevertheless would not have saved Seattle had not the persistence of local entrepreneurs kept the city going. Even when the future looked blackest—with the fire of 1889—the city rallied and rebuilt. Tacoma, which might have become as significant as Seattle, lost out because of the problems of the Northern Pacific and the refusal of the citizens of Seattle to give up.

The study of urban development in the West is handicapped by romance and myth. It is difficult to convince students that city growth need not follow rural foundations, and that the cowboy was a passing role for men who often ended in the city. Oriented as we are to assumptions about our past, we find it hard to conceive of Wyatt Earp repairing sidewalks or Deadwood Dick becoming a Pullman porter. In order to probe Western myths, a study of the cattle towns as seen in Western novels would be an interesting and significant project for students.

The mining cities and the seaport cities of the Pacific are another story. Their development hinges upon accident, luck, and effort. They obtained railway connections even though originally they may not have been located on the roadway. Their shape today, as in the case of Los Angeles, reflects American views of what city life should be and, in the words of Christopher Rand, makes Los Angeles "the ultimate city." Students might be encouraged to compare various Western cities to see if they can derive any generalizations about growth. Did the denial of a rail connection to Denver, Los Angeles, and Seattle prove to be a hindrance, or was it actually a stimulus? Why did Tacoma not outstrip Seattle? What cities in the West had no rail connections and yet became significant? Why?

Bibliography

1. *Geography in an Urban Age,* Unit I: *Geography of Cities* (High School Geography Project, Association of American Geographers: Boulder, Colo., 1968). Three sections here are useful. The first is a rather long section entitled "Portsville," which is a thinly disguised history of Seattle from its founding down to 1900. The project is complete with maps and pictures of Seattle, and students are encouraged to build models of the city at different stages of its growth. The major emphasis is upon the model of the city as applied to Seattle. A disturbing feature of this section, however, is that some of the facts of Seattle's history have been altered. The authors say, "Some of the factual material has been modified to make the activity more manageable as a learning experience." I am not certain this is defensible, particularly since the urban rivalry with Tacoma is only briefly mentioned and the

railroad situation is confused. For this reason, this section can only be used with caution by those interested in historic reality rather than fictional models.

The second useful section is entitled "Time, Place, and the Model." The intent here is to show settlement patterns in the upper Midwest. The maps show towns and cities in upper Michigan, Wisconsin, North and South Dakota, and Montana. In addition, there are representations of town trade areas, city trade areas, and metropolitan trade areas. While the lesson does little with development, it does show urbanization and the influence of the Denver and the Seattle-Portland trade areas.

The third section, "Cities with Special Functions," contains photographs of a number of cities which the student is asked to identify by function. Included are several Western cities—Grand Junction, Colorado; Boulder, Colorado; Salinas, California; Laurel, Montana; and Seattle. The view of Laurel, Montana, is a good one to illustrate that railroads do not necessarily make a city. Laurel has only 4,600 people—and the largest railroad sorting yard between Minneapolis and Spokane. Three railroads run through Laurel from five directions, but the city has little else, and so it has failed to grow.

2. *Ghost Towns of the Great Divide* (Classroom Film Distributors, 1951). The town of Leadville, Colorado, abandoned after the mines proved unprofitable, is the locale. The film shows the Opera House, the Grand Hotel, and private dwellings in the area. Good for junior and senior high school students.

3. *Los Angeles—What Kind of City?* (Kleinberg Films, 1951). A typical day in the life of Angelenos is shown. The history of Los Angeles from a Spanish village to an urban center is also traced, and the problems of smog and automotive clutter are examined. An old but useful film for elementary and secondary classes.

4. *San Francisco—Story of a City* (Walt Disney Productions, Educational Film Division, 1963). An excellent review of the history of San Francisco, including the days of sailing, the trans-

continental railroads, and the lives of farmers, cattlemen, loggers, and merchants. For elementary and secondary students.

5. *City of Gold* (McGraw-Hill Textfilms, 1958). While this movie is composed primarily of photographs of the Klondike Gold Rush and its impact on Alaska, it does help one understand the critical location of Seattle in the 1890's. For junior and senior high school classes.

6. *American Literature—The Westward Movement* (Coronet Films, 1954). The move west is seen through the writings of Washington Irving, Mark Twain, Joaquin Miller, Bess Streeter Aldrich, and Emerson Hough. With the exception of Aldrich, the authors consider the nature of the Far West in its early and middle stages. This is most suitable for senior high school students.

7. *Millionaires of Poverty Gulch* (Indiana University, 1965). This is one in the National Educational Television's Glory Trail series. It shows Cripple Creek, Colorado, as a typical gold mining community in the West. Suitable for junior and senior high school students.

8. *You Can't Get There from Here* (Indiana University, 1965). Another in the Glory Trail series, this film traces the development of transportation and communication facilities in the West. It is good on the impact of the railroad and shows some urban development. For junior and senior high school.

9. *The Real West* (McGraw-Hill Textfilms, 1961). This Project 20 film shows social and economic development in the West from 1849 to 1900. It is narrated by Gary Cooper in one of his last film appearances. While the major thrust is to debunk the myth of the gunfighter and to show the conquest of the plains Indians, the film also shows town development, particularly in mining camps. It is most fruitful for high school students.

10. *Disaster, 1906* (Studio 16 Educational Films, 1961). A recounting of the San Francisco earthquake and fire, and the subsequent reconstruction of the city. Helpful for those interested in city planning and development.

11. Burchard, John, and Albert Bush-Brown, *The Architecture of America* (Boston: Little, Brown, 1961), paperback. The parts on the periods 1860–1885 and 1885–1913 contain comments on architectural landmarks in selected Western areas.

12. Reps, John William, *The Making of Urban America: A History of City Planning in the United States* (Princeton: Princeton University Press, 1965). This is the comprehensive reference work on city planning and should be used in conjunction with this unit.

13. Glaab, Charles N., and A. Theodore Brown, *A History of Urban America* (New York: Macmillan, 1967), paperback. Chapter 5, "The Completion of the Urban Network, 1860–1910," has the best section on Western city development of any urban history text. For advanced students.

14. Green, Constance McLaughlin, *The Rise of Urban America* (New York: Harper and Row, 1965), paperback. There is a little material on cities of the West in "The Impact of Industrialization, 1860–1910," but it is not as well developed as Glaab and Brown. Again, the book should be assigned only to advanced students.

15. Green, Constance McLaughlin, *American Cities in the Growth of the Nation* (New York: John De Graff, 1957), Harper paperback. This book has the best short account of the growth of Seattle.

16. Wakstein, Allen M., ed., *The Urbanization of America: An Historical Anthology* (Boston: Houghton Mifflin, 1970), paperback. Wakstein's anthology contains an essay by Fogelson on Los Angeles which is a good synopsis of why that city is so extended. For special projects.

17. Fogelson, Robert M., *The Fragmented Metropolis: Los Angeles, 1850–1930* (Cambridge, Mass.: Harvard University Press, 1967). This is the best work on the development of this Western city and can be used as the basis for a unit.

18. Pomeroy, Earl, *The Pacific Slope* (New York: Alfred A. Knopf, 1965). Pomeroy's book is the definitive history of that

part of the West beyond the last range of mountains. It is well written and can be handled by senior high school students who want an overall view of this part of the West.

19. Overton, Richard C., *Burlington West: A Colonization History of the Burlington Railroad* (Cambridge, Mass.: Harvard University Press, 1941). Overton's book takes the case of a particular railroad, the Burlington, and considers how it colonized towns through Iowa and Nebraska and west. For special projects.

20. Dykstra, Robert, *The Cattle Towns* (New York: Alfred A. Knopf, 1968). Dykstra's book is one of the first attempts to cut through the romantic haze surrounding the Kansas cattle towns and to introduce some behavioral criteria into the study. The book is suitable for better high school students.

21. Nadeau, Remi A., *City Makers: the Story of Southern California's First Boom, 1868–76* (Los Angeles: Trans-Angelo Books, 1965). This specialized study is a good one to show how an area can be boomed and take off into a period of rapid urbanization. For projects on Los Angeles and other Southern California cities.

22. Streeter, Floyd B., *Prairie Trails and Cow Towns* (New York: Devin-Adair, 1963). Suitable for junior high school and above, particularly for a sense of town location and design.

23. Wolle, Muriel V. S., *The Bonanza Trail: Ghost Towns and Mining Camps of the West* (Bloomington: Indiana University Press, 1953). An excellent study of how towns in the West were founded, grew, and were abandoned. For special projects.

24. Goetzmann, William H., *Exploration and Empire* (New York: Alfred A. Knopf, 1966). Goetzmann's study is one of the best, most comprehensive looks at the West. It is a long book, but highly recommended for supplementary reading.

25. Allen, James B., *The Company Town in the American West* (Norman: University of Oklahoma Press, 1966). Allen studies various lumbering and mining companies which built towns for their employees. He also evaluates the results, including

the Ludlow massacre. The book can be assigned for an in-depth study of this phase of urban development.

26. Durham, Philip, and Everett L. Jones, *The Negro Cowboy* (New York: Dodd, Mead, 1965). This is the definitive work on the Negro cowboy and includes sections on Nat Love and others. It can be understood by senior high students. A more simplified version for juveniles is *The Adventures of Negro Cowboys,* published in 1966.

27. Lord, Clifford L., *Teaching History with Community Resources* (New York: Teachers College Press, 1964). Those in the series that are helpful on the West are:

> *Arizona,* Madeline F. Pare (1968).
> *California,* Andrew Rolle (1965).
> *Colorado,* Carl Ubbelohde (1965).
> *Idaho,* Merle W. Wells (1965).
> *Utah,* Everett L. Cooley (1968).
> *Wyoming,* Lola M. Homsher (1966).
> *Los Angeles,* Andrew Rolle (1965).
> *Denver,* John D. Mitchell (1969).
> *San Francisco,* Moses and Ruth S. Richin (1969).
> *The Sacramento Valley,* Joseph McGowan (1968).

The Industrial City,
1860–1920

A continuing theme in American urban history has been the close connection between urbanization and technological development. The relationship between the two has been dialectical—advances in technology have made possible increased urbanization, increased urbanization has called for new technology. Neither seems possible without the other. Without the social organization and labor potential of the city, industrial development would not occur. Without the technical means to marshal the labor force and to utilize the social organization—transportation and communication—the potential would not be realized. In the period under consideration, 1860–1920, the mutual process of industrialization and urbanization accelerated tremendously, and the popular reaction to the growth of the city and the growth of industry was

Broadway, New York City, in the late 1880's. Cable cars have replaced horse cars for public transportation, and telephone poles have disappeared because the lines now run underground (AMERICAN MUSEUM OF PHOTOGRAPHY)

often connected. Industrialization, which brought together the metropolis and the immigrant, was at once beneficent and malignant; the face of the city became that of the industrial center.

By 1920, after sixty years of the greatest urban growth in our history, more than half of the American people lived in cities. In 1860 Philadelphia had a population of 563,000; by 1890 the population was over 1,000,000. The city grew more in thirty years than it had grown during all of its past. Other cities surpassed Philadelphia in growth rate because of greater industrialization. Pittsburgh, Chicago, Cincinnati, Milwaukee, and Kansas City all benefited greatly from industrial growth. The population growth was in fact surpassed by the growth of industrial productivity. In the years from 1850 to 1900, American production of textiles increased seven times, production of iron and steel increased ten times, processing of agricultural products increased fourteen times, and production of agricultural implements increased twenty-five times.

The growth of industrial cities was in part determined by their ability to specialize or to develop the services necessary to promote specialization in a particular region. Cleveland became significant in this period partly because of the oil boom in Pennsylvania and the subsequent location of Rockefeller interests in Cleveland. Minneapolis became the leading flour-processing center for the great plains, even though the city itself was not very large in the 1870's. Chicago and Kansas City became important meatpacking centers. Milwaukee became an important center for brewing, and Memphis became one for the processing of cottonseed oil. The textile and shoe towns of New England continued to grow as machines replaced craftsmen. Fall River, Massachusetts, became one of the leading producers of cotton goods, while Lowell became identified with carpets. Lynn and Haverhill continued to make shoes. Boston and New York became centers for ready-to-wear clothes. Dayton became the home of the cash register, while Schenectady became a base for General Electric and electrical appliances. Detroit expanded with the coming of the automobile.

The growth of industrial cities was due in part to location, in part to resources, in part to skillful promotion, and in part, as always, to luck. Memphis seemed a logical place for the production of cottonseed oil because of the city's access to the Mississippi River and to the cotton plantations of the Delta region, but other towns further down the Mississippi might have done as well. Minneapolis successfully outstripped St. Louis and Baltimore in flour milling because of technical ingenuity and the exploitation of a peculiar agricultural circumstance. The climate of the northern plains was more conducive to the growing of spring wheat than to the less hardy winter wheat. But spring wheat was hard-kernel as compared with the soft-kerneled winter wheat, and the mills were unwilling to buy it because they had inadequate machinery to process it. Entrepreneurs in Minneapolis adapted Hungarian techniques and were able to process the harder grains and thus to attract more wheat to that city. Milwaukee's advantage in brewing was due in part to the German labor supply with its skills in that art, while European immigrants made possible the garment trade in New York and Boston. The growth of meat-packing in Chicago was also due in part to the available pool of immigrant labor. Cleveland had excellent natural facilities on Lake Erie, but it was the organizational genius of Rockefeller that enabled the city to take a lead in oil processing. Many towns manufactured automobiles, too, but not until Ford located in Detroit did that city become the car capital of the United States.

The growth of cities also acted as a stimulus to the national economy. In 1860 the United States census showed 6 million urban dwellers; in 1900 the total urban population was 30 million; in 1920 it was 54 million. The vast increase in population necessitated expenditures for housing, transportation, and municipal services. The historian Edward C. Kirkland postulated that by 1900, 63 per cent of the construction industry was located in only 209 cities, and that construction done in rural areas amounted to less than 10 per cent of the total. Kirkland indicates that municipal debt, an index of growing services, went from a total of

$200 million in 1860 to $1.4 billion in 1902. (The earlier figure includes money that cities subscribed for railroad securities, investments which by 1902 had become much less significant. Nor do these figures take into account the considerable growth in *private* investment in urban services.) In these ways, then, cities helped develop the industrial society of today. City building became more important than building railroads, and capital was diverted accordingly, thus taking up the slack which could have developed when the nation's rail network was completed.

The growth of the industrial city meant a change in the shape as well as the size of the city. As Charles N. Glaab and A. Theodore Brown have pointed out:

> Although American cities grew rapidly in population in the early nineteenth century, they were still, until about 1850, reasonably compact; a man might walk through all of the neighborhoods of even the larger places in a day. Expanded population was absorbed through a more concentrated use of residential space near the sites of work; this caused a considerable increase in population density and a high degree of congestion in eastern seaboard cities.

Because of this population density and the lack of available housing, social organization was different than it would be later. Slums, while they did exist, were of a different character, and ethnic enclaves were not as common around 1860 as they were to become later.

As Sam Bass Warner, Jr., has shown in his detailed study of Philadelphia, the compact city had a different residential pattern than the sprawling industrial metropolis. In 1860 the poor lived wherever they could in any kind of housing. If they were concentrated anywhere, it was in the outer ring of Philadelphia where land was cheapest and where shacks could be cheaply and hastily thrown up. These poor working-class people located near the source of their work, the textile mills near the perimeter of the city. Immigrants to the city, such as the Irish, were to be found everywhere in the city, in the ring as well as in the core. The

Germans concentrated somewhat on the north side; the free Negro was the most segregated. Warner concludes that Philadelphia before 1860 was settled mainly on the basis of proximity to industry, and that after 1860 this basis was radically changed.

> . . . With the improvement in intracity transportation and the creation of large business organizations, the necessity to hive faded away. As this industrial cause of clustering lapsed, intense segregation based on income, race, foreign birth, and class rose to prominence as the organizing principle of the metropolis.

The period from 1860 to 1920, then, was one in which the population density of cities was lowered. The population density of American cities increased to 1860 but began to drop thereafter. In Chicago the period from 1880 to 1890 saw a spectacular drop in density, from 14,314.5 persons per square mile to 6,343.4. In Philadelphia the movement of population from the center of the city was larger from 1860 to 1910 than it was from 1900 to 1950. What happened in the industrial city was that the outlying areas grew in population and the city became more sprawling.

At the same time new patterns of development became evident. One was the growth of the center city slum, along with the concept of "downtown," and a corresponding increase in suburban living. Workers no longer needed to live next to their work; they could live in any neighborhood which they could afford and which would have them. As they moved to the suburbs, the inner city became the area of dilapidated housing and the home of the most recent migrants to the area.

This pattern of development was made possible technologically by the extension of rapid-transit systems and psychologically by the desire of those in the middle class to emulate wealthier society by living in the country. Hans Blumenfeld has estimated that in the nineteenth century the development of the steamship, railroads, and telegraph facilities made regional control by cities easier, but the lack of technological development in the cities prevented their growth. As he says:

A New York businessman could communicate quickly with his partners in Shanghai by cablegram, but to deliver an order to an office a few blocks away he had to send a messenger. This situation limited cities to a radius of only about three miles from the center. In the absence of elevators the city was also limited in vertical expansion.

Blumenfeld goes on to argue that increasing the radius of travel to twenty miles—easily done with electric streetcars—meant that a city could cover 1,250 square miles with only a third of this space required to house 10 million people living in single family homes. If the radius were increased to thirty miles (which has been done with freeways and the automobile), a city could have 15 million people while still retaining two-thirds of its space for commercial and industrial use.

The latter half of the nineteenth century saw the conversion of the walking city to the riding city. This process is demonstrated best in Sam Bass Warner, Jr.'s *Streetcar Suburbs: The Process of Growth in Boston, 1870–1900*. In his book Warner shows how the city of Boston expanded from a two-mile-radius seaport in 1850 to a metropolitan area with a ten-mile radius, containing thirty-one cities and towns, in 1900. He also shows how the city's population increased from 250,000 to over 1,000,000.

Two elements made Boston's rapid sprawl possible—the invention of the telephone in 1876 and the introduction of streetcars in 1852. The early streetcars were horse drawn and did not push the boundaries of the city out very far: by 1873 the city limits had moved out only a half-mile. Not until the late 1880's did the perimeter of Boston extend four miles, the rapid expansion from this time until 1900 being due in large part to the electrification of the streetcars. By the end of the era, individuals could live ten miles from the center of Boston and commute comfortably to the city's center.

The streetcar lines helped private promoters sell subdivisions, and these promoters made demands on the city for further services—water, sewage, gas, electricity, and telephones. Private and public expenditures met these demands, and the city of Boston grew rapidly. As Warner has shown, all sectors working toward Boston's development shared common assumptions: a belief in equal service throughout the area—the prices on streetcars were the same, the gas rates were the same, the schools were to be the same; a belief that individual initiative should build houses at a profit without public planning; and a view that the dispersal of the urban population was a good idea. The last was a reflection of a rural ideal in a city setting. Moving the immigrant from a crowded tenement to a single-family house in the country would improve his moral as well as his physical health.

The hope proved somewhat illusory. What developed in Boston was a pattern of housing segregated by incomes: the old city became an area of cheap housing for workers, while the new suburban developments housed the new middle class which moved away from the inner city. Housing patterns became quite clear. The rich either bought far out in the country or in Back Bay, the best section in old Boston. The group Warner calls the central middle class—small entrepreneurs, professional people, contractors—went to the suburbs because they knew where they would be working and could easily plan a route to work. This group comprised the first large group—15 per cent of Boston's population—to go to the suburbs.

They were followed by the last group to come, the lower middle class, skilled workers, office and sales personnel, and managers on a lower level. These people had different work requirements, which meant that they could not go as far out in the suburbs as their more prosperous neighbors. They often had seasons when work required extra time, or they had to move from place to place as they plied a skilled trade. It was essential for these people that they be closer to the center of the city and able to utilize crosstown transportation. As a result, these workers bought or rented homes beyond the walking city but not far out in the suburbs. Since the workers in this group outnumbered those in the central middle class—20 or 30 per cent as compared with 15 per cent—

land values in the area just outside the old city exceeded those of land further out.

The poorer classes did not move out until they had become more prosperous. As an immigrant group succeeded, it moved out to the suburbs, and the suburbs reflected successive waves of immigrants. Warner claims that the ethnic composition of the suburbs was similar to that of the old city thirty years earlier.

The pattern of the modern American industrial city thus emerged in the latter half of the nineteenth and early twentieth centuries. The cities not only changed their economic character; their physical shape was altered by different residential patterns of segregation by income instead of segregation by occupation. These changes were made possible by technological developments —streetcars and other rapid-transit systems—but also reflected American views of what life ought to be. Already the metropolis was beginning to be feared, and the city as a home was being replaced by the city as a place of work. The rural ideal of life lived under benign nature prevailed upon many individuals who previously had lacked the means to live that kind of life. But the hope of regeneration by nature was also extended to the immigrant who, it was believed and hoped, could one day also move from the industrial slum to the suburbs.

This era of the industrial city lends itself very well to local research projects by students, particularly those who live in sizable cities. The limits of the older walking city are fairly easily located. Its radius can be plotted and the extension of the city with the advent of streetcars can be traced. Students can project the possible further extension of this radius by buses and trains. Further, the social class and economic circumstances of those who move beyond the boundaries of the older city can be plotted. Warner did this by studying building permits issued in Roxbury, West Roxbury, and Dorchester, Massachusetts, from 1872 to 1901. He then tried to find out who moved in and checked these persons against the state and national censuses of the period. The use of local records and of other materials can also reveal social groupings. While Warner was quite sophisticated in his techniques, the student need not be so thorough and may be content with a smaller segment of a city.

Finally, since the pattern of suburbanization which typifies American cities developed in this era, it is important to discover what factors contributed to this development. Far too many urbanologists are ahistoric enough to claim that modern urban problems are unique and that the suburbs are relatively new. A cursory glance shows this is not the case. Further, the growth of the industrial city lends itself to generalizations and to graphic presentations. The income segregation of residential units, the changes in land use, the change in worker residences, and the growth of the city in the direction of transport routes can all be mapped.

Bibliography

1. *Geography in an Urban Age:* Unit I: *Geography of Cities* (High School Geography Project, Association of American Geographers: Boulder, Colo., 1968). The section "A Tale of Three Cities," which details the growth of Boston, New York, and Philadelphia from their beginnings to 1860, can be used in conjunction with Warner's *Streetcar Suburbs* to analyze Boston's growth before the introduction of streetcars.

2. *Middle Atlantic Seaboard Region, The Great Cities—Megalopolis* (McGraw-Hill Textfilms, 1963). The life and problems of the urbanized seaboard region from Boston to Washington, D.C., are the subjects of this film, a part of the United States Geography Social Studies series. The film shows the end result of the industrial city and enables viewers to see the problems engendered by sprawl and suburban development. For junior and senior high school students.

3. *Chicago Fire* (McGraw-Hill Textfilms, 1956). Walter Cronkite narrates this film, part of the You Are There series, on the great Chicago fire of October 8, 1871. Chicago emerged from the fire to become a great industrial city. While this film is more concerned with the causes and consequences of the disaster than

with the development of Chicago, the patterns of growth can be seen. The film is an elementary one.

4. *Dawn of a New Era—America Enters the Twentieth Century* (S. L. Film Productions, 1966). The period 1897–1905 is the focus of this film, which utilizes cuts from films of the era and shows some of its notable people—inventors, political leaders, and entertainers. The film gives the flavor of the times and offers some firsthand views of cities. Suitable for senior high school students.

5. *Chicago—Midland Metropolis* (Encyclopedia Britannica Films, 1963). This film touches on the factors of growth, immigration, industrialization, and transportation in Chicago, and how these have affected its citizens. Useful in contrasting the city's growth to others in the same time span. For junior high school.

6. *The Changing City* (Coronet Films, 1963). The growth of the metropolis and the impact of this growth on the people of the city are the themes of this film, which outlines historical patterns of development and the implications of these patterns in land use and urban renewal. A useful film for an overall, general view. Recommended for junior and senior high school students.

7. *Third Avenue El* (Contemporary Films, n.d.). This film provides a nostalgic ride through old New York City on the elevated railroad, which has since been torn down. Not the least of the film's attractions is the sound track—the music of Haydn played by Wanda Landowska on the harpischord. The film conveys a sense of the city as might have been experienced by a commuter at the turn of the century. Highly recommended for mature students.

8. Glaab, Charles N., and A. Theodore Brown, *A History of Urban America* (New York: Macmillan, 1967), paperback. Chapter 6, "Transformation and Complexity: The Changing City, 1860–1910," is an excellent introduction to the development of the industrial city. For better students.

9. Green, Constance McLaughlin, *The Rise of Urban America* (New York: Harper and Row, 1965), paperback. Chapter 4,

"The Impact of Industrialization, 1860–1910," is a summary of the impact of industrial development on urban life. For better students.

10. Callow, Alexander B., Jr., ed., *American Urban History* (New York: Oxford University Press, 1969), paperback. The fourth section on "The City in the Age of Industry" contains three good articles which are provocative and which furnish ideas for understanding the development of cities. The essays can be handled by better students.

11. Wakstein, Allen M., ed., *The Urbanization of America* (Boston: Houghton Mifflin, 1970), paperback. Part 4, "Urbanization and Industrialization," has four essays which duplicate some of those in Callow. For the same students.

12. Mohl, Raymond A., and Neil Betten, eds., *Urban America in Historical Perspective* (New York: Weybright and Talley, 1970). Chapter 4, "The Industrial City," includes two articles on industrial cities and others which detail the impact of urbanism on the church, politics, and immigrants. For more sophisticated students.

13. Green, Constance McLaughlin, *American Cities in the Growth of the Nation* (New York: John De Graff, 1957), Harper paperback. This book considers individual cities and their relation to manufacturing, and presents valuable case studies. It should be assigned to those who wish to see examples of urban development centered on industrial specialization.

14. McKelvey, Blake, *The Urbanization of America, 1860–1915* (New Brunswick, N.J.: Rutgers University Press, 1963). A classic in the field of urban history, and justly so. It should be the point of departure for students who wish to understand the era and the major themes in urbanization.

15. Kirkland, Edward C., *Industry Comes of Age: Business, Labor, and Public Policy, 1860–1897* (New York: Holt, Rinehart and Winston, 1961), Quadrangle paperback. Kirkland's book is a specialized one which should be assigned only to those interested in and competent to understand economic development.

Kirkland does consider the impact of cities on economic growth and the extent to which cities were a product of that growth.

16. Jaher, Frederick C., ed., *The Age of Industrialism in America* (New York: Free Press, 1968), paperback. The essays in this collection include material on the reciprocal relations between industrialization and urbanization. Jaher has an article on Boston between 1870 and 1940, and John Cawelti writes on the World's Fairs of 1876, 1893, and 1933. Sophisticated and recommended only for teachers.

17. Warner, Sam Bass, Jr., *Streetcar Suburbs: The Process of Growth in Boston, 1870–1900* (New York: Atheneum, 1969), paperback. Warner's book is well illustrated and not difficult. It is basic to understanding the beginnings of urban sprawl, the interconnection between transportation and suburbs, and the process of residential segregation by income groups. Highly recommended for senior high students.

18. Warner, Sam Bass, Jr., *The Private City: Philadelphia in Three Periods of Its* Growth (Philadelphia: University of Pennsylvania Press, 1966). The last period of growth which Warner studies is from 1920–1930, the period of industrialization. Warner shows how the housing patterns shift in this period from occupational grouping to income grouping. A significant and important book. For better students and teachers only.

19. Pierce, Bessie L., *A History of Chicago* (3 vols., New York: Alfred A. Knopf, 1937–57). The last volume covers the period 1871–93 when Chicago became a modern industrial city. Useful for projects and cross-city comparisons.

20. McKelvey, Blake, *Rochester* (3 vols., Cambridge, Mass.: Harvard University Press, 1945–1956). The later volumes contain the story of the impact of Eastman Kodak on the city and can be used as a case study of industrial growth.

21. Still, Bayrd, *Milwaukee: The History of a City* (Madison: State Historical Society of Wisconsin, 1965). Still's book is useful in showing how the unique skills of the Germans in Milwaukee helped the beginnings of the brewing industry. For research projects.

22. Chapman, Edmund H., *Cleveland: Village to Metropolis* (Cleveland: Western Reserve University Press, 1965). Chapman shows how Cleveland expanded greatly in this era, partly from its natural location and partly from its connection with Rockefeller interests. For research projects.

23. Buder, Stanley, *Pullman: An Experiment in Industrial Order and Community Planning, 1880–1930* (New York: Oxford University Press, 1967), paperback. Buder's book is the first volume in a series edited by Richard C. Wade and entitled Urban Life in America. Pullman was a suburban development planned by the sleeping car company; it collapsed in 1894 after labor-management difficulties. The community then became another suburban area. Recommended as an example of a unique development in industrial cities. For those with an interest in company towns.

24. Hilton, George W., and John F. Due, *The Electric Inter-urban Railways in America* (Stanford: Stanford University Press, 1960). Although they have passed from the American scene, the inter-urbans have a devoted following of antiquarians. Inter-urbans did not directly change the patterns of city life, but they did tie cities together and affected city design. This is the history of the movement. Recommended for special projects and for railroad buffs.

25. Wiebe, Robert H., *The Search for Order, 1877–1920* (New York: Hill and Wang, 1967), paperback. Wiebe's theme is that the decentralized small-town community which typified the American scene in 1877 was supplanted by a new order which was the product of an urban middle class. This class wanted a rational, secular, bureaucratic society to go along with industrialization and urbanization. Useful and provocative on the impact of the industrial city. For teachers primarily.

26. Schlesinger, Arthur M., Sr., *The Rise of the City* (New York: Macmillan, 1933). The Schlesinger volume in The History of American Life series is often cited as one of the first attempts at modern urban history. Schlesinger, the academic father of many Harvard social historians, still is worth reading for his

original and penetrating insights. The book is most suited for the teacher's library.

27. Thernstrom, Stephan, *Poverty and Progress: Social Mobility in a Nineteenth-Century City* (Cambridge, Mass.: MIT Press and Harvard University Press, 1964), Atheneum paperback. Thernstrom's study of Newburyport is mainly concerned with social mobility, but the mobility of workers sheds much light on industrialization and suburbanization, for the major goal and achievement of workers was the ownership of a home. For better students and teachers only.

28. Lord, Clifford L., *Teaching History with Community Resources* (New York: Teachers College Press, 1964). The pertinent volumes in this series are:

Cincinnati, Louis L. Tucker (1968).

Houston, Joe B. Frantz (1968).

Los Angeles, Andrew Rolle (1965).

New York City, Bayrd Still (1965).

Raleigh–Durham–Chapel Hill, William S. Powell (1968).

Boston, Walter Muir Whitehill (1969).

Denver, John D. Mitchell (1969).

Milwaukee, Charles N. Glaab (1969).

San Francisco, Moses and Ruth S. Richin (1969).

Chicago, Clement M. Silvestro (1969).

The Immigrant and the City,
1860–1920

The history of the United States has been called a history of immigration. Indeed, much of our history is involved with the impact of the immigrant upon American life and the impact of American life upon the immigrant. This is no less true in urban history, and for several reasons.

The first is that the processes of immigration and urbanization went hand in hand. In the experience of members of the "new immigrant" groups from southeastern Europe who formed the bulk of migrants after 1890, coming to America meant coming to the city. While earlier immigrants—Germans, English, and Scandinavians—had been lured west by land offered by states such as Wisconsin, Minnesota, or Iowa, or by railroads such as the Burlington, the Northern Pacific, or the Santa Fe, the later waves were not as successfully solicited for the settling of Western lands. Not by choice but by design, Austro-Hungarians, Italians, Poles, Russians, Greeks, Rumanians, and Turks became part of the American city. The vast majority of them were unskilled laborers—81.9 per cent, compared with 18.9 per cent who were skilled; and they wanted to continue their agricultural pursuits.

Why did these migrants come to America, then, and why did they end up in the city? First of all, they came because it was now easier to come. Regular steamship schedules were widely advertised, and passage was both safe and relatively cheap. Countries which had previously forbidden migration now either repealed such laws or failed to enforce them. The unification of Italy in 1860 meant emigration was possible for Italians. In 1867 Austria-Hungary decided to permit emigration. The Balkan states, which emerged from Turkish rule in 1877, allowed emigration which the Turks had forbidden.

The second reason the immigrants came was primarily a social one, with economic overtones. Eastern Europe had undergone a great change in agricultural practice; the European peasant was being displaced. The end of feudal obligations and the resultant division of land made many agricultural workers surplus and forced them off the land. Hence Austro-Hungarians, Italians, and Poles left a European peasant society to enter an urbanized America. The shift was traumatic, from an agricultural, medieval, village life to an urban, modern, city life. The psychic costs, as Oscar Handlin has shown, were exceedingly high.

One fact should be made clear, however, and that is that most of the new immigrants had come from villages in the Old World; they had not lived in the kind of single farmsteads that existed in the United States. In 1910, 78.6 per cent of those who entered the United States had lived in a village before migrating. The new immigrants rarely were able to become farmers. They could not, for they lacked both the skills and capital necessary for American large-scale farming. Some became truck farmers,

Baxter Street Court, New York City, in the late 1880's, photograph by Jacob Riis (JACOB RIIS COLLECTION, MUSEUM OF THE CITY OF NEW YORK)

others migrant laborers, but most chose to live and work in cities with their own ethnic groups.

The new immigrants from southeastern Europe moved into areas of the city previously occupied by the older immigrants. The Irish and the Germans moved to the suburbs or just beyond the walking city in Boston and in New York. The Italians and the Russian Jews supplanted them. The core of the older city became identified with the exotic, foreign immigrant, and neighborhoods became ghettos. Many a large city had its "Little Russia," its "Little Poland," or its "Little Italy." These ethnic enclaves were further divided into smaller units reflecting parochial elements. Various Russian groups would congregate together, as would Poles, Italians, and people from the many districts and provinces of the Austro-Hungarian empire.

The ghettos reflected a social organization that was European and a vision of the metropolis that was, as Herbert Gans has put it, that of "an urban village." As it expanded, the industrial city also fragmented, so that it became a collection of small towns and villages within an urban milieu. Each ethnic neighborhood became self-contained with its own version of European institutions. The local church became a center for religious observance, the local foreign-language newspaper became the sole source of information, the mutual-aid society became the welfare agency the immigrant looked to, and the family ties of the Old World were perpetuated in the New. Indigenous American institutions were strained by the different visions of the new immigrants. The Catholic Church was under attack from Poles and Italians because of its Irish and German base. The public schools were filled with children whose parents often were suspicious of education. The neighborhood saloon became the social center for the ethnic male, and the prevailing approval of drinking added to its attractiveness.

Urban pressures and a European tradition of private settlement of personal grievance contributed to the supposed high crime rate and the violence of the ghetto. Unfamiliar with municipal, state, and national laws, the immigrant often preferred immediate action rather than the slower procedures of the courts. Often lower class, the new immigrant, like the older Irish immigrant, was accused of being lazy, drunken, and prone to crime. Indeed, the Italians, as Daniel Bell has shown in "Crime as an American Way of Life," became associated with crime because of three factors in the urban situation which the Italians exploited. These were (1) the success of Italians in politics in several large cities— Chicago, New York, Kansas City, and Los Angeles—at about the same time, (2) the appearance of Italians in criminal organizations, and (3) the seeming interrelation of the two—politicians and criminals—with the influence of the criminals apparently significant.

The new immigrant often found his path of mobility blocked by the older immigrant. Consequently he had to find other means of achieving wealth and social status. In the case of the Italians, the Irish had pre-empted two of the paths which had previously been open—the Catholic Church and urban politics. As Bell points out, in the 1950's there was no Italian bishop in America though the Catholic Church had a hundred bishops, and there was no Italian archbishop although there were twenty-one American archbishops. Therefore, while the Italian was nominally Catholic he could not achieve the highest offices of the Church— they were controlled by the Irish. He could become a priest, but again his chances for a good parish were slim.

The same situation prevailed in the case of urban politics. The Irishman was assuming control about the time the new immigrant arrived. The first Irish mayor of Boston, Hugh O'Brien, was elected in 1883. In New York City, Tammany Hall was becoming an Irish preserve. Not until after the 1930's did the Italians gain top political positions and names like Fiorello La Guardia and Vito Marcantonio became well known in New York City. The Italian association with crime was somewhat accidental and, Bell argues, no more reprehensible than the early practices of the Irish nor those of the Anglo-Saxon capitalists who preceded them. Once the Italians had succeeded in obtaining "respectability," they became overwhelmingly involved in professional and legitimate business endeavors like other earlier migrant groups. But the old reputation lingered on.

The close connection between the immigrant and the city was partially responsible for the native American revulsion against the metropolis. Earlier the city had not been so closely identified with Catholicism, the immigrant, and alcohol, and hence had been mistrusted less for its inhabitants than for its unhealthy atmosphere. The later city became a cesspool of corruption and a fountain of vice for the native American. Nowhere was corruption more noticed than in city government and in bossism. The political arrangements developed by immigrants in the city became the target of reformist zeal. The Tweed Ring in New York City, Boss Cox in Cincinnati, Frank Hague in Jersey City, Mayor Curley in Boston, and the Pendergasts in Kansas City all came to typify bad government, and all were closely related to immigrant groups, primarily the Irish.

Bossism, of course, filled a political need. In the rapidly expanding industrial city, the technological tools necessary to bind the city together were lacking. Someone needed to operate as a kind of broker or communications supervisor, to tell one part of the city what another was doing, and thus to provide jobs for an area in which there were job seekers, contracts in an area where there were contractors, and necessary facilities—sewers, streetcars, lights, gas, water—where these were needed. The boss knew what was being done, and he circulated the information mainly to his cronies. Had the boss not been present, another kind of system would have been necessary. Seymour Mandelbaum, in *Boss Tweed's New York,* makes quite clear how vital Tweed's services were in this regard.

The second function of the political machine in the city was an ameliorative one. The machine acted as a kind of welfare agency, dispensing economic favors in return for political support and smoothing the way of the immigrant in an alien society. The machine found jobs for the immigrant and his children or, if the immigrant was unable to work, provided charity for him. In so doing, the machine workers fit into the immigrant's world, personalized that world by attending weddings and funerals, and helped hold it together.

The third function of the political machine was educative—demonstrating a new role for the immigrant and familiarizing him with American political practices. In the first function the political leader showed the immigrant how it was possible to climb the ladder of social mobility. The politician was often himself an immigrant or a second-generation American whose ties with the old country were still obvious. If the Fitzgeralds in Boston could produce a mayor, why not the O'Reillys or the Kennedys? The political machine and its workers provided role models for aspiring young men and showed them how the system operated. The immigrant was taught which forms to fill out, how to fill them out, where to look for a job, how to vote, which areas were likely to look most kindly upon the immigrant as a neighbor, which areas should be avoided, where he should go with a complaint about municipal services, what his rights were when the police arrested him, and, in general, how to survive in a modern industrial city. The immigrant went through what would now be called a process of political socialization, and the urban political machine was the socializer.

Finally, the machine acted as a mediator between those persons who had economic and social power and those who had the most votes. The bosses were supported by white Anglo-Saxon Protestant businessmen who were either too involved with making money to practice the necessary political rituals and thus left the sordid bit to others, or who agreed with the educative function of the machine and the conservative social control which it afforded. The major difficulty with this connection between old and new America was the problem of the visibility of power and the failure to admit the new American to the clubs and organizations of the city.

The phenomenon of bossism can be illustrated in a number of cities, but perhaps one that seems atypical is best—Pendergast's machine in Kansas City as described by Lyle W. Dorsett. Kansas City was primarily a nonimmigrant city with only 6 per cent of its voters foreign-born, yet Pendergast's machine is regarded as a classic case of bossism. The machine grew and served the citizens of Kansas City even though only a minority of those citizens were new Americans. Its history shows why this type of government seemed necessary.

Jim Pendergast was born of Irish parents in Ohio and came to Kansas City in 1876 when he was twenty years old. He worked in packing houses and in an iron foundry until he won enough money on a horse to buy a hotel-saloon in 1881 in an industrial area, West Bottoms, populated by low-income Negroes, Irish, German, and native laborers. This area was bounded by another, the North End, which was populated by a large number of Italians and was called "Little Italy."

Pendergast entered politics in 1884 as a Democratic party delegate from the Sixth Ward, the "Bloody Sixth," so-called because of the commonplace of election-day fights there. After the Sixth was remade the First Ward, Pendergast was elected alderman in 1892 to serve in the lower house of the city council, a position he held until 1910. As alderman, Pendergast was for better garbage collection, lower telephone rates, and against lowering firemen's salaries. His extra-curricular activities also furthered his political career: he put up bail for men of his district charged with swindling, and he cashed workers' checks in his saloon. He later closed his first saloon but opened several others which also functioned as gambling centers with police protection despite their illegality.

Pendergast moved into the North End district with one of his saloons and followed it in 1896 with political organization. He came to terms with the leaders of the district who were afraid of a reform prosecuting attorney, and by 1898 he was in control of the North End and the police department in Kansas City. He used the control to reward his followers with jobs and to ease restrictions on gamblers and saloons. In 1900 he campaigned for alderman with an eye to the ethnic vote—the "King of Little Italy" spoke for Pendergast in Italian, German voters got free beer, and Negro gamblers were assured that the police would look the other way. By this time Pendergast had gained control of enough city hall jobs so that he had more patronage than ever to dispose. His brother became street superintendent with two hundred jobs to fill; another lieutenant became head of the fire department. In 1902 Pendergast lost control over the police department and suffered a temporary setback to his political fortunes. He reinforced his reputation in 1903, however, when he was a one-man relief agency for flood victims in Kansas City.

From 1906 on, Jim Pendergast, because of failing health, began the transfer of power to his brother Tom, who had served as street superintendent from 1900 to 1902 and as county marshal from 1902 to 1904. In both positions Tom had gained friends through favors, among Negroes as well as whites. When Jim Pendergast died in 1911, Tom was prepared to take over. His first move was to win Jackson County, in which Kansas City was located, through control of the county court. This would give him control of the road fund and a selection of county offices from which he could extend his patronage. In 1912 his men won a majority in the county and gave Pendergast the county patronage.

Tom Pendergast continued his welfare programs, granting jobs and money to his loyal followers and workers. This money was obtained from a number of sources—a wholesale liquor company, a house of prostitution in a hotel he owned, and from a thirty-year franchise for the Metropolitan Street Railway Company, received from Kansas City in 1914. This franchise enabled the company to increase its rates and lower its taxes, thus adding to its profitability. The excuse for the franchise was that the extension of streetcar lines into suburbs cost money and that increased funds were needed to provide for the expansion of municipal services.

By 1916 Pendergast had achieved almost complete control of Kansas City and Jackson County. His men were in the most lucrative offices in the city and county, and the Ross Construction Company, which was obtaining many city contracts, was owned by a political subordinate of Pendergast. By the end of World War I Pendergast seemed to be in firm control of the whole area. But the early twenties proved to be a more difficult time. In 1922 a Pendergast candidate, Harry Truman, became a county judge, and after his election proved to be an honest official. Consequently the amount of county graft was reduced. In the same year Pendergast lost the police department, though he still was able to win an honest election for control of the city because of his appeal to Negro and women voters. In 1924, however, a reform movement to institute a new city charter and nonpartisan government began. Pendergast did not oppose the charter because it had such extensive support, and in 1925 it was approved by the voters. But in the election of that year Pendergast controlled the city council—five out of nine members—and thus was able to hire the city manager. In fact he achieved more power through reform than he had had previously.

Pendergast thereupon expanded his techniques of machine politics to include all of Kansas City. He still catered to the ethnicity of the Italians and the black voters, but he also created bridge clubs and baseball and bowling leagues as adjuncts of the ward political clubs. He began a newspaper, the *Missouri Democrat,* which became an organ of the machine and publicized his many beneficent activities. The new city manager, a Pendergast man, had a reservoir of 3,700 jobs to be given to loyal Democrats. The city now rebated taxes to a number of businesses in return for their political and economic support, as well as protecting the illegal sale of liquor by night clubs, hotels, and saloons.

When the depression of the 1930's brought electoral success for the Democrats, Pendergast seized the opportunity to influence the state party machinery and was able to elect his candidate for governor. With this coup, Pendergast extended his patronage and his illegal activities state-wide. In one instance he received $750,-000 for settling an insurance case to the advantage of the company and the disadvantage of the state.

Pendergast's influence had a national side as well. His help made possible Roosevelt's nomination in 1932; in return, Pendergast intervened with the new President to pardon Conrad Mann, an associate of Pendergast who had been convicted of violating the federal anti-lottery law. Pendergast also gained patronage through federal projects—the Civil Works Administration and the Works Progress Administration. Finally, the successful campaign of Harry Truman for the United States Senate in 1934 redounded to Pendergast's advantage by indicating that the boss could still get out the vote.

The Pendergast machine had always padded voting lists. In 1934 it went a step further and employed Italian hoods to strong-arm the elections. They killed four people. Not until 1936, when the election frauds were brought to court, did the public become alarmed. The governor of Missouri, Lloyd Stark, decided that the best way to be elected U. S. Senator was to attack Pendergast, despite the fact that he had won the gubernatorial nomination with Pendergast's help. The governor began with the police, which the legislature put under state control in 1939. Upon this transfer, investigation of the police department showed widespread corruption. Organized crime was rampant in Kansas City, and the police either ignored the criminals or cooperated with them. The governor also helped instigate a federal investigation into Pendergast's tax records. In the 1938 elections he openly challenged Pendergast and, by using his patronage, defeated Pendergast's candidate. This helped turn Roosevelt toward the governor and against Pendergast. When the President ordered five federal agencies to investigate Pendergast, they uncovered evidence of income tax evasion. Pendergast was convicted on this charge in 1939 and sent to prison. The subsequent investigation and publicizing of the graft and corruption in Kansas City caused the downfall of the machine in 1940. The only bright spot that year was the re-election of Harry Truman to the Senate. Truman, a Pendergast man, went from the Senate to the presidency, and represented perhaps the last significant gasp of the older city politics.

Pendergast's career is a superb example of how the city boss worked and how he gained widespread support from business groups, members of the opposition party, and various ethnic groups. He served the city and its inhabitants—albeit at a high price. He ran what amounted to welfare and employment agencies in a pre-federalized social security era. He ventured into illegal activities and consorted with criminals, but he also furthered ethnic participation in the political life of Kansas City.

The study of bossism in American cities is one that lends itself to comparative treatment. Where did bosses occur and why? What elements made possible the growth of a city without a machine? Why did the old boss system die out? Did federalized social security turn people away from the ward politician, or were they outraged by the machine's shady deals? What role did reformers play in eliminating bossism, and were these reformers really practical political men?

Bibliography

1. *Metropolis* (Encyclopedia Britannica Films, 1963). This film is part of the NBC television course entitled "The Structure and Function of American Government" and concerns various ways of organizing city government. It is sophisticated and theoretical but does provide a base for further study of alternate ways of running city government. For better students.

2. *Innocent Years, 1901–1914* (McGraw-Hill Textfilms, 1965). While the name seems a misnomer for this unit, this Project 20 film shows the significant events of the era, including immigration, industrialization, and the growth of cities. Helpful, and highly recommended for high school students.

3. *America the Melting Pot* (Hearst Metrotone News, 1964). The mutual impact of the immigrant on America and of America

on the immigrant forms the basis of this film which is part of the Screen News Digest series. Suitable for high school students.

4. *The Golden Door* (Encyclopedia Britannica Films, 1963). Another in the Structure and Function of American Government series, this film analyzes the nature and causes of anti-alien sentiment which results in anti-city attitudes and in legislation to restrict immigration. For better students.

5. *Uprooted and the Alien-American* (Encyclopedia Britannica Films, 1963). This is also part of the Structure and Function of American Government series which closely relates to the preceding film. The conflict between immigrant and American values is the basis of the discussion. The film sheds light on the problems of urbanization and Americanization. The films in the series are all about the same level of difficulty.

6. *Our Immigrant Heritage* (McGraw-Hill Textfilms, 1966). Rather than concentrating upon the problems inherent in immigration, the film emphasizes the immigrant contribution to American society. For junior and senior high school students.

7. *Balkanization of Urban Life* (Encyclopedia Britannica Films, 1963). Arthur Naftalin, who was mayor of Minneapolis in 1963, discusses the problems of unifying city government in this film which is one in the Structure and Function of American Government series. The views of someone on the inside are especially stimulating.

8. *Good Night, Socrates* (Contemporary Films, 1963). An American of Greek descent reflects on his boyhood in a Greek neighborhood as the section is being torn down. Recommended for its human appeal and impact. For junior and senior high school students.

9. Glaab, Charles N., and A. Theodore Brown, *A History of Urban America* (New York: Macmillan, 1967), paperback. Chapter 8, "Bosses and Reformers," is an excellent summary of the interrelation among immigrants, industrial development, and city bossism. Recommended for better students.

10. Green, Constance McLaughlin, *The Rise of Urban America* (New York: Harper and Row, 1965), paperback. Chapter 5 covers political changes and developments in American cities from the Civil War to 1910, but in much less detail than Glaab and Brown.

11. Callow, Alexander B., Jr., ed., *American Urban History* (New York: Oxford University Press, 1969), paperback. Callow's collection includes a fine variety on the social and political problems of the industrial city. The book has Daniel Bell's article as well as ones by Ostrogorski, Handlin, Glazer, and Moynihan. Better students will find these articles an excellent place to begin.

12. Wakstein, Allen M., ed., *The Urbanization of America* (Boston: Houghton Mifflin, 1970), paperback. Wakstein's section on "The Impact of Urbanization" touches on boss rule and immigration, and includes two articles on Chicago and one on New York City.

13. Mohl, Raymond A., and Neil Betten, eds., *Urban America in Historical Perspective* (New York: Weybright and Talley, 1970). This anthology does not contain a separate section on the immigrant, but the section on the industrial city has useful articles on Cincinnati and on Italians in America.

14. Strauss, Anselm, *Images of the American City* (New York: Free Press, 1961). Included in the images which Strauss describes are those held by the immigrants who come to the city. Strauss shows how it is possible to view cities in a number of different ways. For better students only.

15. Gans, Herbert, *The Urban Villagers* (New York: Free Press, 1962), paperback. Gans, a sociologist, argues that the Italians in Boston view their area as a village with definite physical and cultural features. The thesis is provocative, and the book can be assigned for advanced projects.

16. Jones, Maldwyn Allen, *American Immigration* (Chicago: University of Chicago Press, 1960), paperback. One in the Chicago History of American Civilization series. It is eminently readable and is the best survey of the subject. The chapter entitled

"Immigrants in Industrial America" is an excellent summary of the problems of urban life.

17. Shannon, William, *The American Irish* (New York: Macmillan, 1963). Shannon writes well and the book is exciting. It details the Irishman's paths of mobility in the Catholic Church and the city machine. Highly recommended.

18. Callow, Alexander B., Jr., *The Tweed Ring* (New York: Oxford University Press, 1966), paperback. This is the most readable account of the Tweed Ring in New York City. It explains why the immigrants supported Tweed and what his function was.

19. Mandlebaum, Seymour, *Boss Tweed's New York* (New York: John Wiley, 1965), paperback. Mandlebaum's thesis is that Tweed was an essential link in the communications chain which held New York City together, and that his fall was a result of improved alternatives. Recommended for special projects only.

20. Dorsett, Lyle W., *The Pendergast Machine* (New York: Oxford University Press, 1968), paperback. This book in Oxford's Urban Life in America series is an excellent brief summary of the lives and careers of the Pendergast brothers. Recommended as a case study in bossism.

21. Miller, Zane L., *Boss Cox's Cincinnati: Urban Politics in the Progressive Era* (New York: Oxford University Press, 1968), paperback. Also in the Urban Life in America series. The city of Cincinnati grew rapidly in the latter half of the nineteenth century, and developed machine politics similar to other cities. Like Kansas City, Cincinnati did not have the largest percentage of immigrants but did have a city boss. Recommended for cross-city comparisons of political machines.

22. Holli, Melvin G., *Reform in Detroit: Hazen S. Pingree and Urban Politics* (New York: Oxford University Press, 1969). Pingree was not a boss, he was a reform mayor; but the problems of Detroit were similar to those of other cities of the time. The conditions which led to bossism existed in Detroit, and the city suffered government by cronies. Another volume in the Oxford Urban Life in America series, useful for a view of the Motor City.

23. Keller, Morton, *The Art and Politics of Thomas Nast* (New York: Oxford University Press, 1968). The crusading cartoonist who exposed the Tweed Ring with his acid cartoons is the subject for this book which contains more than two hundred of his drawings. A useful reference tool for those students who wish to see history visualized and who are interested in cartooning.

24. Wilson, James Q., ed., *City Politics and Public Policy* (New York: John Wiley, 1968). Wilson, a noted political scientist, has edited a collection which shows the interrelation between politics and policy. Recommended for better students who want to know how the system works.

25. Leinwand, Gerald, ed., *City Government* (New York: Washington Square Press, 1970), paperback. A volume in the Problems of American Society series designed for secondary schools. The curriculum committee of the Trenton, New Jersey, public schools provided editorial assistance for the books, which contain both text and readings. Recommended for general use.

26. Terkel, Studs, *Division Street: America* (New York: Pantheon, 1967), Avon paperback. Studs Terkel's forte is interviewing people. In this book he looks at his city, Chicago, through the eyes of many persons of varying ethnic backgrounds. The book is eminently readable and can be assigned to senior high school students.

27. Lavine, David, *The Mayor and the Changing City* (New York: Random House, 1966). This is the second volume in the American Birthright series. Its topic is New Haven and its mayor at that time, Richard C. Lee. Lee gained a reputation as a progressive mayor who urged extensive urban renewal for his community. The book is aimed at young readers and can be understood by junior high school students. Illustrated.

28. Maier, Henry W., *Challenge to the Cities: An Approach to a Theory of Urban Leadership* (New York: Random House, 1966), paperback. Maier, who was mayor of Milwaukee, outlines his program for successful government. His formula is to know the problems of the city, to research solutions, and to under-

stand the structure of government. The book is nontechnical, so high school students can manage it.

29. O'Connor, Edwin, *The Last Hurrah* (Boston: Little, Brown, 1956), Bantam paperback. This famous novel about boss politics in Boston is a fascinating account of an Irish politician. Highly recommended for high school students.

30. Banfield, Edward C., and James Q. Wilson, *City Politics* (Cambridge Mass.: Harvard University Press, 1963), Vintage paperback. A standard work by two political scientists, the first of whom heads President Nixon's task force on Model Cities. For reference only.

31. Lord, Clifford L., ed., *Teaching History with Community Resources* (New York: Teachers College Press, 1964). There are six volumes in the series on immigrant groups which are recommended. These include:

The Star of Hope: The Finns in America, John I. Kolehmainen (1968).
The Germans in America, Carl Wittke (1967).
The Greeks in America, Theodore Saloutos (1967).
The Irish in America, Carl Wittke (1968).
The Mexicans in America, Carey McWilliams (1968).
The Norwegians in America, Elinor Haugen (1967).

The Black Man and the City,
1865–1970

The civil rights revolution of the post–World War II era and black militancy are both a product of the urbanization of the Negro in America. Just as black abolitionists before the Civil War clustered in Northern cities, so do the new abolitionists. The city has provided a population base, a training ground for leadership, and the social structure necessary for the organization of protest and pressure groups.

The urbanization of the black man has been largely a twentieth-century phenomenon. August Meier and Elliott Rudwick, in their *From Plantation to Ghetto,* say this:

> After the Civil War and Emancipation, the major watershed in American Negro history was the Great Migration to Northern cities that began during the First World War. According to

Marcus Garvey's uniformed guard in Harlem, 1924 (JAMES VANDERZEE, COURTESY REGINALD MCGHEE)

the census of 1910, Negroes were overwhelmingly rural and Southern; approximately three out of four lived in rural areas and nine out of ten lived in the South. Today Negroes are mainly an urban population, almost three fourths of the 20,491,000 nonwhites being city-dwellers, according to the 1960 census.

The movement of blacks to the city accelerated in the 1960's, and today there are cities in the North which have more blacks than whites. These include Gary, Indiana, and Washington, D.C. Demographers predict that this trend of a black majority will continue, because the black migration is coupled with another political phenomenon, the growing inability of cities to annex suburbs since the 1920's. Those who try to forecast future trends argue that by the 1980's many major Northern cities will have black cores ringed by white suburbs.

How did this situation come about? Is the black man only another in the wave of immigrants to the city, and will his experience be the same as the experience of those southeastern Europeans who preceded him? Some social scientists argue this position, claiming that the black man is the "new" immigrant of the twentieth century. Just as the Polish peasant was forced to move from a rural folk culture to an urban one, so the black man must move from the rural South to an urban, Northern culture. This is essentially the argument of Daniel Patrick Moynihan when he compares the Irish stereotype of Paddy with the black stereotype of Sambo. This analogy, however, overlooks the three hundred years of black history that led to urbanization and fails to account for the cultural Americanization of those three hundred years. The Polish and Irish peasant needed to become both American and urban; the black sharecropper needed only to become urban. The pattern of black settlement was different, and the black ghetto was not the same as the Irish or Polish ghetto.

The process of urbanization and ghettoization can be illustrated best in New York City. Two recent books, *Harlem: The Making of a Ghetto* and *Negro Mecca: A History of the Negro in New York City* have made clear the historic forces that led to the concentration of black citizens in Harlem in Manhattan and in the Bedford-Stuyvesant area of Brooklyn.

The black man came to New Amsterdam in 1626, and has persisted throughout the history of New York City. By 1860 Negroes were living in three major areas of the city—Greenwich Village, the west Twenties, and the east Eighties. By the 1870's and 1880's Italians were replacing black renters in Greenwich Village. These displaced blacks moved to the Tenderloin district— so-called because of its crime rate—and to San Juan Hill and Harlem. Harlem grew in the 1900's because of its quiet residential character and because it was not associated with the lowly immigrant. There is evidence that blacks moved away from Italians and toward the Irish.

In all areas of New York City, housing conditions for blacks were poor and white property holders resisted their influx. The black man paid a higher rent, even though he may have been considered a better risk than the newly arrived immigrant. Most blacks were renters in apartments rather than in single-family dwellings, and had a higher population concentration than did white tenants.

The problem of black housing led to the formation of the National Urban League in 1910. Originally called the League on Urban Conditions, the agency at first had a dual housing function. The first was to create a housing list containing recommended and nonrecommended housing. The second was to stimulate community pride and neighborhood betterment. The Urban League was also interested in upgrading the employment status of black citizens.

The job problem of black New Yorkers was unique. Contrary to the usual immigrant pattern—replacing the native American in the hardest and most distasteful jobs—the black was displaced by the immigrant in the service sector, which was relatively better. The Irish became domestic servants; the French, German, and Irish took over hotel work. The Italians became barbers and boot-blacks. Despite this displacement, the black man did not move up to skilled trades, though his percentage increased in the professions.

By 1910 half of the black men were still employed in domestic service, and 86 per cent of black women were employed in the same area.

The attraction of jobs in New York City proved to be consistent, however. The black population, which ranged from 1.4 to 1.9 per cent of the total population, grew after World War I. By 1960 the percentage was 13.9. New York gained 51 per cent in black population from 1900 to 1910, but the large increase was brought on by the coming of World War I, natural disasters in the South—the boll weevil infestation of cotton and floods—and the demands of Northern industry. The influx from the South was increased by the migration from the Caribbean of West Indian blacks who hoped for greater economic advantage in the United States.

The results of this increase of blacks, hemmed together into a ghetto in Harlem, were both political and cultural. On August 1, 1914, Marcus Garvey began the first black political movement to have grass-roots support—the Universal Negro Improvement Association. Garvey was a Jamaican who came to New York City and had his greatest success there preaching black pride and a Back-to-Africa movement. He emphasized black nationalism and solidarity and proposed to free both black Africans and black Americans. Garvey created an African Legion, a Black Star Steamship Line, and a number of black-owned and -operated enterprises. He attacked the NAACP and other Negro leaders of the time for their integrationist policies. When his steamship line failed, Garvey was convicted of using the mails to defraud; he was jailed and ultimately deported. Much of Garvey's technique can be found in today's black nationalist movements; his appeal to the depressed black citizen was emotional and direct.

The cultural reaction to ghettoization was the "Harlem Renaissance." A consciousness of race pride emerged, along with an interest in black and African history. Black bookstores specialized in these areas, and stores began selling African artifacts as well as black dolls. Alain Locke, the first black Rhodes scholar, used the term the "New Negro" in a collection of his writings published in 1925. The "New Negro" was proud of being black, he demanded his rights, he considered his cultural contribution to America significant, and he wanted equality. Other writers such as Claude McKay, Countee Cullen, and Langston Hughes lived in Harlem at the same time. Black musicians and novelists also blossomed in Harlem, capturing the attention of the white community. The ghetto became a tourist attraction, and the black creative artist became a fixture in the fashionable salons of the day. The idea grew that black culture had much to offer white America.

One of the most widely regarded features of black culture was music—jazz, ragtime, and blues. Paul Whiteman and George Gershwin used blues or jazz themes in their popular and symphonic performances. The black tradition in music came from the rural work chant and the spiritual, but it also drew from the urban milieu. W. C. Handy, the father of the blues, had gone from Florence, Alabama, to Chicago in 1892 to sing in a quartet at the Columbian Exposition. When the Exposition was postponed for a year, the quartet went to St. Louis. The St. Louis experience became part of Handy's music, and the "St. Louis Blues" became a classic. Scott Joplin, the king of ragtime, was born in Texarkana and traveled over the Southwest. He spent time in Sedalia, Missouri, a railway hub, working as a piano player in a bar, then worked in Kansas City. He migrated to New York City in 1904 and remained there until he died. Composer of the "Maple Leaf Rag," Joplin, like Handy, was an urban product. The city, with its market for popular music, made possible Joplin's career.

New Orleans, of course, was a center of black musical creativity. "Jelly Roll" Morton is perhaps a good example of the urban bluesman. Born in New Orleans, Morton at the age of sixteen left his middle-class home to become a piano player in a bordello on Rampart Street. He played solos or in combos with others throughout the South during the early 1900's. In 1910 he went to Chicago and stayed until 1918. There he played to the growing numbers of black workers who had come from the South to find work with the advent of World War I. When he left Chicago, Morton went to Los Angeles, where he formed several musical groups, then to St. Louis, New York, and Washington, ending his days as an itinerant musician playing jazz.

Blues, ragtime, and jazz, because of their association with the seamier side of urban life—prostitution, gambling, and liquor— were at first as rejected by middle-class Negroes as by middle-class whites. But by the 1920's black music was becoming accepted by more and more middle-class people regardless of color.

In *Urban Blues,* Charles Keil argues that blues music is the vehicle for understanding urban lower-class Negro culture. Keil presents an interesting and controversial thesis—that the contemporary bluesman best expresses basic black urban culture. His role combines the ability to win in verbal contests, the concept of the con man, and the view of a man as one who dresses well and who has considerable social poise. Whether Keil is right or wrong, the role of the blues and the bluesman reveals much about the problems of the black man in the city as well as his adaptation to and manipulation of the environment. Today, rock music evolving from black rhythm and blues has become the contemporary sound and still has very evident black roots. Because of this heritage, black urban experience has become part of American cultural history. In this ironic way, black lower-class values have captured white men as well as blacks.

The 1930's brought a shift in black culture, manifested sometimes religiously, sometimes politically. The depression which gripped the larger society in the thirties had been familiar to the black man years before, but worsening conditions in the United States magnified the problems of blacks in New York, Chicago, Philadelphia, and other cities with substantial black populations. In black communities religious sects sprang up which gave hope to the hopeless and often served as social welfare agencies. The best known of these was that of Father Divine (George Baker). Baker grew up in the Savannah River rice-growing area but migrated to Long Island where he opened a free employment agency which also served as a private relief agency. He had early conceived of himself as touched with Divinity and had called himself "The Son of Righteousness." In 1932 Father Divine moved to Harlem where he continued to proclaim his Divinity and began to serve expensive free meals to destitute individuals, finding or making jobs for them and, in general, serving a needed and useful function as a community organizer.

In Detroit at the same time, a new religious group was founded which combined a welfare orientation with the nationalistic ideas of Marcus Garvey. This group was the Black Muslims, and the nominal founder was a man named W. D. Fard who sold fabrics and raincoats on the streets of "Paradise Valley." Fard worked in Detroit only about three years, from 1930 to 1933 or 1934. In addition to selling his wares to black customers, Fard taught them his religious ideas, which included the belief that the black man was the original man and the white man was a devil; the white man had taken the black man's religion—Islam—from him, and the black man must give up his white religion and ways and turn to Islam. When he did, he would receive a new name. Fard established the first Temple of Islam, which by 1934 had eight thousand members. He disappeared in 1933 or 1934, but he had already designated his successor to be Elijah Muhammad (Robert Poole). Poole had been born in Sandersville, Georgia, in 1897, and had migrated to Detroit in 1923. He met Fard while both were working for General Motors and became a follower and friend. Under Elijah Muhammad's direction, the Muslims expanded despite a hiatus caused by Muhammad's three-year imprisonment for draft evasion during World War II. Today the Muslims are a force in black ghetto life, and their religion owes its existence to Northern urban conditions, its frustrations and problems.

The Black Muslims' most famous convert was Malcolm X, who has become a folk hero to the black civil rights movement. Malcolm X (Malcolm Little) was born in Omaha, Nebraska, in 1925. His father was a Baptist minister and a follower of Marcus

Garvey. After the family moved to Lansing, Michigan, Malcolm
saw his home burned by the Ku Klux Klan and his father killed
by a streetcar. Malcolm moved to Harlem where he became a
pusher, a gambler, and a procurer. Converted to Islam by his own
brother while both were in prison in 1947, Malcolm X joined the
Mosque in Detroit, worked for a time as a minister in Philadelphia,
and then was assigned to Harlem. In Harlem he was a spectacular
success, but he became disaffected with the Lost-Found Nation of
Islam and broke with it in 1964 to form his own Muslim Mosque.
Less than a year later, Malcolm X was assassinated by persons
identified as Muslims—though Elijah Muhammad denied the
connection.

The NAACP (National Association for the Advancement of
Colored People) also continued its work in urban areas during the
depression. It had previously relied heavily upon legal action and
propaganda measures, appealing to Negroes who had migrated to
Northern cities, but it now turned to an economic program because
of the depression in the cities. It was not a sufficiently radical program for the long-time worker and co-founder of the NAACP, W.
E. B. DuBois, who resigned. In the 1940's the NAACP was joined
by two new movements—the March on Washington Movement led
by A. Philip Randolph, which forced Roosevelt to issue an execu-
tive order setting up a Fair Employment Practices Commission,
and CORE (Congress of Racial Equality), which came out of the
Fellowship of Reconciliation, a pacifist organization, through
the offices of Bayard Rustin and James Farmer. The March on
Washington, unlike earlier civil rights movements, was all black,
had a broad base of support, and involved economic demands.
CORE, though more white than black at its inception and into
the 1960's, adopted a method—the sit-in—which was taken from
the sit-down strike, and shared a nonviolent philosophy. All three
of these movements, NAACP, the March on Washington, and
CORE, used the ideas and methods of mass movements of the
time and capitalized on the concentrated urban populations in
order to win what victories they could.

In the 1950's another urban-based movement, this time with roots in the South, spurred the cause of civil rights. Dr. Martin Luther King, Jr., was able to galvanize the black community and to bring changes through boycotts in such cities as Montgomery, Birmingham, and Tuskegee. The Southern Christian Leadership Conference (SCLC), founded in 1957 by King, was urban based, as befitted an organization led by a thoroughly urban man. King's father had left rural Georgia, where he was born, and migrated to Atlanta. After graduating from Morehouse College, he married the daughter of the pastor of the Ebenezer Baptist Church, whom he succeeded. His son was born in Atlanta in 1929, attended Morehouse and Crozer Theological Seminary in Philadelphia, and finished his Ph. D. in systematic theology at Boston University. Martin Luther King, Jr., then returned to the South to become pastor of Dexter Avenue Church in Montgomery, Alabama. It was at this point that King became involved with Rosa Parks and the bus boycott in his capacity as president of the Montgomery Improvement Association. King's charismatic appeal was typical of the black minister who served as a leader of political and social movements.

The 1960's saw a proliferation of black civil rights and protest groups. These ranged from SNCC (originally the Student Nonviolent Coordinating Committee), begun in Raleigh, North Carolina, in 1960, and first aimed at putting together sit-in movements, to such revolutionary nationalist groups as RAM (Revolutionary Action Movement), the Republic of New Africa, and the Black Panthers. The latter three are also associated with cities—Detroit, New York, Philadelphia, and Oakland. RAM and the Republic of New Africa want a separate black nation inside the United States, while the Panthers and other militant groups urge community control by black people and aim their appeal at an urbanized black generation.

Before members of the younger black generation became radicalized, they tried to work through the political apparatus of the cities. Black wards had their own ward heelers who were black. In

return for support of the city machine, these political function-
aries were given jobs to dispense or were encouraged themselves
to run for office. They then became members of the city council,
the state legislature, or, as in the case in Chicago in 1928, Congressmen. As the black man became more and more active in
governmental affairs, Northern cities gave him his political education. Unfortunately, his political participation did not extend much
beyond marshaling the vote during municipal elections and token
control over community decisions.

The mass movement of the black man into the city finally
precipitated social friction and conflict. Prejudice and overt violence were the common reactions to black attempts to achieve
equality in recreation, jobs, and homes. Among the most violent
of the race riots in twentieth-century America were those in
Atlanta in 1906, in Springfield, Illinois, in 1908, in East St. Louis
in 1917, in Washington and Chicago in 1919, in Detroit and
Harlem in 1943, in Los Angeles in 1965, and in Newark and
Detroit in 1967. These instances of violence followed no real
pattern. The altercation in Atlanta was primarily a case of whites
attacking blacks who did not retaliate. In Chicago in 1919 blacks
did resist and more nearly proportionate numbers of blacks and
whites were killed. The riots of the 1960's, like those earlier,
saw many more blacks than whites killed, but a new ingredient was
added—the destruction of property in the ghetto by blacks.
Clearly, the friction which accompanied the numerical increase
of blacks in the city has not eased.

This unit may be expanded almost indefinitely. The teacher
can concentrate on several relevant problems and can encourage
the formation of generalizations about the mutual relations of
blacks and the city. Some such generalizations have been suggested—the patterns of black migration to the city; the impact
of the city on the personality and culture of the black man as
seen in his music; the relation of civil rights movements to the
city; the relation of black voters to city government; and the racial

violence that has accompanied urbanization. Materials are plentiful and are available at a reasonable price.

Bibliography

1. "Poor People's Choice" (Academic Games Project, Center for Study of Social Organization of Schools, Johns Hopkins University). This simulation game concerns economic and social mobility in the ghetto, and the interaction of the community and the individual. Recommended for junior and senior high school students.

2. "Sunshine" (Interact, Lakeside, Calif. 92040). In this simulation game, students assume the roles of different races in a mythical city, and work through solutions to a number of problems. The game can be played by elementary as well as high school students.

3. *Geography in an Urban Age,* Unit I: *Geography of Cities* (High School Geography Project, Association of American Geographers: Boulder, Colo., 1968). The second section in the Student Resources workbook is on "Models of City Form," using Chicago as an example. While there is no mention of race as influencing patterns of settlement, features such as population density, age distribution, median income, median school years completed, and percentage of male workers in white-collar occupations reveal the places where immigrants and blacks live. With only a little more information, the pattern of black settlement could be derived.

4. *The Cities and the Poor* (Indiana University, 1966). This two-part film is one of National Educational Television's America's Crises series. Topics covered include problems of the urban poor and the rise of militant groups. Recommended for senior high school students.

5. *The Future and the Negro* (Indiana University, 1965). Ossie Davis narrates this film in the History of the Negro People series from National Educational Television. There is a good

panel discussion, but the film is long—seventy-five minutes—and so much has happened since 1965 that the film seems dated.

6. *Free at Last* (Indiana University, 1965). Another in the History of the Negro People series, this one covers the period from 1865 to 1945. Ossie Davis narrates. The film shows glimpses of Frederick Douglass, Booker T. Washington, Marcus Garvey, W. E. B. DuBois, and others. It is excellent on the growth of Harlem and the Negro renaissance of the 1920's. Highly recommended for junior and senior high school students.

7. *New Mood* (Indiana University, 1965). The third film in the History of the Negro People series specifically concerns civil rights movements from 1954 to 1964. Martin Luther King, Jr., Malcolm X, and Medgar Evers, among others, appear and their programs are described. Highly recommended for junior and senior high school students.

8. *Harlem Wednesday* (Storyband, 1959). Paintings by Gregorio Prestopino and jazz by Benny Carter liven this film which purports to show activities on an ordinary mid-week day in Harlem. For junior and senior high school.

9. *Uptown—Portrait of a New York City Slum* (Danska Films, 1966). The camera takes the viewer on a tour of Spanish and Negro Harlem. The film is descriptive and can be used in junior and senior high school classes if the students are not too sophisticated.

10. *Black Heritage: A History of Afro-Americans* (Holt, Rinehart and Winston, 1970). The entire series has 108 half-hour lectures on black history. They cannot be rented but must be purchased. Those pertinent to urban history include E. U. Essien-Udom's lectures on "Marcus Garvey and His Movement," four lectures on the "Harlem Renaissance," Horace Mann Bond's "Urbanization: The Expansion of the Ghetto," and the lectures contained in "The Freedom Movement: America and Beyond," in "Protest and Rebellion in the North," and in "The Cultural Scene: From 1954 to the Current Mood." Holt, Rinehart and Winston also has a series of twenty-seven paperbacks under the

same title with film transcripts, illustrations, and a questions and projects section. It is a comprehensive collection, but expensive. For advanced students only.

11. *Civil Disorder: The Kerner Report* (Indiana University, n.d.). The format of this three-part film is a discussion of the report among James Baldwin, Charles V. Hamilton, Bayard Rustin, and Kenneth Clark. Not visually stimulating, but the participants do analyze the report quite well. Recommended for senior high school students.

12. Meier, August, and Elliott M. Rudwick, *From Plantation to Ghetto* (New York: Hill and Wang, 1966), paperback. The last chapters in this survey of Negro history are invaluable for the relation of the black man to the city. This is the best interpretive history to date and is highly recommended for high school students as well as teachers.

13. Bontemps, Arna, and Jack Conroy, *Anyplace But Here* (New York: Hill and Wang, 1966). Originally published in 1945, this book has been updated for the American Century series. It treats black music, Black Muslims, Marcus Garvey, and Malcolm X, as well as tracing the history of black communities in Detroit, Chicago, Philadelphia, and Los Angeles. Invaluable, and highly recommended for senior high school students.

14. Bennett, Lerone, Jr., *Confrontation: Black and White* (Baltimore: Penguin Books, 1965), paperback. This popularly written book concentrates on the civil rights movement. Bennett evaluates and discusses such leaders as William Monroe Trotter in Boston, A. Philip Randolph in New York City, and Martin Luther King, Jr. His insights are keen and his prose pungent. Useful for high school students.

15. Meier, August, and Francis L. Broderick, eds., *Negro Protest Thought in the Twentieth Century* (Indianapolis: Bobbs-Merrill, 1965), paperback. This book in the American Heritage series is the best reader on civil rights movements down to 1965. The selections are original statements by black leaders. Highly recommended for high school students.

16. Bracey, John H., Jr., August Meier, and Elliott Rudwick, eds., *Black Nationalism in America* (Indianapolis: Bobbs-Merrill, 1970), paperback. This reader should be used to supplement the one above. It is also part of the American Heritage series but concentrates on black solidarity. The book covers the entire American experience, but approximately half of it is devoted to the twentieth century. Representative selections have been taken from the works of Alain Locke, Kelly Miller, A. Philip Randolph, Elijah Muhammad, Malcolm X, Eldridge Cleaver, Stokely Carmichael, and others. Comprehensive and informative. For better students and special projects.

17. Malcolm X and Alex Haley, *The Autobiography of Malcolm X* (New York: Grove Press, 1965), paperback. Malcolm X's autobiography has become a classic. The topics he writes about are controversial, but the book offers enormous insights into urban black life and black power movements. Black students in particular are impressed by it.

18. Cleaver, Eldridge, *Soul on Ice* (New York: McGraw-Hill, 1969), Delta paperback. Cleaver's best-selling book is also very controversial in view of his prison record and association with the Black Panthers. It reflects the anger of a black man with American society. Recommended for mature students.

19. Cruse, Harold, *The Crisis of the Negro Intellectual* (New York: Morrow, 1967), Apollo paperback. Cruse's book has deservedly won acclaim. Its theme is that the 1920's was a watershed for the black community in Harlem, and that the Marxists prevented the community from becoming culturally conscious. Cruse's book is difficult and should be assigned only to better students.

20. Keil, Charles, *Urban Blues* (Chicago: University of Chicago Press, 1966), paperback. Another classic, this book attempts to show the relation between blues and the black urban style of life. It has been widely read and admired. Recommended for students interested in music and in life styles.

21. Zinn, Howard, *SNCC: The New Abolitionists* (Boston: Beacon Press, 1964), paperback. This is the best study of the

founding of SNCC, though it is dated. Useful for the teacher and for student projects.

22. King, Martin Luther, Jr., *Why We Can't Wait* (New York: Harper and Row, 1964), Signet paperback. This book can be assigned to students who are interested in an insight into King's ideas. The book makes a case for immediate improvement in racial relations as well as for nonviolent means to attain equality. Recommended for special projects and for research.

23. Cronon, E. David, *Black Moses: The Story of Marcus Garvey and the Universal Negro Improvement Association* (Madison: University of Wisconsin Press, 1955), paperback. Cronon's book is the definitive study of Garvey's Back-to-Africa Movement. It shows the interrelationship between Harlem and the Garveyites. Useful for research and special studies.

24. Essien-Udom, E. U., *Black Nationalism: The Search for an Identity in America* (Chicago: University of Chicago Press, 1962), Dell paperback. Essien-Udom is an African who has studied the Black Muslims, among others, and is on the whole sympathetic to the idea of a black identity. For research projects.

25. Clark, Kenneth, *Dark Ghetto* (New York: Harper and Row, 1965), paperback. The noted black director of the Social Dynamics Research Institute of the City College of New York did this study of Harlem which covers such areas as the social dynamics, psychology, pathology, and power structure of the ghetto. Recommended for research into ghetto life.

26. Spear, Allan H., *Black Chicago: The Making of a Negro Ghetto, 1890–1920* (Chicago: University of Chicago Press, 1967), paperback. This is a specialized study of the beginnings of the sizable black community in Chicago at the beginning of significant migration from the South. Students will find the book useful in special projects.

27. Osofsky, Gilbert, *Harlem: The Making of a Ghetto* (New York: Harper and Row, 1966), paperback. This book is the best history of Negro Harlem, but it is specialized and probably should be used only in student projects.

28. Waskow, Arthur I., *From Race Riot to Sit-In* (Garden City: Doubleday, 1966), paperback. This is a study in the strategy of civil rights movements and a comparison of the riots of 1919 with the technique of the 1960's. It is a provocative book which can be handled by better senior high school students.

29. *Report of the National Advisory Commission on Civil Disorders* (Washington, D.C.: Government Printing Office, 1968), paperback. The Kerner Report, as this is called, has a wealth of information on urban disturbances and black-white relations. It can be used for special projects.

30. Wilson, James Q., *Negro Politics* (Glencoe, Ill.: Free Press, 1960), paperback. Wilson's book is a standard one in political science. This book tries to develop a framework for understanding the operation of black politics. Recommended for research only.

31. Skolnick, Jerome, *The Politics of Protest* (New York: Ballantine Books, 1969), paperback. This study was a task force report to the National Commission on the Causes and Prevention of Violence, and concerns the strategy, techniques, and presumed effectiveness of protest movements. For teachers' libraries and for reference.

32. Jacobs, Paul, *Prelude to Riot: The Urban Condition from the Bottom Up* (New York: Random House, 1968), paperback. An excellent study of the conditions which lead to urban uprisings. Popularly written, and can be handled by senior high school students.

33. Meier, August, *Negro Thought in America, 1880–1915: Racial Ideologies in the Age of Booker T. Washington* (Ann Arbor: University of Michigan Press, 1963), paperback. Meier is one of the foremost historians of the black man in America. In this study he touches on the competing ideas of the period. His conclusion is that the "New Negro" movement had its roots in an earlier period which already had developed ideas. The book is good for research and for talented students.

34. Armstrong, Louis, *Satchmo: My Life in New Orleans* (Englewood Cliffs: Prentice-Hall, 1954). Louis Armstrong's

story can be used to supplement a course in urban history. His recollections of his youth are interesting as well as informative. Suitable for junior and senior high school students.

35. Ellison, Ralph, *Invisible Man* (New York: Random House, 1953), Signet paperback. Ellison's superb novel attempts to re-create the experience of the black man in America. The book can be used in English and in history classes.

36. Wright, Richard, *Native Son* (New York: Harper, 1969), paperback. *Native Son* has become a classic. Based on Wright's own experience in Chicago, the book tells the story of Bigger Thomas, a black boy who grew up in the ghetto and went wrong. It can be used in English as well as in history classes to give the flavor of black urban life.

37. Brown, Claude, *Manchild in the Promised Land* (New York: Signet Books, 1965), paperback. Brown grew up in Spanish Harlem; his life reflects both the problem of Puerto Ricans and blacks in the city. The book talks of sex and drugs and their use in the ghetto. It uses strong language, but can be assigned to high school students.

38. Hoover, Dwight W., ed., *Understanding Negro History* (Chicago: Quadrangle Books, 1968), paperback. This collection of articles attempts to set a theoretical base for the study of Negro history. The book is selective and provides a framework for further work. Recommended for senior high school students.

39. Meier, August, and Elliott Rudwick, eds., *Black Protest in the Sixties* (Chicago: Quadrangle Books, 1970), paperback. The latest collection put together by Meier and Rudwick is the most up to date in the area of recent civil rights movements. Highly recommended for senior high school students.

Reaction to the City, 1860–1920

The impact of the city in the decades following the Civil War elicited a variety of responses. In some cases the city provoked a change in such institutions as churches and schools. In other cases the response was to rationalize existing bureaucracies or to create new professions such as public administration, urban planning, and social work to help control problems of the city. The new professionals would replace party hacks, volunteers, and amateurs, and, with their knowledge, create an urban setting in keeping with the highest American ideals. The problem of the immigrant in the city—the European or the American black—stimulated the reformist urge.

The usual compartmentalization of American history serves to blind the teacher and the student from seeing that reform and

First public playground in Chicago, started by Hull-House in 1893 (JANE ADDAMS MEMORIAL COLLECTION, UNIVERSITY OF ILLINOIS AT CHICAGO CIRCLE)

reaction do not necessarily follow each other in a pattern. Too often the era after the Civil War is portrayed as an era of big business, greed and corruption, and little social concern. The major reform impulse of the period is attributed to disgruntled farmers who were reacting to industrialization. This simplistic view does not hold up if one looks closely at the forces at work. Reformers did attack social evils in the 1880's and 1890's, and many of them lived in cities and attacked urban evils. The attitudes, goals, and techniques of the Progressives were anticipated by these urban reformers.

What did the reformers want? They wanted more than anything else to improve the environment of the cities, particularly the housing of the poor. They were for more equal treatment of women, Negroes, and immigrants. They wanted an eight-hour day and higher pay for workers. They wanted more responsible government, more relevant schools and churches, and new institutions such as settlement houses to cope with urban ills. While the reformers ranged from conservative to radical, they agreed upon the urgency of these problems and the need to solve them.

Perhaps one of the first of the important post–Civil War reformers was Charles Loring Brace, whose *The Dangerous Classes of New York* was published in 1872. Brace, a Congregational minister, worked in New York City with poor children and established projects to send these children to rural settings. He was much concerned about the failure of the church and society to educate and care for the children of the city's poor and, as the title of his book indicates, felt that this neglect might result in revolution in the streets. Brace had founded the Children's Aid Society, a pioneer welfare agency, in New York in 1853. His books and his descriptions of city life helped rouse Americans to conditions in the slums. Despite his early emphasis upon moving children from the city, Brace eventually became convinced that the city itself had to be reformed. He devoted his later years to that task.

Another Congregational minister, who was even more successful in calling attention to the evils of the city, was Josiah Strong.

His book *Our Country: Its Possible Future and its Present Crisis* (1885) has been called by Henry F. May "the *Uncle Tom's Cabin* of city reform." Published by the American Home Missionary Society, this best-selling book combined an expansionist optimism with an anti-city prejudice. Strong feared the city because it embraced Catholics, the urban poor, and large numbers of immigrants, and because it accentuated class divisions in American society. The city dweller was particularly susceptible to the siren songs of socialists and revolutionaries. Strong, like Brace, believed the city could be reformed, but it should be accomplished by Christians through the agency of the church.

The Social Gospel movement which began in the 1870's was in part directed at urban ills. It attempted to align American churches with social reform. The ministers involved in the movement—Walter Rauschenbusch, George Herron, Shailer Matthews, Washington Gladden, and others—stressed the insights of Brace and Strong. Modern industrial society, by concentrating people in cities, magnified class differences, increased social strife and revolutionary violence, and damaged social sympathy and social unity. The Social Gospel ministers, never in the majority, came from urban parishes of the larger Protestant denominations—Episcopalians, Congregationalists, Methodists, and Baptists. A typical career was that of Washington Gladden, who lived in North Adams, Massachusetts; Springfield, Massachusetts; Brooklyn; New York City; and Columbus, Ohio. In these cities Gladden worked as a minister and as an editorial writer. A less typical example was George Herron, who went from Minneapolis to Burlington, Iowa, to Grinnell College, and from there to the Socialist party. While they never succeeded in converting even their own denominations to the Social Gospel, these clergymen at least spread the ideas that society needed help and that Christians had duties to their fellows in the city.

The concern of the churches was expressed in other more tangible ways as well. They tried to attract more of the urban poor to their congregations through revival activity in the neighborhoods and through the addition of new facilities to their existing buildings. The churches built gymnasiums, opened kitchens and club rooms, and began new groups and organizations to fill the needs and the vacant hours of the less fortunate members of the urban community. In addition, the churches often helped to develop settlement houses through the mediation of their ministers.

Other agencies were part of the reform picture. The Salvation Army, begun in England, came to the United States in 1880 and attacked urban problems through welfare and evangelistic efforts. Three years earlier an English Episcopal minister, S. Humphreys Gurteen, helped establish the Buffalo Charity Organization Society. Patterned after the London Society for Organizing Charitable Relief and Repressing Mendicancy, the Buffalo Society prided itself on a scientific approach which emphasized managerial efficiency, the gospel of work, and friendly visitors who were volunteer workers. Within five years, charity organizations had been created in twenty-two cities. The settlement house came later and was also an English import. The first one in this country, Neighborhood Guild in New York City, was founded in 1886 and patterned after Toynbee Hall in London. In 1890 Hull-House in Chicago was begun by Jane Addams and Ellen Gates Starr. Five years later there were fifty settlement houses located in American cities throughout the land. The houses attempted to ease the immigrant's adjustment to a new land and provided an amazingly varied number of services to immigrants and their families. These included serving hot lunches, providing bathhouses, gymnasiums, lecture halls, and music rooms, teaching courses in homemaking, and educating the immigrant in the ways of obtaining municipal services. The settlements owed their founding to the altruistic impulses of charitable individuals who were imbued with the spirit, if not the letter, of the Social Gospel.

The schools also became involved in the reform effort, in part because of the settlement houses. Lillian Wald, who was identified with New York's Henry Street Settlement, successfully persuaded the City Health Department to employ school physicians in 1897. Another worker at Henry Street started the first classes for handicapped children sanctioned by the Board of Education. The schools, like the settlements, found themselves giving baths and teaching citizenship and good health habits as well as beginning English. The experience with the immigrant and with American urban society led in the direction of progressive education. Innovation in education, according to John Dewey, was necessary because of the central theme of industry in American society. The schools must teach those subjects which are necessary in an urban age and develop those instincts which formerly had been developed by rural environment. In Gary, Indiana, the plan of education was Deweyism applied in an urban setting. The emphasis was upon community in the schools; for participation in the industrial life of the household, the Gary Plan substituted the industrial activities of the school. In the social sciences, units quite often involved the city. One such unit was "The City: A Healthful Place in Which to Live." Progressive education, as Dewey visualized it, was the instrument for bridging the gap between a rural and an urban society. The long-run solution to American urban ills was to be found in the schools which would transform society. No less than the churches, the schools were to be revitalized and were to lead the fight to save the cities. Progressive education, like the Social Gospel, however, failed to achieve what its most ardent promoters hoped.

Reaction to the impact of the city was greatest in the reform of municipal government. The movement to change city government has by now become encapsulated in an historical cliché. As Samuel Hays puts it:

> The reform ideology which became the basis of historical analysis is well known. It appears in classic form in Lincoln Steffens' *Shame of the Cities.* The urban political struggle of the Progressive Era, so the argument goes, involved a conflict between public impulses for "good government" against a corrupt alliance of "machine politics" and "special interests."

The methods of the reformers consisted of throwing the rascals out and replacing political appointees with those chosen on merit, exchanging professionals for amateurs. Instead of political cronyism, civil service lists would be used. Instead of mayors, commissions or city managers would run cities. Instead of local community school boards, one board would serve the entire city. All of these reforms were accomplished amid declarations of high moral purpose and in the name of the American dream. Like progressive education, municipal reform claimed to be scientific; like the Social Gospel movement, municipal reform relied upon social science techniques to determine the facts. The social science instrument most often used was the survey, and the agency was the municipal research bureau. The first such bureau was begun in New York City in 1906 with money donated by Andrew Carnegie and John D. Rockefeller.

The proponents of city reform, however, had motives beyond altruistic ones. Largely business and professional people, including a good many upper-class individuals, the municipal reformers wanted to win the city back from alien, lower-class hands. In a sense, they were taking Josiah Strong seriously. As Hays has said, "They objected to a structure of government which enabled local and particularistic interests to dominate." The city was run by men who represented local interests and lower- and middle-class people. The reformers wanted to centralize city government under the direction of a group with larger interests and broader connections. Although they were admired for their democratic instincts, the reform movements actually diminished the contact of many persons with government. It was not incongruous that organized labor consistently opposed the institution of manager-type city government.

While city-manager and commission government did not become a standard form, the proponents of centralized city government won their battle to diminish ward power on city councils and school boards. School boards became centralized and the preserve of the "better people" in the community. Quite often this was accomplished by nonelectoral means. State legislatures passed acts or city governments voluntarily switched to new forms. The leaders of the business community, by attacking the immorality of the political machine, were able to substitute a system that was supposedly more efficient, less immoral, and more scientific. The reforms also made city government more responsive to the needs of business, less responsive to the needs of the immigrant.

The move toward professional government during the Progressive era also emphasized public administration. The ideas of the period soon became institutionalized, and now almost every university offers courses or curriculums in public administration, which reflect their historical source. They emphasize the efficiency of private business practices and the desirability of unified public authority. Power ought to come from the top: the city manager should propose changes which popularly elected city officials may accept or reject. Despite this approach, public administration is still couched in the language of the American democratic ethos, and more and more students become public administrators on all levels of government, from municipal to federal.

In still another area, that of planning, the same process of historical development can be seen. The origins of regional and urban planning go back to the nineteenth century; its first proponents were reformers at heart. Planning and municipal reform went hand in hand—the planner came to use the bureaus of municipal research and to claim credit for his work as being scientific. And planning, like municipal reform, though it was couched in terms of progress and the democratic faith, had a conservative face as well.

The first Colonial cities had been planned, but the rapid growth of American cities in the nineteenth century outstripped the will or ability of Americans to control it. In the latter part of the century, however, there was a fresh effort to re-establish control of growth, and to limit private avarice in favor of the public interest. Just as the reformer of municipal politics sought to fight corruption, so the planner sought to combat sprawl and physical ugliness. Planning, like the Social Gospel and municipal reform, would redeem the American city from the plight into which it had fallen.

Two groups converged to develop planning into a profession and a way of life. These were landscape architects and housing reformers. The first group included such persons as Frederick Law Olmsted, Daniel Burnham, H. W. S. Cleveland, and Charles Eliot. The second included such men as Lawrence Veiller.

The landscape architects tried to combine nature with urban life. In a kind of romantic way, they hoped that an improved urban environment would change the moral tone of the city's inhabitants. By providing public areas suitable for the poor and for children, they hoped to drain away some of the tension connected with urban life. The park movement is usually dated from 1851 when Frederick Law Olmsted began the construction of Central Park, though other cities had had parks prior to this time. From 1870 to 1890 the park movement was in full swing. The park movement also involved bureaucratization, in that typically a park commission would be created to acquire land and to supervise its usage. Thus agencies like the Boston Metropolitan Park Commission can be considered the forerunners of modern planning agencies.

The Chicago World's Fair provided a tremendous impetus to architectural planning as well as to the career of the architect Daniel Burnham. Burnham, along with Frederick Law Olmsted (a son of the creator of Central Park), was appointed to the Senate Park Commission in 1901 to develop a park system for the city of Washington. The two men hired Charles Follen McKim and proceeded to build the Mall in Washington. Burnham also proceeded with his plan for Chicago, "the first comprehensive modern plan for an American city." Begun in 1896 and not completed until 1909, Burnham's plan included not only the lakefront boulevard and park with a boat lagoon, but also proposals for an area sixty miles in radius that included new streets, traffic regulation, a civic center, and additional parks.

Housing reformers also sought to uplift the quality of urban life by improving the physical environment. Like the advocates of the Social Gospel, they believed that improved housing would serve to allay unrest and prevent revolution while it raised the level of public health. The pioneer housing reformer Lawrence Veiller was instrumental in getting the Tenement House Law of 1901 approved by the New York State Legislature and Governor Odell. Although Veiller felt the law was a compromise and believed that only a fire or some other natural catastrophe would make New York City aware of poor housing, other reformers were more optimistic. The law required that the population density of apartments be reduced and that each apartment have its own bathroom. Veiller later founded the National Housing Association and, through the Russell Sage Foundation, saw his ideas on housing restriction widely circulated. Despite his interest in reform, Veiller surprisingly did not advocate public housing nor constructive legislation to raise building standards.

In 1909 the first national planning conference was held in Washington, D.C., and as a result of it the National Conference on City Planning was organized. This was succeeded in 1917 by the American City Planning Institute. The earlier members of the planning movement were meanwhile being replaced. Architects and housing reformers who used planning as an adjunct to their other social roles gave way to the professional planner. The professional was likely to have been trained in a university and to regard his function as that of a technician. The reformist impulse was dying out.

The major tool of the planner became the zoning ordinance, a means of providing for certain kinds of homes or businesses in certain areas. First adopted by New York City in 1916, zoning ordinances rapidly spread throughout the country. In 1922 a dozen California communities passed zoning enactments. Three years later cities in the Midwest, Northeast, and South were caught up in the fervor to rationalize land use. The ordinances were generally overseen by planning boards which were advisory and nonpolitical and which utilized the services of a professional planner. More than seven hundred city planning boards were operating in 1934, at the beginning of Franklin Roosevelt's first administration, as well as eighty-five county and regional planning boards.

Perhaps the most famous regional plan of the time was that of New York. The Russell Sage Foundation granted enough money in 1922 to finance a ten-year study, which was carried out by economists and sociologists whose findings were published in ten volumes. The study also resulted in the formation of the Regional Plan Association, which has carried on the work of research and planning. An organization with a similar name, the Regional Planning Association, called the study inadequate. Its members were theorists of the first order, including Benton MacKaye and his disciple Lewis Mumford. Impressed with the Garden City idea of Ebenezer Howard, an Englishman, the Regional Planning Association from its inception in 1923 advocated the creation of new towns, extensive community planning, and the rehabilitation of existing municipalities. Its planned city of Radburn, New Jersey, did not develop as scheduled, but the decentralization preached by the group remained part of the new cities movement. Despite its ideas and contributions, the Regional Planning Association dissolved only ten years after its founding.

Planning continues in our own time, though its reformist element is almost completely gone. The demand for the professional planner continues to expand, partly because of federal grants which specify that cities requesting aid must have planners. Despite the increase, planning has fixed the city in a pattern of development that has sometimes aggravated rather than solved its problems. Zoning made neighborhoods uniform, but it also has tended to segregate them by income. Further, the inadvertent combination of zoning and accelerated suburbanization in the 1920's, and the inability of the city to annex these suburbs, meant that the new migrants to the city lived in areas which were homogeneous and uniform, and had little contact with other areas. Zoning has made the city more rational, but it has also made it physically possible for the city to be polarized.

Finally, among reform elements, social work, like urban planning and public administration, became a profession with its own ethos and its own technical outlook and reliance on the scientific knowledge of human behavior. This knowledge, exercised through casework techniques, could enable the poor to survive in an urban setting; the larger idea of reforming the whole society gradually died among social workers. Social work also possessed a conservative side: the amelioration of social ills and the maintenance of the indigent family on welfare prevented social revolution.

Early attempts at welfare emphasized friendly visiting. The worker was to serve as a moral example for the poor, to show how the poor could better themselves, to educate the poor in the virtues of middle-class society—hard work, thrift, cleanliness, and sobriety. As social work became professionalized, social workers claimed a special body of knowledge which held that the poor were not morally inferior but were rather the product of their circumstances. Social workers went into hospitals and schools, and into psychiatric social work. The pioneer social worker Mary Richmond, in two books, *Social Diagnosis* (1917) and *What Is Social Case Work?* (1922), noted the basic skills in the profession: the social worker collected all of the facts pertaining to a case and then arrived at a decision regarding the social difficulty.

The founding of the National Committee for Mental Hygiene in 1909 by Clifford W. Beers gave impetus to the element of psychiatry in social work. Gradually social workers changed from an emphasis on the social environment to one emphasizing mental illness. This change is illustrated by the growth of child-guidance clinics. Sponsored by the Division on the Prevention of Delinquency of the National Committee for Mental Hygiene, the first clinic was opened in St. Louis in 1922. The Commonwealth Fund provided needed funds until 1927, after which the clinics continued on their own. The clinics had considerable impact and spurred the growth of the psychiatric approach. The major social work argument in the 1930's came to be which psychiatric school possessed the truth—Freud (diagnostic) or Rank (functional)—rather than whether psychiatric treatment of the individual was more effective than social diagnosis of a community problem.

As social workers became psychiatrically oriented, they also became conscious of their need to create professional organizations. The first national organization was the American Association of Hospital Social Workers, founded in 1917. Two other groups followed, the American Association of Visiting Teachers in 1919 and the American Association of Psychiatric Social Workers in 1926. The major group, however, was the American Association of Social Workers, created in 1921. These organizations, like the American Institute of Planning and those organizations concerned with public administration, stressed graduate work in professional schools plus work experience as qualifications for membership. These standards were constantly raised until amateurs were no longer eligible.

As social workers became professionalized, welfare agencies became centralized and bureaucratized. Federated financing, which came upon the scene during World War I and which anticipated the Community Chest, made fund raising a collective, community enterprise. Denver had a society for this purpose as early as 1887, but the movement did not gain impetus until later. Federated financing, like city planning, relied upon studies of community need, scientific management, and economy. The boards of community chests quite often represented primarily the business community, which is understandable in view of the fact that this community gave the largest share of the money. Like municipal reform, the control of money for private agencies tended to fall into the hands of the "better people."

A study of the 1865–1920 era reveals an attempt by native Americans to regain control of the cities. This was accomplished in a number of ways. Churches and schools were changed. New professions emerged to run municipal government, to plan the city, and to administer charity. Originally these groups were composed of persons with a sensitive social concern and a desire to reform society, but the professions came to rely upon technical skills and bureaucratic organization to the neglect of social reform. Once again, in the process, control became centralized, and the immigrant's voice in the city and schools was diminished. In a larger sense, the move to professionalism was a move to circumvent political control of the cities by suspect groups—immigrants, Catholics, and Negroes.

This unit has attempted to do several things: to point to the possibility of careers in urban service—urban and regional planning, public administration, and social work; to show the growth of bureaucratization, and professionalism; to go behind the political rhetoric of the period to see what actually happened; to demonstrate that reform was not cyclical but can be found throughout the period; and to show how solutions to problems—such as zoning to upgrade neighborhoods—in turn create new problems such as income segregation.

Bibliography

1. *Geography in an Urban Age,* Unit I: *Geography of Cities* (High School Geography Project, Association of American Geographers: Boulder, Colo., 1968). Activity 2, "New Orleans," and Activity 3, "Models of City Form," can be used to show the impact of zoning and planning. The idea of planned development is shown, as is the difference in areas due to residential segregation.

2. *The Rise of New Towns* (Indiana University, 1966). This film details the rise of totally planned communities. Planners, government officials, and other urban specialists discuss the social and economic implications of the movement. Several planned cities, including Foster City and Irvine, California, are shown. A good film to illustrate what planners now consider to be the best features of a city. For senior students.

3. *Lewis Mumford on the City* (Sterling Educational Films, 1963). The noted urbanologist can be seen in six films. They are:

a. *The City and Its Region*
b. *The City and the Future*
c. *The City—Cars or People?*
d. *The City—Heaven and Hell*
e. *The City as Man's Home*
f. *The Heart of the City*

All illustrate to some degree Mumford's ideas on how cities should be planned. The first treats of regional planning and how the city should fit into the country. The second concerns a choice between urban sprawl and a new regional city. The third argues for an alternative to automotive transportation. The fourth is historical. The fifth involves urban phenomena such as slums, suburbs, and housing complexes, with suggestions for improvement. The last shows the drabness of the central part of the city and how to overcome it. The films can be shown to senior high school students and are important in showing what is involved in planning.

4. *Challenge of Urban Renewal* (Encyclopedia Britannica Films, 1966). Taken from an NBC special entitled "America the Beautiful," this film shows urban and suburban sprawl and modern thinking on planning. Suitable for high school students.

5. *Harlem Crusader* (Encyclopedia Britannica Films, 1966). The subject of this NBC study is a social worker in Spanish Harlem who worked with Puerto Ricans over a five-year period. The film shows how this particular social worker operated and is useful in understanding the problems and goals of the profession. For senior high school students.

6. *The Green City* (Stuart Finley Films, 1963). This film contrasts those cities which have grown up without much planning to those which have been planned to preserve green and open spaces. It is useful for junior and senior high school students,

particularly as they are reminded that modern urban planning began with parks.

7. *How to Look at a City* (Indiana University, 1964). Eugene Raskin, architect and author, discusses the standards used by architects and planners to judge the quality of city neighborhoods. Among these standards are population density, scale, and variety. This production of National Educational Television is in The Metropolis—Creator or Destroyer series. Sophisticated but useful.

8. *The Mural on Our Street* (Contemporary Films, 1964). Judith Crist narrates this film, which shows how the members of the Henry Street settlement house made a ceramic tile mural. The film can be understood by high school students and is an interesting introduction to the operation of a settlement house in our time.

9. *Robert Moses* (Encyclopedia Britannica Films, 1960). Robert Moses is interviewed by Gilmore Clark, designer of the court and gardens of the United Nations. Moses, who was a city planner and New York City park commissioner, describes his planning ideas. The film is recommended for senior high school students.

10. Tunnard, Christopher, and Henry H. Reed, *American Skyline* (Boston: Houghton Mifflin, 1955), Mentor paperback. The two sections of this book that pertain to the era under consideration are "The Expanding City" (1880–1910), and "The City of Towers" (1910–1933). The book is excellent on city design and is not too difficult for senior high school students.

11. Tunnard, Christopher, *The Modern American City* (New York: Van Nostrand, 1968), paperback. This book contains both narrative and readings. Tunnard, who was Professor of City Planning at Yale, has useful chapters on plans and planning down to 1930. Recommended for teachers and for better students.

12. Reps, John William, *The Making of Urban America* (Princeton: Princeton University Press, 1965). Reps's book is the standard reference work on city plans. It should be used by

those who are design-oriented and wish to compare various cities. Reps's work concludes in 1910.

13. Glaab, Charles N., and A. Theodore Brown, *A History of Urban America* (New York: Macmillan, 1967), paperback. Chapters 7, 8, and 9 have sections devoted to welfare, government, and planning. For advanced undergraduates.

14. Green, Constance McLaughlin, *The Rise of Urban America* (New York: Harper and Row, 1965), paperback. Chapters 5 and 6 contain useful sections on attempts to reform the city. The book's interesting detail ought to engage the attention of students.

15. Callow, Alexander B., Jr., ed., *American Urban History* (New York: Oxford University Press, 1969), paperback. The section entitled "The City in National Affairs" includes Hays's important article. While it focuses primarily on political change, the section sheds light upon the entire reaction to the city.

16. Wakstein, Allen M., ed., *The Urbanization of America* (Boston: Houghton Mifflin, 1970), paperback. Wakstein has the best section on the attempt to control the city in his "The Rising Concern for Urban Life." He includes selections on politics, planning, and religion, but nothing on social work. The articles can be understood by better students and are a must for teachers.

17. Mohl, Raymond A., and Neil Betten, eds., *Urban America in Historical Perspective* (New York: Weybright and Talley, 1970). Chapter 4, "The Industrial City," contains several pertinent selections, including one on Boss Cox of Cincinnati who made social reform a feature of his bossism. The book can be handled by advanced students.

18. Hirsch, Werner Z., ed., *Urban Life and Form* (New York: Holt, Rinehart and Winston, 1963). Hirsch's collection of readings ties design and planning together and is useful for design-oriented teachers and students.

19. Lynch, Kevin, *The Image of the City* (Cambridge, Mass.: MIT Press, 1960), paperback. Lynch uses theories of perception to explain how people visualize cities. An excellent book for design theory. Recommended for special projects.

20. Tager, Jack, and Park Dixon Goist, eds., *The Urban Vision* (Homewood, Ill.: Dorsey Press, 1970), paperback. This collection of readings is concerned with the twentieth century and has excellent sections on social reformers, architectural reformers, and regional planners of the 1920's. The book contains Burnham's discussion of his pioneer plan for Chicago. Highly recommended for reference.

21. McKelvey, Blake, *The Urbanization of America, 1860–1915* (New Brunswick, N.J.: Rutgers University Press, 1963). McKelvey's history is a general one, but it does touch upon city reform movements, particularly in their political aspects. For senior high school classes.

22. Warner, Sam Bass, Jr., *The Private City: Philadelphia in Three Periods of Its Growth* (Philadelphia: University of Pennsylvania Press, 1968). The last period Warner discusses is from 1920 to 1930. In the consideration, Warner indicates the beginnings of planning and governmental reform. The book ought to be read by teachers and can be assigned to better students.

23. Lubove, Roy, *The Professional Altruist: The Emergence of Social Work as a Career* (New York: Atheneum, 1969), paperback. An interesting account of the transition of social work from voluntarism to professionalism. The book may be assigned to students interested in a social work career.

24. Lubove, Roy, ed., *The Urban Community: Housing and Planning in the Progressive Era* (Englewood Cliffs, N.J.: Prentice-Hall, 1967), paperback. This volume in the American Historical Sources series contains an introduction on urban planning as well as selected primary sources from the period. Recommended for those who like to go directly to sources.

25. Lubove, Roy, *The Progressives and the Slums: Tenement House Reform in New York City, 1890–1917* (Pittsburgh: University of Pittsburgh Press, 1962). The roots of urban planning from social reformers such as Lawrence Veiller are traced by Lubove in this book. Some of the sources used in here also appear in the preceding volume. For special projects.

26. Lubove, Roy, *Community Planning in the 1920's: The Contribution of the Regional Planning Association of America* (Pittsburgh: University of Pittsburgh Press, 1963), paperback. Lubove's is the definitive book on this phase of planning. Again, for special study.

27. MacKaye, Benton, *The New Exploration: A Philosophy of Regional Planning* (Urbana: University of Illinois Press, 1962), paperback. MacKaye was a leader in the Regional Planning Association of America. His book, originally published in 1928, expresses quite well his theories of how regions should be developed. Useful for teachers and for advanced student projects.

28. Mann, Arthur, *Yankee Reformers in an Urban Age: Social Reform in Boston, 1880–1900* (New York: Harper and Row, 1966), paperback. This book treats reform movements, including those in religion and education, in Boston. His conclusion that there was an active reform movement before the Progressive era is an important one. The book is recommended for special projects.

29. Warner, Sam Bass, Jr., *Streetcar Suburbs: The Process of Growth in Boston, 1870–1900* (New York: Atheneum, 1969), paperback. Warner's book shows how informal zoning preceded formal zoning, and how the park movement affected suburban growth in Boston. A useful book to use with Mann's.

30. Bremner, Robert H., *From the Depths: The Discovery of Poverty in the United States* (New York: New York University Press, 1956), paperback. This is a period study of the beginning of the realization that poverty was not necessarily a transitory stage for everyone but was instead a permanent condition for some. The book can be assigned for special projects.

31. Abell, Aaron, *The Urban Impact on American Protestantism* (Cambridge, Mass.: Harvard University Press, 1962). Abell's history is general, but it does describe the beginnings of the Social Gospel movement. For reference work.

32. Davis, Allen F., *Spearheads for Reform: The Social Settlements and the Progressive Movement, 1890–1914* (New York:

Oxford University Press, 1967), paperback. Davis' book, another volume in the Urban Life in America series, is a study of the connection between settlement houses and the Progressive movement. Among those individuals considered are Jane Addams, Lillian Wald, Robert Wood, and Graham Taylor. For special projects.

33. Altshuler, Alan, *The City Planning Process: A Political Analysis* (Ithaca: Cornell University Press, 1965), paperback. Altshuler's work takes into account the various pressures operating upon the planners in a city. An excellent book, but probably too sophisticated an analysis for most students.

34. Warner, Sam Bass, Jr., ed., *Planning for a Nation of Cities* (Cambridge, Mass.: MIT Press, 1966), paperback. This collection of articles is oriented around the theme of urban America. Specialized, but a good teacher resource.

35. Makielski, Stanislaw, Jr., *The Politics of Zoning: The New York Experience* (New York: Columbia University Press, 1966). This is a history of zoning in New York City from 1916. In the first period, from 1916 to 1938, zoning was decentralized and was administered on the borough level. After 1938 zoning was administered throughout the city by the City Planning Commission. Like Altshuler's book, Makielski's shows how political factors prevent rational zoning. For special projects.

36. Scott, Mel, *American City Planning* (Berkeley: University of California Press, 1969). Scott's history of planning, commissioned by the American Institute of Planners, is comprehensive, beginning in 1890. The book describes ideas, events, individuals, and institutions. Recommended for reference work.

Images of the City,
1860–1970

The growing awareness of the city in the late nineteenth century, and the attempts of some Americans to recapture it, produced new visions of the city, some optimistic and others gloomy. Architects, novelists, and utopian thinkers had in some way to accommodate themselves to the city. This unit attempts to assess that accommodation.

The city was the focus of literary attention early, but Edward Bellamy intensified that focus in 1888 with *Looking Backward.* Bellamy's book became a best-seller and Nationalist clubs sprang up to put Bellamy's ideas into practice. Whatever Bellamy's purpose in writing the book—to create fantasy or to urge social reform—the end result was a model of the future which contained both promising and frightening prospects.

"Splinter Beach," a study of New York painted in 1913 by George Bellows
(FROM THE MASSES MAGAZINE)

The protagonist of *Looking Backward,* Julian West, discovers a technologically advanced urban society in 2000 A.D., complete with radios, air transport, and labor-saving devices. The society provides adequately for everyone's needs, but it is rigid and authoritarian. The work is done by an industrial army composed of all citizens who serve until they are forty-five. After forty-five, the citizen may follow his own desires. All divisions in the society —race, sex, class—are healed by the common devotion to the tasks of the urban nation.

It is difficult to categorize Bellamy's ideas or to account for his popularity. He was not an orthodox socialist, as witness his fondness for a military society. He wrote well, though his earlier novels did not arouse much interest. Bellamy seems to have capitalized upon the intense interest in America's future noticeable at the time.

Another novelist of the period, who was influenced by Bellamy, was William Dean Howells. In 1895 Howells' *A Hazard of New Fortunes* appeared. Unlike *Looking Backward, A Hazard of New Fortunes* was not fantasy but a realistic novel. It analyzed the social structure of New York City, contrasting the poor and the rich and taking the side of the urban poor. Howells' novel was reformist in tone, though he was too skilled to write a polemic.

Not all the realistic novels of the late nineteenth and early twentieth centuries contained moral overtones or reformist views. Quite often they reflected the seamier sides of the city. Stephen Crane's *Maggie: A Girl of the Streets* (1893) traced the downfall of a girl gone wrong. Theodore Dreiser's *Sister Carrie* (1900), *The Financier* (1912), and *The Titan* (1914) all portray the city as a jungle. Sister Carrie wins in the jungle, but her lover, George Hurstwood, loses. Frank Cowperwood wins and loses in Philadelphia and Chicago. Overall, despite cutthroat competition, poor living conditions, and sin and evil, the city emerges in the literature of the period as an attractive place to live. As Glaab and Brown point out, the city had magnetic power, it had culture, and it represented freedom and the energy of a dynamic society.

In Dreiser and Crane there are visions of a vigorous and exciting life in the city. The city crushes its victims, to be sure, but life is that way.

The literature of the early twentieth century is replete with examples of those who shunned the small town yet ended their lives there. The twenties in particular saw an attack upon the Midwestern small town led by such authors as Sherwood Anderson and Sinclair Lewis. Anderson's first novel, *Windy McPherson's Son* (1916), relates the village experiences of Sam McPherson and contrasts this life to his business success in Chicago. While Sam fails, the message of the book is that it is better to be a failure in Chicago than to stay at home in the village. *Winesburg, Ohio* (1919), Anderson's collection of short stories, concerns life in a small Ohio town. The picture of the town is not especially flattering, but the question persists whether the characters would have been any different in another locale. Anderson is not as much anti-urban as pro-people. The same may be said of Sinclair Lewis, whose novel *Babbitt* (1924) is often used to document the horrors of small-town life with its conventionalities and rigid patterns of social behavior. Yet Lewis regarded George F. Babbitt sympathetically; the novel ends with Babbitt content with his town of Zenith and his real estate business. There is part of the American dream in Babbitt's promotional schemes, and the barren lives of Zenith's citizens could be favorably contrasted to those of the farmers close by.

One of the best novels of the 1920's, *The Great Gatsby* (1925), also has an urban theme. James Gatz came from the Midwest and became Jay Gatsby, owner of an estate on suburban Long Island. He moved from a simple society to a complex one, and was driven to attain status, culture, and acceptance in the biggest city, New York. Gatsby retained some of his nostalgia for the rural past, but the character created by F. Scott Fitzgerald was archetypical in his hegira. "Making it" meant the city, and while the city was often crass and disappointing, it was where the action was.

The depression and the war years brought forth social protest literature as well as that recounting martial deeds. John Steinbeck, Ernest Hemingway, John Dos Passos, and Norman Mailer recounted the lives of American Okies, expatriates, soldiers, and ex-soldiers. While their themes were not confined to urban settings, the protagonists of their novels moved easily in and out of the city. The city had become a familiar, if not a friendly, place.

The outpouring of black literature which began in the 1920's and reached a peak in the 1960's was also urban oriented. Richard Wright's *Native Son* (1940) and Ralph Ellison's *Invisible Man* (1952) recount the experiences of black men in the ghettos of Chicago and New York. Both reflect the terrible quality of life in an urban society full of racial prejudice, yet both go beyond the city in assessing blame. The city is only the locale; the root causes are elsewhere. The city lacks community, but racial prejudice there is no worse than in Mississippi. It only takes different forms.

In the 1950's and 1960's the city became a way of life. Utopian speculation on the future of the city can be found in the science fiction of our own time. Typical of these novels is *The City and the Stars* (1953) by Arthur C. Clarke, regarded by many as the most impressive writer in this genre because of his *2001: A Space Odyssey*. In *The City and the Stars* Clarke extends Bellamy's utopia to the limit. Diaspor, the locale of the story, is the ultimate city where there is no change and no death. The city is run by machines whose stored images of the city constantly keep it the same. The end of Diaspor comes when the sterility of this existence is broken. In this book Clarke reverses Bellamy and argues for spontaneity rather than hierarchical order. The smoothly running society is the one to be feared.

The novels of the 1950's and 1960's have also echoed the Jewish experience in America. The creativity of sons and grandsons of immigrants, as funneled into literature, has treated the city as a fact of life. Examples of Jewish novels are Saul Bellow's *Herzog* (1964), Bernard Malamud's *The Assistant* (1957); and

Philip Roth's *Goodbye, Columbus* (1959). The heroes are all urbanites, though not all second- or third-generation Americans. They accept the city and its ethnicity. There is little question that this is where men live and where life is fullest. The city has become the norm rather than the exception.

The images of the city in literature range from realistic to utopian. Perhaps the anti-utopian temper of most contemporary literature prevents anyone but the science-fiction writer from speculating on the future; the fact is that the city as a stage for action in imaginative literature has lost its mystery and exoticism. It has become commonplace as the home of the scholar, the pawnbroker, and the plumbing parts dealer as well as the businessman and real estate promoter. No longer are novels concerned with those whom the city uses up; they also involve those whose natural habitat is the city and whose success involves the manipulation of the urban environment.

Just as the American novelist has attempted to come to terms with the city either by creating an idealized model or by accepting the city as necessary, so too have architects. Architects became professionalized sooner than did city planners or social workers, when the American Institute of Architects was founded in 1857. At the time, buildings were still being designed by mechanics and engineers. In addition, what architectural designs were created were primarily for private clients. Attention to problems of city design was scant.

After the Civil War the pattern changed. Professional architectural courses grew, and the city became more important to designers. Massachusetts Institute of Technology, founded in 1861, offered an independent course in architecture in 1866, the first in the United States. The University of Illinois established a school of architecture in 1870 and Cornell in 1871. Both of these were in departments of engineering.

At the same time, new building techniques and new technology were making possible considerable change in the physical design of cities. Wooden structures had been supplemented by the use of

cast iron in the form of columns and façades before the Civil
War. Iron provided more structural strength, but the fullest use
of iron and steel were not made until the first true iron skeleton
building was constructed in 1871 in France. The possibilities inherent in iron were to become real in the age of the city.

Two other developments furthered building design. One, like
the use of iron, pre-dated the Civil War. This was the elevator.
Steam-powered elevators were a familiar sight in businesses and
factories by the 1850's, but the impetus for passenger elevators
was provided by Elisha Graves Otis' demonstration of his safe
elevator at the New York Crystal Palace Exhibition of 1853. The
other development was the gradual increase in the use of electricity,
a source of power and light for city buildings. Generation of electricity was also demonstrated at a fair, the Philadelphia Centennial
of 1876, and by the turn of the century electricity was becoming
more and more commonplace in homes and offices.

By the time of the rapid growth of American cities, then, both
professional skills and technology were available to facilitate that
growth. When the first skyscraper was built in Chicago, it marked
a major innovation in American architecture. The fire of 1871
decimated much of the city, making rapid rebuilding necessary.
Major William Le Baron Jenny, in constructing the Home Insurance building in 1883, used steel framing for the upper part
as load bearing, rather than using layers of bricks for this purpose as had been done previously. Bricks were then used as a
veneer. Two reasons for Jenny's action have been given. The first
was a bricklayers' strike; the second was that he got the idea
when he saw a book placed on a wire birdcage. In any event, the
skyscraper was born. Practitioners of the Chicago school of architecture, such men as Louis Sullivan and Frank Lloyd Wright, now
had the opportunity to develop the typical American city edifice.
Sullivan did so with his Wainwright Building in St. Louis and
his Prudential Building in Buffalo, and Wright followed with his
Larkin Building in Buffalo.

Despite the beginnings of the new city form with its skyline of giant buildings, the period 1880–1910 was marked by the City Beautiful movement which looked to the past rather than the future. A revival of the historical spirit in American architecture, under the aegis of such men as Richard Morris Hunt, founder of the American Institute of Architects, and Henry Hobson Richardson, had as its purpose to make American cities beautiful. This urge might take Gothic or Roman forms, but it was motivated by an image of America as a country worthy of great cities.

The City Beautiful movement was stimulated by the World's Columbian Exposition, the Chicago World's Fair of 1893, which used a classical theme. The Fair, with its White City, was bitterly attacked and just as strongly defended. Louis Sullivan did not like the overall concept, though he and Adler designed the Transportation Building. He felt it was too foreign and too Eastern. Those who defended the Fair spoke in terms of America's coming of age in architectural matters, of no longer being mere copyists but adapting European forms to American reality.

The City Beautiful movement continued after the Fair with the work of Daniel Burnham and others. Their emphasis was on the building of civic centers in the heart of the cities, and monumental gateways to the city in the guise of massive railway stations—St. Louis' Union Station (1894), New York's Pennsylvania Station (1910), and New York's Grand Central Terminal (1913). Burnham's firm designed civic centers for Cleveland, Manila, and Chicago. He also designed Union Station in the course of his work in Washington.

The City Beautiful movement visualized the city as an imperial center. It was no accident that Washington's Union Station and New York's Pennsylvania Station borrowed from Roman forms. Union Station's waiting room resembled the Imperial baths, while Pennsylvania Station specifically replicated the Baths of Caracalla. The civic center also echoed the theme of the new Romans. Government was to dominate the city, and the city was to dominate the hinterland. The architecture of the period, no less than the government, was to demonstrate that Americans once more were in control of their cities and their destinies. The embodiment of this control was in the City Beautiful.

By 1910 the City Beautiful movement appeared to have run its course. The skyscraper had won, and the future belonged to those who designed it. The greatest of the regional school of architects and, according to many critics, the greatest American architect, Frank Lloyd Wright, was by now openly anti-urban in his preferences. Born on a farm in Wisconsin, Wright first went to Chicago in 1887. While he continued to design public and private buildings, he also fulminated against their location in the cities in books like *The Disappearing City* (1932) and *The Living City* (1958), his last effort. In these books Wright argued that cities were unnatural and nonorganic, that they were in a process of decline, and that they would decay and disappear. The skyscraper would be in the country, surrounded by greenery and free from other such edifices. In his plan for Broadacre City, shown at Rockefeller Center in 1935 and at the Museum of Modern Art in 1940, Wright took four square miles of land as his base for homes, government and cultural buildings, businesses, industries, and farms. Each was separate, connected by highways and private automobiles. His goal, as he put it in 1958, was to get everyone their acre of land, to decentralize the city, to make the city the country. Wright's vision of the city as the country was as utopian as Clarke's view of the ultimate city. But it was not labeled as fantasy, and it affected architectural images of what the city should be.

The years from 1910 to 1933 witnessed startling city growth. Major skyscrapers became the norm in cityscapes. Chicago's Tribune Tower, and in New York the RCA Building, McGraw-Hill, Chrysler, Rockefeller Center, and the Empire State Building were built during this era. But no rationale for city design accompanied this construction, though some designers and city planners either criticized the lack of a rationale or proposed rationales

of their own. Lewis Mumford commented on the social usefulness
of skyscrapers as early as 1927, but his ideas went unheeded.
The forces behind the urban skyscraper were economic; commercial interests vied with each other to construct office buildings.
The image of the city, more unconsciously assumed than consciously stated, had become the metropolis as trading city. The
metropolis as imperial city was gone.

The period from 1933 to the present reflects disagreement about
the design of cities. Conflicting schools of architecture have de-
bated the ideas of Le Corbusier, Mies van der Rohe, Walter
Gropius, and Wright. There is no underlying unity in architectural
theory and hence no unity about the relation of architecture to
the city. It is obvious that the city's image is as important today
as it was in the 1880's, but no unifying vision has come. Architects accept the city in a qualified way. This acceptance seems,
like the novelist's, a recognition that the city has many images
and that complexity rather than unity may be the key.

This unit lends itself to a core approach. The integration of
literature and history can be accomplished by discussing the
image of the city as it appears in realistic novels, in black literature, or in science fiction. The integration of art and history can
be accomplished with units on the City Beautiful, the city of
towers, and the modern city. Changing ideas of what the city
is or should be reflect changes in what Americans are or feel they
ought to be. The Roman architecture of the City Beautiful satisfies
the conception of an imperial nation, just as the RCA and Empire State buildings reflect the business orientation of the 1920's
and 1930's.

Finally, while creativity may be inherent in some of us, it can
also be stimulated and drawn out of others. We need images of
what the city should be, both in the sense of community and in
the sense of physical design. Students can be encouraged to study
other people's dreams as well as to project their own. While few
will become novelists or architects—although we need more of
both—all ought to have some idea of what a city should be.

Bibliography

1. *The New Age of Architecture* (Fortune Magazine, 1958). This film was released by the American Institute of Architects. With city planners and builders, architects discuss the aesthetic, moral, and economic implications of architectural design and its relation to city problems. Recommended for senior high school students.

2. *Los Angeles from the Air* (Gary Goldsmith, 1965). This film of Los Angeles from a helicopter provides a good view of the Civic Center and the Coliseum. It also shows the impact of the freeways on this scattered city. The film can be used to illustrate architectural design and scale.

3. *Toward the Gilded Age—Inventions and Big Business* (Graphic Curriculum, 1966). This is one in the CBS Story of America film series. It relates the impact of electrification, the telegraph and telephone, and the elevator. The film fits in well with this unit and can be used for junior and senior high school students.

4. *Disaster, 1906* (Studio 16 Educational Films, 1961). This film shows the ravages of the San Francisco earthquake and fire of 1906 and the reconstruction following the disaster. Recommended for junior and senior high school students.

5. *Chicago Dynamic* (United States Steel, 1957). United States Steel produced this film, which is a history of the use of structural steel in frame and curtain-wall construction. It is useful in showing how technological change affects architecture.

6. *Kazin: The Writer and the City* (Chelsea House, 1969). In this film the literary critic Alfred Kazin examines the city as an aesthetic force, a presence, and an inspiration in American literature from Walt Whitman to Norman Mailer. Highly recommended.

7. Andrews, Wayne, *Architecture, Ambition and Americans* (New York: Harper, 1955), Free Press paperback. Andrews' history of architecture is popularly written and focuses upon why

people built the kinds of houses they did. The book is profusely illustrated and is spritely reading. There is less on city architecture than there might be, but on the strength of its other qualities the book could be assigned to better students.

8. Burchard, John, and Albert Bush-Brown, *The Architecture of America* (Boston: Little, Brown, 1965), paperback. The American Institute of Architects commissioned this illustrated history which has a wealth of information. The paperback abridgement concentrates on post–Civil War buildings. A useful reference tool.

9. Tunnard, Christopher, *The Modern American City* (Princeton: Van Nostrand, 1968), paperback. This book is most useful for the period under consideration. It contains two sections, one narrative and the other readings. It combines planning and architecture and is recommended as a good brief survey of the field.

10. White, Morton, and Lucia White, *The Intellectual versus the City* (New York: New American Library, 1962), paperback. This book centers on the anti-urbanism of American intellectuals. It contains a short chapter on Frank Lloyd Wright as well as chapters on William Dean Howells, Frank Norris, and Theodore Dreiser. For teacher reference and special projects.

11. Glaab, Charles N., and A. Theodore Brown, *A History of Urban America* (New York: Macmillan, 1967), paperback. Chapter 9, "The Urban Community Examined," is an excellent one on literary and sociological responses to the city. It is a useful summary for better students.

12. Callow, Alexander B., Jr., ed., *American Urban History* (New York: Oxford University Press, 1969), paperback. Callow has an excellent section on "The City in the American Mind" which includes an article on the poet and the rise of the city as well as articles by the Whites, Anselm Strauss, and Scott Greer. For better students only.

13. Tager, Jack, and Park Dixon Goist, eds., *The Urban Vision* (Homewood, Ill.: Dorsey Press, 1970), paperback. The editors

have included a section on architectural reformers which gives the flavor of the period and the thinking behind civic art and the City Beautiful movement. Recommended for teachers and for special projects.

14. Tunnard, Christopher, *The City of Man* (New York: Scribner's, 1953). Tunnard describes the periods of city design in this book which is easy to read and can be assigned to high school students.

15. Tunnard, Christopher, and Henry H. Reed, Jr., *American Skyline: The Growth and Form of Our Cities and Towns* (Boston: Houghton Mifflin, 1955), Mentor paperback. Similar to the other two Tunnard books listed, this one includes some readings used in *The Modern American City*.

16. Scully, Vincent, *American Architecture and Urbanism* (New York: Frederick A. Praeger, 1969). Scully's book is the most successful attempt to tie together architecture and urbanism. Recommended for research units and for teacher resources.

17. Hirsch, Werner Z., ed., *Urban Life and Form* (New York: Holt, Rinehart and Winston, 1963). This collection of essays centers upon the design element in urban life. Useful for reference.

18. Dunlap, George A., *The City in the American Novel, 1789–1900* (New York: Russell and Russell, 1965). The latter part of this survey is pertinent to the period under consideration. The book is a standard one and can be recommended as a starting point for study of the city in the novel.

19. Strauss, Anselm, *Images of the American City* (Glencoe, Ill.: Free Press, 1961). While Strauss does not stress imaginative literature, he includes reactions of individuals to the cities in which they lived. Better students will find this book provocative.

20. Wilson, William H., *The City Beautiful Movement in Kansas City* (Columbia: University of Missouri Press, 1964). Wilson's study of Kansas City shows how the city was changed by conscious architectural design. Recommended for special projects.

21. Condit, Carl W., *The Rise of the Skyscraper* (Chicago: University of Chicago Press, 1952). Condit's study is the standard work on the history of the steel-framed skyscraper. An interesting book which can be read with profit by better students.

22. Condit, Carl W., *The Chicago School of Architecture* (Chicago: University of Chicago Press, 1964). Condit here recounts the history of such architects as Sullivan and Frank Lloyd Wright. An interesting book, valuable for understanding the pioneers of urban skyscrapers. The book ought to be available for reference.

23. Cook, David Miller, *The Small Town in American Literature* (New York: Dodd, Mead, 1969). This is a general discussion of the treatment of the small town in novels. Up to date and definitive for reference purposes.

24. Doxiades, Konstantinos A., *Between Dystopia and Utopia* (Hartford, Conn.: Trinity College Press, 1966). Doxiades is a Greek designer and planner who is one of the most imaginative of modern city theorists. His visionary ideas and his planning techniques are suggested in this compilation of his lectures at Trinity. For teachers primarily.

25. Doxiades, Konstantinos A., *Ekistics: An Introduction to the Science of Human Settlement* (New York: Oxford University Press, 1968). This is the most important exposition of Doxiades ideas. At $35 the book can only be afforded by libraries.

26. Crosby, Theodore, *Architecture: City Sense* (New York: Reinhold, 1965), paperback. Crosby examines cities in the United States and England with an eye to developments since 1945. The book is a personal view.

27. Nairn, Ian, *The American Landscape: A Critical View* (New York: Random House, 1965). Nairn takes a hard look at American cities based upon his travels in this country from 1940 to 1960. He has sharp things to say about architecture and the lack of planning. Highly recommended for teachers and good students.

28. Weimer, David R., ed., *City and Country in America* (New York: Appleton-Century Crofts, 1962), paperback. Weimer's collection of readings shows how these two areas have been visualized differently at different times in American history. A good collection for this particular problem.

29. Fitch, James Morston, *Architecture and the Esthetics of Plenty* (New York: Columbia University Press, 1961). Fitch discusses American architecture in terms of what is American about it. He claims that abundance leads to vulgarity. For special projects only.

Metropolis and Megalopolis, 1920–1970

The census of 1920 revealed that, for the first time, more Americans lived in cities than in rural areas. Each succeeding census has showed increasing urbanization, but also a changing pattern of urban settlement. From 1900 to 1920 the central city grew faster than the suburbs or satellite cities, but since 1920 the latter have grown faster. Each census since 1920 shows increasing suburbanization. By 1975, according to some projections, 57 per cent of those who live in metropolitan areas will be in the suburbs.

While suburbanization has been a continuing feature of American urban life, the "new" movement since 1920 has been of a different character. In the first place, annexation of the suburbs by the central city has become increasingly difficult since about 1920. Before this time, the city may have been decentralized, but its political autonomy was unchallenged. Now the flight to the suburbs means a flight to a different political community, supposedly self-sufficient, but dependent upon the city for the employment of its citizens. Moreover, since those who leave the city are usually in the higher income brackets, the central city loses a class of citizens whose level of ability to support it is high. Part of the reason for leaving, of course is to avoid the higher tax burden of the city. The failure to annex the suburbs, coupled with the loss of its more affluent citizens, has impoverished the city and forced taxes up. It is a vicious cycle.

The second difference in the suburban movement since 1920 is racial. White people are moving to the suburbs to avoid the black migration to the cities. The population of the core of the largest American cities has become increasingly black. In 1910, 73 per cent of the black population lived on farms, mainly in the South. World War I, the depression, World War II, and the mechanization and industrialization of agriculture all contributed to the exodus to cities in the North and South. By 1970 the percentage of blacks living in cities was almost equal to those living on farms in 1910. Indeed, the black population is more urban than the white. Moreover, the black migration has been to the central city and not to the suburb as has white urban migration. In the 1960's ten blacks moved to the cities for every one who moved to the suburbs. Only recently has the black movement to the suburbs increased; it is still too early to tell whether this is a long-range trend or only a temporary reversal of the prevailing pattern.

The mixture of these two new ingredients in American urban development since 1920 has proved to be explosive. Central cities have lost a tax base and population, or have managed only to hold their own, while the demands on the city have grown geometrically. The movement of blacks to the city has meant a greater need for jobs, education, and welfare. Poorly equipped because of poverty and discrimination in the rural South, blacks coming to the city have encountered frustration, unemployment, poor living conditions, and urban decay. These factors have contributed

John F. Kennedy Expressway, Chicago (ILLINOIS DEPARTMENT OF HIGHWAYS)

to the racial unrest and tension of the 1960's and have often seemingly divided the American city into two armed camps.

The National Advisory Commission on Civil Disorders estimated in 1968 that by 1985 thirteen cities would have black population majorities. These cities and the projected times include Washington, D.C., Gary, Newark (all three of which have already reached this status), New Orleans (1971), Richmond (1971), Baltimore (1972), Jacksonville (1972), Cleveland (1975), St. Louis (1978), Detroit (1979), Philadelphia (1981), Oakland (1983), and Chicago (1984). The Commission also indicated that ten other cities would have black majorities in their schools by 1985—Dallas, Pittsburgh, Buffalo, Louisville, Indianapolis, Kansas City, Cincinnati, Harrisburg, Hartford, and New Haven. Thus the center of a number of major cities will be black while their environs are white.

Another feature that has become part of urban America has been brought about by the accelerated military expenditures of the Second World War, the Cold War, and the wars in Korea and Vietnam. This is the concentration of aircraft and space manufacturing in certain cities in the South and West and the concentration of electronics manufacturing in "strip cities" in the same areas as well as on the fringes of such cities as Boston. The decision as to the location of these facilities was in part a political one, but it was also a decision dictated not by the traditional availability of transportation, land, and other resources so much as it was a function of the availability of certain talents. The electronics skills located at MIT and Cal Tech became a focus for development. Traditional reasons for industrial location—adequate transportation (usually by rail), adequate working force (usually a pool of unskilled laborers), and proximity to natural resources (usually coal and iron ore)—were supplanted. New reasons seem more impelling—nearby pools of university talent, a salubrious climate (physical and social) to attract this talent, and a connection with either the Defense Department or Congress.

The trends toward suburbs, toward a center city composed of those outside the dominant white middle-class culture, and toward industrial satellites and "strip cities" are not new. Similar conditions have been a part of city growth in the past. The suburbs of the 1890's were created by street railways; the central city in the same period was becoming Italian and Jewish; and the new industrial towns were those like Pullman and Gary outside of Chicago. The characters were different, but the process seems similar. Why then did the city come to be regarded as such a problem in the 1960's?

In the first place, better communications have acquainted Americans with the conditions of urban life. Economists estimate that 20 per cent of the residential areas in large cities are slums, and that these slums are homes to one-third of the urban population in the central city. However much slums have been a part of urban life, they have never been as infamous as they are today. Largely through the medium of television, Americans have witnessed the living conditions of the urban poor. While perhaps the proportion of slums to decent residential areas is lower than in the past, the visibility of today's slums has made their existence much more real than earlier ones. In any event, the slums are an obvious blight on American society.

Another reason for the present concern with urban problems is their connection with race. The racial division in America has become a function of city life. The blacks' expanded drive for equality has taken root in the Northern city, and it is there that frustrations have given rise to disturbances. The race riots in Chicago in 1919 and in Detroit in 1943 reflected the dislocation of war; the racial conflict waned in both cities with the end of the war. The problems of the 1960's allow no such hope. The riots in Watts in 1965 were followed by those in Newark and Detroit in 1967, and each succeeding year has seen its share of death and property destruction. Because the riots are also television spectacles, they have entered into the minds of middle America. A larger feeling of pessimism about American society has become evident, and the locale of this disappointment is in the cities.

Despite this recent pessimism, the half-century from 1920 to 1970 was marked by a constant variety of reforms, each with its own group of supporters and its own program to save the cities. Some of the programs have been local, some regional, and some national. All have had, at best, only limited success.

One of the reform devices has been to attack municipal problems with boards, agencies, or commissions. This movement, which dates far back into the period, is an attempt to get around the splintering effect of suburban decentralization with its many units of government. The growth of suburbia has meant the growth of small-unit government. As an example: in 1900 the New York region had 127 governments; in 1920 it had 204; in 1954 it had 1,071. In order to cope with problems that extended beyond governmental boundaries, special organizations were created to handle specific problems. Municipal transit authorities became common, as did port authorities and metropolitan commissions to build and operate bridges, tunnels, airports, and toll roads. Some of these agencies were more than municipal, they were regional in concept and organization. They worked with greater or lesser efficiency, but they did not solve—or even attempt to face—the real problem of proliferating governments.

Like the reforms sponsored by the Progressives earlier, the use of special authorities bypassed the political process and moved in the direction of administrative government. The commissioners were appointed officials who quite often owed their allegiance to the state and who were not accountable to a municipal electorate. These commissioners ran effective, business-type agencies whose main goal was to provide the best services at the lowest possible costs. But these services were not often coordinated with others, nor did the agencies concern themselves with general urban welfare. In this sense, then, the attempt to solve urban problems with special agencies was also a conservative approach designed not to disturb the American preference for local government as expressed in suburban communities.

The same generalization can be made with other programs designed to save cities. As Jack Meltzer has said:

> The programs to "save our cities" were predicated on three base points: the reinforcement of commercial, industrial, and institutional property commitments for tax and allied purposes, the retention and attraction of middle- and high-income individuals and families, and community stability. The expressway, urban renewal, and public housing programs were all created and administered to achieve those ends.

The expressway was first proposed by Benton MacKaye in an article in *Harper's* in 1931. He argued for limited-access roads and for continuous nonstop travel on these roads. His townless highways would avoid urban centers, whether they were large or small. The expressway became a reality and grew tremendously after World War II. In 1956 President Eisenhower stimulated the building of interstate highways with increased federal aid. The principle of using federal funds for highway construction had been established with the Federal Highways Act of 1916, which started the system of dollar matching, but by the 1960's the federal government was paying 90 per cent of the costs for expressway construction.

Contrary to MacKaye's hopes, the expressway did not avoid the city. It came to the city to help commuters go to work, made it possible for the middle classes to live in the suburbs but work in the city, and thus accelerated the trend that was already apparent in the 1950's. While half of the daytime population in the five largest American cities in 1950 was concentrated within two miles of their centers, the nighttime population of the same areas was less than 15 per cent of the total. In Newark, New Jersey, the daytime population was twice the census figure for resident population. The expressway made possible the continued use of the city as a place of business, but it increased the separation of work from residence.

This use of the city comes at a high price. Urban land is expensive and construction costs are high. Despite federal funding, the building of urban expressways involves direct and indirect expense to the city. New parking must be provided; arteries leading into and away from expressways occupy land that has been taxed but can no longer be counted upon to produce revenue. Quite often the expressway cuts through the poorer areas of the city, dividing the community and displacing the urban poor. These displaced persons often congest other areas and create new housing problems. Finally, the expressway has increased the tendency of the city to expand and decentralize. By increasing the effective radius of the commuter, it has made possible the growth of new bedroom communities to take advantage of the radius. Thus, while expressways have helped to maintain the economic dominance of the city, they have also intensified its problems.

The same mixed record applies to public housing and urban renewal. While the idea of public housing is not new, actual construction of public housing did not occur until federal legislation in 1937. The law provided that local housing authorities could demolish slum buildings and build public housing for low rental, with the federal government supplying subsidies to make the scheme workable. The Housing Act of 1937 was a landmark in that the nation assumed responsibility for the elimination of slums. In 1949 the second important federal housing act was passed, and became the basis for urban renewal. The 1949 act promised every American family decent living conditions, and provided public housing money and moving expenses for persons displaced by slum clearance. The major construction was to be done through private firms with federal assistance. Still, urban renewal did not become a significant force in urban life until after 1954, when experts discovered that it could serve everyone's needs. Local agencies could use eminent domain to tear down slums with federal funds; real estate developers could buy land more cheaply; taxes would be raised on the new apartments which would house middle-class citizens. All of this was made possible by a major difference between the Housing Act of 1937 and the Housing Act of 1949: the former mandated that the cleared land be used for low-rent or subsidized housing, while the latter permitted local agencies to decide what use should be made of such land.

In the years since 1954, urban renewal has been attacked and defended mainly on the basis of what cities have done with the slum areas they have cleared. There has been little discussion of whether slums ought to be torn down, though some critics have maintained that not only unsound buildings have been razed. The major question has been the kind of housing provided for those displaced, and the major problem has been that public housing has not kept pace with relocation. Indeed, in 1954 Congress cut the number of authorized public housing units from 135,000 to 35,000. The question of where displaced families move becomes more significant when we note that up to 70 per cent of those who have had to relocate because of urban renewal are nonwhite. For some critics, urban renewal has meant Negro removal.

The black man has again been caught in a vise. Forced from his urban home, he has had to seek housing elsewhere, but he has been unable to move to the suburbs because of lack of funds. Thus his only alternative has been to move into other areas within the city. There is contradictory evidence whether the move has been to poorer or to better quarters, but no one can deny that urban renewal has meant more problems for the black community.

Besides dislocating black people, critics charge, urban renewal does so to make way for luxury apartments. Using statistics furnished by the Urban Renewal Administration, Martin Anderson in his book *The Federal Bulldozer* claimed that the median monthly rental for new living units erected under urban renewal was $192 in 1962. Those who defend the building of such high-rise apartments point out that it raises the tax revenues of the cities and attracts the richer white citizen back into the center of things. Critics of the scheme ask how many black families moved into the new units.

To be sure, the experience in urban renewal has its brighter side. The need for more community participation, especially by those who may be most directly affected, has been emphasized to such an extent that the Office of Economic Opportunity and the Model Cities programs rely heavily upon it. Today's programs at least verbalize a concern for community planning and community goals, and attempt a more comprehensive attack on poverty and other city problems. But overall the high hopes for urban renewal have not been realized. New Haven, Connecticut, which received more urban renewal funds and more publicity than almost any other city under its mayor Richard Lee, has not been without racial and other difficulties. Other cities do not seem to have solved their problems through urban renewal, and the slums persist.

Despite obvious reasons for concern, some social critics do not regard the city as a disaster area and have hope for the future megalopolis. These individuals argue that we are not losing the fight with poverty but simply that our goals are too high, that our expectations have risen faster than our ability to meet them. In general they agree that intervention in the city has been too rigid, that we need to modify zoning regulations to help end income segregation, that we must somehow encourage mixed-income occupancy. In presenting such views, these critics have faith in the city as the best place to live, as an exciting, disorderly place where things happen. They are not utopian, they do not believe there will be no problems; they do believe that men prefer to live in cities and will continue to do so.

This unit on urban development, like the other units, could occupy a whole semester. The media are full of material on urban problems; the major difficulty is in selecting appropriate information for the student. Most of the media approach today's urban problems ahistorically. Thus the problems seem more ominous because they seem to be new. An acquaintance with the history of the American city will help to allay our fears and make the future appear less threatening.

Bibliography

1. *Geography in an Urban Age,* Unit I: *Geography of Cities* (High School Geography Project, Association of American Geographers: Boulder, Colo., 1968). Since the emphasis in this project is on contemporary city development, there is much useful material for the teacher. Three sections are of particular value: "Models of City Form," which concentrates upon the development of Chicago and its environs; "Time-Distance," which studies a hypothetical city which has a freeway built around it; and "Megalopolis," which concerns the rapidly industrializing Northeastern seaboard of the United States. All of the sections are useful, but the last is perhaps the best. The "Time-Distance" section graphically shows how freeways reduce the time to get to areas in the city but does not pay much attention to human or social costs. The same holds true for "Models of City Form," which has little value orientation. But on balance the project is a valuable one and is highly recommended. The teacher can use the data as a basis for further work.

2. "City I" (Urban Systems Simulations, 1717 Massachusetts Ave., N.W., Washington, D.C. 20036). This simulation game utilizes an urban center and three suburbs. The players assume various roles and make social, economic, and political decisions. Suitable for high school seniors and adults.

3. "Region" (Urban Systems Simulations, Washington, D.C.). The problems of an urban region are the subject of this game. The emphasis is again on economic and political decisions and their consequences. Recommended for high school seniors and adults.

4. *Law and Order* (Warren Schloat Productions, 1970). This series includes six color filmstrips, of which the last two, *Violent Dissent* and *The Establishment Responds,* are most pertinent to this unit. The first discusses campus disorders and the second urban riots, including the police response at Berkeley's People's Park demonstration and Chicago's 1968 Democratic National Convention. Recommended for junior and senior high school students.

5. *Problems of Cities* (New York Times, 1968). This set includes two records and two filmstrips. The subject is treated in a current and detailed fashion. For senior high school students.

6. *Megalopolis—Cradle of the Future* (Encyclopedia Britannica Films, 1963). Based upon the ideas of Jean Gottmann, this film shows the problems implicit in the urbanization of the Northeastern seaboard from Boston to Washington, D.C. It advocates better political and economic organization. Recommended for senior high school students.

7. *America's Crises* (Indiana University, 1966). This series consists of three films—*The Rise of New Towns, Crime in the Streets,* and *The Cities and the Poor* (2 parts)—all of which first appeared on National Educational Television. The last two are especially pertinent to this unit.

8. *Lewis Mumford on the City* (Sterling Educational Films, 1963). This series includes six films: *The City and Its Region, The City and the Future, The City—Cars or People?, The City—Heaven and Hell, The City as Man's Home,* and *The Heart of the City.* The first proposes regional planning with integrated city and country; the second attacks low-grade urban sprawl; the third advocates a carless city; the fourth is a history of cities; the fifth is a plan to eliminate slums and to improve living standards; and the last is a study of the drabness of the central city. Mumford is always stimulating, and these films are important for better students.

9. *Challenge of Urban Renewal* (Encyclopedia Britannica Films, 1966). This was an NBC production called "America the Beautiful." It discusses urban and suburban sprawl and pleads for better design, but does not analyze urban renewal insofar as its social costs are concerned. For junior and senior high students.

10. *Balkanization of Urban Life* (Encyclopedia Britannica Films, 1963). Arthur Naftalin, then mayor of Minneapolis, describes the overlapping of governmental units and operations. The film is useful in showing how the government of an urban area is split into many competing jurisdictions. For better students only.

11. Green, Constance McLaughlin, *The Rise of Urban America* (New York: Harper and Row, 1965), paperback. The last three chapters concern urban developments since 1911.

12. Callow, Alexander B., Jr., ed., *American Urban History* (New York: Oxford University Press, 1969), paperback. The section entitled "The City in Modern Times" in this collection of readings is an excellent one. It contains a criticism of urban renewal by Herbert Gans as well as a rebuttal. It also contains a thoughtful article by Scott Greer, an excellent urban political scientist. For sophisticated students and for teachers' resources.

13. Wakstein, Allen M., ed., *The Urbanization of America: An Historical Anthology* (Boston: Houghton Mifflin, 1970), paperback. Sections 7 and 8, "Metropolitanization" and "Contemporary Urban Problems," are comprehensive and contain a variety of viewpoints and themes. Highly recommended.

14. Mohl, Raymond A., and Neil Betten, eds., *Urban America in Historical Perspective* (New York: Weybright and Talley, 1970). Chapter 5, "The Modern Metropolis," is an excellent treatment of the problems of modern American cities. The selections are on the same level of sophistication as the two preceding volumes.

15. Tager, Jack, and Park Dixon Goist, eds., *The Urban Vision* (Homewood, Ill.: Dorsey Press, 1970), paperback. Part 3, "An Urban Nation, 1945–1965," contains nine thoughtful essays on the metropolis and the megalopolis. It is highly recommended for an analysis of urban problems. For projects and special use.

16. Tunnard, Christopher, *The Modern American City* (Princeton: Van Nostrand, 1968), paperback. This book is slim, but it does have two concluding chapters on urban development, primarily from a planning and design perspective. For students who have this interest.

17. Wood, Robert C., *Suburbia: Its People and Their Politics* (Boston: Houghton Mifflin, 1959), paperback. Wood is a professor of political science at MIT and director of the Harvard-MIT Joint Center for Urban Studies. He has also served as chair-

man of the President's Task Force on Metropolitan and Urban Problems. In this book he analyzes the suburban population and finds it motivated by an older, small-town ideology out of keeping with American metropolitan growth. Recommended for teachers and for independent reading.

18. Gottmann, Jean, *Megalopolis: The Urbanized Northeastern Seaboard of the United States* (Cambridge, Mass.: MIT Press, 1961), paperback. Gottmann, a French geographer and professor at the University of Paris, popularized the Greek word *megalopolis* in this book which was commissioned by the Twentieth Century Fund. An important book, it can be assigned to better students. Its theoretical base should be understood by teachers as well.

19. Jacobs, Jane, *The Death and Life of Great American Cities* (New York: Random House, 1961), paperback. Mrs. Jacobs is highly critical of urban renewal. She argues for diversity and for the idea of mixed neighborhoods (commercial, residential, etc.). A controversial but significant book.

20. Weaver, Robert C., *Dilemmas of Urban America* (Cambridge, Mass.: Harvard University Press, 1965), Atheneum paperback. Weaver, a Negro, was the first Cabinet officer specifically named to handle urban affairs. In his book he is critical of certain aspects of urban renewal but recognizes that the race problem is crucial in cities. A valuable book for special projects.

21. Lowe, Jeanne, *Cities in a Race with Time* (New York: Random House, 1967), paperback. This book discusses the twin problems of race and poverty. Miss Lowe maintains there is only a short time left for Americans to solve these problems before the cities explode. Her book is easy enough for high school students to handle.

22. McKelvey, Blake, *The Emergence of Metropolitan America, 1915–1966* (New Brunswick, N.J.: Rutgers University Press, 1968). McKelvey's book is a standard work in the field and ought to be the starting place for those who wish to understand city growth in historical terms. For outside reading assignments.

23. Greer, Scott, *Urban Renewal and American Cities: The Dilemma of Democratic Intervention* (Indianapolis: Bobbs-Merrill, 1965), paperback. In this book Greer looks at urban renewal with a somewhat critical eye. He is good at pointing to problems and future prospects. The book is necessary for any study of the process of urban renewal. Can be handled by better students.

24. Anderson, Martin, *The Federal Bulldozer: A Critical Analysis of Urban Renewal, 1949–1962* (Cambridge, Mass.: Harvard University Press, 1964), McGraw-Hill paperback. The most critical book on urban renewal, it stimulated much controversy. Indispensable for an in-depth study of the topic. Recommended for units on urban renewal.

25. Abrams, Charles, *The City Is the Frontier* (New York: Harper and Row, 1965), paperback. Abrams, an urban sociologist, analyzes urban problems in this book, particularly those connected with housing and urban renewal. He has an excellent historical perspective as well as a keen insight into the problems. For reference.

26. Ginger, Ray, ed., *Modern American Cities* (Chicago: Quadrangle Books, 1969), paperback. This book contains selections from the *New York Times,* divided into three parts: "Boomtowns and Placid Places," "Some Characteristics of Cities," and "Toward the Future of Cities." It is a good collection which can be handled by senior high school students.

27. Glazer, Nathan, ed., *Cities in Trouble* (Chicago: Quadrangle Books, 1970), paperback. Another *New York Times* book which focuses on the current crisis by concentrating primarily on New York City. The selections are astute ones and the level is the same as the preceding book.

28. Gans, Herbert J., *People and Plans* (New York: Basic Books, 1968). Gans pleads for better planning to take into account human needs. For better students.

29. Wilson, James Q., ed., *Urban Renewal: The Record and the Controversy* (Cambridge, Mass.: MIT Press, 1967), paper-

back. A well-balanced presentation of the pros and cons of urban renewal. Useful for reference and for special assignments.

30. Starr, Roger, *The Living End* (New York: Coward-McCann, 1966). Starr's book examines the critics of the city and their overly simplistic solutions to its problems. He identifies five areas which are the most significant trouble spots and suggests solutions. For better students.

31. Greer, Scott, *The Emerging City: Myth and Reality* (New York: Free Press, 1965), paperback. Greer predicts the future by projecting from today's metropolis. He analyzes the contemporary urban crisis and the changes occurring in the cities. A stimulating book which is suitable for teacher resources and special student projects.

32. Gruen, Victor, *The Heart of Our Cities* (New York: Simon and Schuster, 1964), paperback. Gruen's book is a plea for more planning and for better methods of handling traffic through metropolitan centers. It is a well-written book which has deservedly won popular attention. For better high school students.

33. Kaitz, Edward M., and Herbert Harvey Hyman, *Urban Planning for Social Welfare: A Model Cities Approach* (New York: Frederick A. Praeger, 1970). The authors were consultants to the Human Resources Administration of New York City. The book concerns the experience of the Model Cities program in New York. The major difficulty emphasized is the problem of informing and working with area residents. For special projects only.

34. Banfield, Edward C., *The Unheavenly City* (Boston: Little, Brown, 1970). Banfield, who heads President Nixon's task force on Model Cities, argues in this book that urban society is not deteriorating, that we are not losing the war on poverty. He recommends that we abolish the minimum wage, reduce the school-leaving age to fourteen, and institutionalize the incompetent poor. These conservative proposals are calculated to shock, as are the other ideas in the book. It should be read to counterbalance those pessimists who cry the doom of the city.

35. Sennett, Richard, *The Uses of Disorder: Personal Identity and City Life* (New York: Alfred A. Knopf, 1970). This is another argument for the city. Sennett believes that association with others of like identity develops a personality that has little tolerance or ambiguity. Therefore, city areas ought to be composed of people of mixed incomes and mixed occupancy. Sennett advocates vertical streets with stores, bars, and laundromats on various building levels. To accomplish all this, Sennett would eliminate centralized authority and zoning laws. His work is interesting and provocative and can be recommended for better students.

36. Von Eckhardt, Wolf, *A Place to Live* (New York: Delacorte Press, 1967), Delta paperback. Von Eckhardt is architecture critic for the *Washington Post* and writes for the *Saturday Review*. In focusing on architecture, he criticizes a number of buildings for not meeting the needs of the citizen of the city. Recommended for design-oriented students.

37. Leinwand, Gerald, ed., *Problems of American Society* (New York: Washington Square Press), paperback. These urban text materials are aimed at the secondary school student. They consist of narrative and readings, and were developed in collaboration with the curriculum committee of the Trenton, New Jersey, public schools. The titles are:

> *The Negro in the City.*
> *The City as a Community.*
> *Air and Water Pollution.*
> *City Government.*
> *Slums.*
> *The Traffic Jam.*
> *The People of the City.*

Index

Authors and Titles

281

A Note on the Author

Dwight W. Hoover was born in Oskaloosa, Iowa, and did not move to a large city until he went to Philadelphia at the age of twenty-two to do graduate work at Haverford College. He subsequently received a Ph.D. in history from the University of Iowa. Mr. Hoover's main concerns have been with the writing of American history, with the history of the Negro in America, and with the history of American cities particularly. This interest in urban history, combined with his rural background, gives him an unusual vantage point from which to explain the material in this book. Mr. Hoover is now Professor of History at Ball State University, and a member of the American Historical Association and the Organization of American Historians. His other books include *Understanding Negro History* and *The 21st Century: Dimensions in Social Change.*

DATE DUE
